"Jim Newheiser continues to be a wealth of biblical wisdom. Whatever he writes I buy because I know it will be wise, insightful, biblical, and fleshed out in the trenches of real ministry with real people. As a pastor and counselor myself for over thirty years, I'm always looking for biblical resources like this. *Marriage, Divorce, and Remarriage* will serve the church well because the questions that leaders face today have become increasingly complicated. Jim cuts through the fog with the light of God's Word and the heart of a real shepherd that has been forged side by side with people who are hurting and looking for answers. This little book can be the guide that takes you by the hand and leads you through the forest of winding, twisting turns, plowing through the underbrush of today's questions about sex, marriage, divorce, and remarriage. Get a copy to read and reread, as well as one to give to any church leader or counselor who is working with people today."

—**Brad Bigney**, Pastor, Grace Fellowship, Florence, Kentucky; author, *Gospel Treason*

"Jim Newheiser offers wise biblical counsel and tackles very difficult (but sadly common) issues in a way that pastors, elders, and those preparing to serve in the church will benefit from and greatly appreciate. I wish I had had a copy of *Marriage, Divorce, and Remarriage: Critical Questions and Answers* before I started out in ministry in the local church. I would have been better equipped to help and better prepared for the kinds of issues I would encounter. Above all, Dr. Newheiser seeks to be faithful to Scripture and summons us to a caring fidelity, even when it means that we have to deny self and take up our cross (Luke 9:23). We find here a call and plan to support God's grand design for marriage through the counseling ministry of the church."

—**Ligon Duncan**, Chancellor/CEO, Reformed Theological Seminary; John E. Richards Professor of Systematic Theology, RTS Jackson

"Not many people have spent as many hours opening the Bible to help couples experiencing difficulties as my friend Dr. Jim Newheiser.

D1519258

The answers he offers in this very helpful guide flow out of years of experience and a deep love for Christ and his church. I heartily recommend it!"
—**Elyse Fitzpatrick**, Author, *Counsel from the Cross*

"Jim Newheiser has had decades of counseling experience, much of it in the field of marriage, divorce, and remarriage. He is now my valued colleague at Reformed Theological Seminary. His book is the most thorough and cogent treatment I know on these subjects. I cannot think of any question in this area that he has not discussed with biblical wisdom, applied to real-life situations. I hope that many couples will use this book in their premarital counseling and that churches will use it in dealing with marriage problems in their congregations."
—**John M. Frame**, Professor Emeritus of Systematic Theology
   and Philosophy, Reformed Theological Seminary, Orlando,
   Florida.

"Jim Newheiser combines careful biblical thinking, decades of marriage counseling experience, and practical pastoral sensitivity to bring thorough wisdom to a surprisingly wide number of questions and sub-questions, including thorny and painful ones. While not every reader will agree with every aspect of every answer, the reader hungry to think carefully and practically about these matters will be richly rewarded with this concise yet comprehensive resource."
—**Robert D. Jones**, Biblical Counseling Professor, Southern
   Seminary; author, *Uprooting Anger* and *Pursuing Peace*

"As I read the table of contents for *Marriage, Divorce, and Remarriage*, I couldn't wait to read Jim's answers. Then when I actually started reading Jim's rich engagement with each of these forty vital questions, I had to wait—to slow down, ponder, reflect, and learn from the wisdom of a seasoned pastor and biblical counselor. *Marriage, Divorce, and Remarriage* is an excellent book for pastors and counselors—not simply for its thorough and relevant answers, but perhaps even more for its example of how to relate God's Word to the tough issues of daily life."

—**Bob Kellemen**, Chair, Biblical Counseling Department,
　Crossroads Bible College; author, *Gospel-Centered Counseling*

"Sooner or later, marriage touches all our lives. It is therefore one of the most important and most debated realities in the universe. That fact makes Jim Newheiser's book one of the most crucial for Christians to read. I am aware of no resource on marriage that is as comprehensive and yet as accessible as this book. Every issue addressed here is debated by someone, but Newheiser's careful and compassionate arguments require thoughtful engagement from everyone. I am happy to commend it to any scholar, pastor, or layperson seeking to understand the biblical teaching on marriage."

—**Heath Lambert**, Assistant Professor of Biblical Counseling,
　The Southern Baptist Theological Seminary; Executive
　Director, Association of Certified Biblical Counselors (ACBC)

"This book about marriage is different from most other books about marriage. It is different in that it provides biblically based answers to a great variety of current questions that are not answered in any other marriage book that I have ever read. In that sense it is unique, and I recommend it wholeheartedly. And it is also unique in that Dr. Newheiser's answers are not just his opinion or the opinion of certain so-called experts, but drawn from an exegesis of Scripture. Jim seeks to ground all his answers in what God says in his Word, the Bible. As a pastor and marriage counselor, I am glad to have such a book to which I can refer people for solid information on critical questions that are being asked in this twenty-first century."

—**Wayne Mack**, Director, Professor, Counselor, Strengthening Ministries Training Institute; Association of Certified Biblical Counselors (ACBC), Member of the Academy; Director, ACBC Africa

"Jim Newheiser has written an exceptional resource on marriage. It is carefully organized, thoroughly researched, and very well written. This book is going to be the gold standard for pastors, biblical counselors, and other Christians who want to glorify God on the issue of marriage. I highly recommend it."

—**Martha Peace**, Biblical counselor, conference speaker, best-selling author of *The Excellent Wife*

"Basic questions are comfortable questions. Jim Newheiser leads us beyond the comfortable basics of marriage to where real ministry often forces us—the unstable edges of this vital topic. Is abuse grounds for divorce? When is remarriage a bad idea? Does forgiveness always mean reconciliation? Newheiser answers risky questions such as these with delicacy and conviction, providing biblical footing for the edges."

—**Jeremy Pierre**, Associate Professor of Biblical Counseling, The Southern Baptist Theological Seminary; author, *The Dynamic Heart in Daily Life*

"There may not be a more difficult set of questions for Christians than those raised regarding marriage, divorce, and remarriage. Complex issues in these incredibly important areas abound, yet in Jim Newheiser's new book, these many questions receive fair, helpful, and, most importantly, biblical answers. My hat is off to the author for tackling so many questions and providing much-needed clarity in the midst of a fog of confusion surrounding these critical matters. The graciousness and skill with which he does so is a lesson for us all in handling what appear to be vexing uncertainties about, for instance, whom to marry, how to stay married, and what the bases are if you don't. As a pastor, I for one am always looking for helpful treatments on critical concerns for members of my congregation, and we surely have it here in this most valuable and eminently readable volume. May it receive wide acclaim as a trusted source for the church's singles and couples alike."

—**Lance Quinn**, Senior Pastor, Bethany Church, Thousand Oaks, California

"With his astute biblical wisdom and his years of experience, Jim Newheiser provides for us an exceptional question-and-answer tool for growing in our knowledge of marriage and in the topics related to marriage. Since we hold the marriage relationship in honor (Heb. 13:4), we make every effort to grow in our knowledge of biblical marriage, to practice biblical marriage, and to help others do the same, leading to the cultivation of marriages that proclaim the excellencies of God. We do this well by knowing what questions to ask and how to answer them biblically. This book will help us do just that."

—**Andrew Rogers**, Soul Care Pastor, College Park Church, Indianapolis, Indiana

"Over the past forty years, I have counseled hundreds of couples who were struggling with questions that this book answers with clarity. But unlike most books that cover a similar subject, this volume by Jim Newheiser handles these questions with biblical precision and grace. When there has been passionate love in marriage, there is also the potential for passionate hate. When this is true, it is difficult for those involved to think objectively, much less biblically. This book will provide a clear direction as it unfolds God's wonderful Word concerning marriage, divorce, and remarriage. Someone has wisely remarked, 'A good Christian wedding always involves two funerals.' A husband and wife must first learn to die to self; then they are ready to do things God's way. Anyone who has questions about marriage, divorce, or remarriage from a thoroughly biblical perspective must carefully study this book with the Bible alongside!"

—**John D. Street**, Professor, The Master's University and Seminary; President, Association of Certified Biblical Counselors (ACBC)

"*Marriage, Divorce, and Remarriage* by Jim Newheiser brings needed clarity to contemporary confusion over this foundation of society. Newheiser evaluates fairly those with whom he disagrees, making this book a real treasure. He answers the knotty questions from God's Word, making this volume valuable for a pastor bringing counsel, or a spouse caught up in a difficult marriage. Newheiser's pastoral insight, lucid analysis, and biblical focus make this book a must-read for people with questions about marriage and a valuable resource for a pastor's bookshelf."

—**Tedd Tripp**, Author, conference speaker

"In *Marriage, Divorce, and Remarriage*, Jim Newheiser humbly tackles some of the tough issues often connected to marriage. He acknowledges that good people may differ and then encourages the reader to search the Scriptures, not rely on man's opinion. Jim doesn't stop there, however. He blesses the reader with the result of his own scriptural conclusions and provides wise guidance for those who want to please the Lord in their approach to this topic."

—**Steve Viars**, Senior Pastor, Faith Church, Lafayette, Indiana

MARRIAGE DIVORCE AND REMARRIAGE

MARRIAGE
DIVORCE AND
REMARRIAGE

Critical Questions and Answers

JIM NEWHEISER

P U B L I S H I N G

P.O. BOX 817 • PHILLIPSBURG • NEW JERSEY 08865-0817

© 2017 by Jim Newheiser

All rights reserved. No part of this book may be reproduced, stored in a retrieval system, or transmitted in any form or by any means—electronic, mechanical, photocopy, recording, or otherwise—except for brief quotations for the purpose of review or comment, without the prior permission of the publisher, P&R Publishing Company, P.O. Box 817, Phillipsburg, New Jersey 08865–0817.

Scripture quotations marked (ESV) are from the ESV® Bible (*The Holy Bible, English Standard Version*), copyright © 2001 by Crossway, a publishing ministry of Good News Publishers. Used by permission. All rights reserved.

Scripture quotations marked (HCSB) are taken from the Holman Christian Standard Bible®, Used by Permission HCSB ©1999, 2000, 2002, 2003, 2009 Holman Bible Publishers. Holman Christian Standard Bible®, Holman CSB®, and HCSB® are federally registered trademarks of Holman Bible Publishers.

Scripture quotations marked (KJV) are from the Holy Bible, King James Version (Authorized Version). First published in 1611.

Scripture quotations marked (NIV) are taken from the Holy Bible, New International Version®, NIV®. Copyright © 1973, 1978, 1984, 2011 by Biblica, Inc.™ Used by permission of Zondervan. All rights reserved worldwide. www.zondervan.com The "NIV" and "New International Version" are trademarks registered in the United States Patent and Trademark Office by Biblica, Inc.™

Italics within Scripture quotations indicate emphasis added.

Printed in the United States of America

ISBN: 978-1-62995-316-8 (pbk)
ISBN: 978-1-62995-317-5 (ePub)
ISBN: 978-1-62995-318-2 (Mobi)

Library of Congress Cataloging-in-Publication Data

Names: Newheiser, Jim, author.
Title: Marriage, divorce, and remarriage : critical questions and answers / Jim Newheiser.
Description: Phillipsburg : P&R Publishing, 2017. | Includes bibliographical references and index.
Identifiers: LCCN 2017000245| ISBN 9781629953168 (pbk.) | ISBN 9781629953175 (epub) | ISBN 9781629953182 (mobi)
Subjects: LCSH: Marriage counseling. | Marriage--Religious aspects--Christianity. | Church work with married people.
Classification: LCC BV4012.27 .N49 2017 | DDC 261.8/3581--dc23
LC record available at https://lccn.loc.gov/2017000245

With thanks to God, who gave me Caroline as my wife. It must be because he knew how weak I would be that he gave me such a gracious and patient companion. Her love helps me to comprehend the gracious love of Christ for me. She has been a helper who has done me good all the days of my life and with whom I have shared surpassing joy.

CONTENTS

Contents

PART 2: DIVORCE AND REMARRIAGE

A. The Foundations of Divorce and Remarriage

B. Divorce and Remarriage Controversies

C. Practical Questions

FOREWORD

When you understand something, you know what questions to ask. For example, if you understand the book of Obadiah, you can ask lots of questions. If you do not understand it, you are reduced to, "Is that a book in the Bible?" When you can ask forty important questions, it means that you understand the issues well.

Then comes the equally challenging part. Once you ask the questions, you hope to give clear, cogent, scriptural answers in which you make your case but recognize that there are other perspectives, and you are respectful toward them.

Dr. Newheiser does both. He asks the important questions about marriage, divorce, and remarriage, and he gives biblically reasoned and very practical answers. You would think that he must be a 110-year-old to accrue that kind of wisdom. But somehow, he has accrued it in much less time. He has accrued it through loving God, pastoring a church, loving his family, being quick to receive advice and critique, living under Scripture and feeding on it, listening before he speaks, and loving others.

As I read the book, my first thought was that this is the perfect book for pastors, elders, and church leaders. Jim succinctly covers the matters that they will encounter in everyday ministry. It is perfect for them, but there is more.

Even though the book is in a question-and-answer format, after I read a dozen or so entries, I discovered that the book was teaching me how to use Scripture to think about our modern questions. In other words, Jim prepares you to ask forty more questions and consider forty wise answers. That's what a good book should do.

And one more benefit: When I read the book, I simply engaged in more conversations about marriage, divorce, and remarriage. That, too, is what a good book should do.

Edward T. Welch
Counselor and Faculty Member
Christian Counseling & Educational Foundation

PREFACE

It has been my privilege to teach about marriage and to engage in marriage counseling for more than thirty years. It has been my greater privilege to be in a very blessed marriage for over thirty-seven years. Both experiences have taught me much.

As I have faced some very difficult and challenging marriage counseling questions, I have been most thankful for the inerrancy and the sufficiency of God's Word (2 Tim. 3:16–17), which contains timeless truth that applies in all ages and cultures. The Bible offers powerful, authoritative, and helpful answers for every issue and question we may face in our own lives or when offering counsel to others. My hope in writing this book is to shed light on these answers for those who are eager to know God's wisdom.

I envision this book as being used in a few different ways. Some may read it straight through to obtain an overview of how Scripture addresses various matters concerning marriage, divorce, and remarriage. The question-and-answer format will make this helpful to others who may use it as a reference, which will help them to answer challenging issues as they arise. I also anticipate that counselors may assign particular chapters to their counselees as they face particular situations (e.g., how single people can know whether it is God's will for them to marry, or how a married couple can resolve conflicts and improve their communication).

The first half of the book deals with questions that tend to be more pastoral and less controversial (at least in Bible-believing evangelical circles)—the nature of marriage, entering into marriage, having a successful marriage, and facing challenges in marriage. The second half of the book deals with what the Bible teaches about divorce and remarriage—issues that many Christians in our day sharply disagree on. While those who differ with me may not be satisfied with all my answers, my hope is that they will be able to acknowledge that I have sought to understand their position and have treated it with respect and fairness. It additionally has been my intention not to duck the difficult questions and, on those issues that I am not sure about, to present different perspectives while admitting my uncertainty.

ACKNOWLEDGMENTS

I am very thankful to Benjamin Merkle, who encouraged me to write about these issues. Ben is a godly husband and father, an excellent scholar, and a dear friend. I also thank God for John Hughes and Ian Thompson, of P&R Publishing, for their help and encouragement as we brought this project to completion. I am particularly indebted to Pat Kuhl, Ann Maree Goudzwaard, and Christina Henson, whose help in proofreading and editing made this a much better (and more readable) book. In addition, I am grateful to God for Don and Darlene Downs, who gave me a place of beauty and respite from which to write. I pray that our work will be a blessing to the church, the bride of Christ, to his glory.

INTRODUCTION

Marriage is important. The Bible begins with a marriage—of Adam and Eve (Gen. 2:18–25)—and it ends with a marriage—of the Lamb and his bride, the church (Rev. 19:7–9). Marriage is designed by God as a picture of his loving covenant relationship with us. Marriage is the most intimate of all human relationships, in which a man and a woman have opportunity to love each other as God has loved them. Through marriage, we learn more about God's love for us. As we strive to grasp the dimensions of God's love for us, we learn how to love one another in marriage.

Because God is the Creator of humankind and of marriage, his Word is the authoritative source for what we are to believe and how we are to live. As Ray Ortlund writes, "Marriage did not arise from historical forces. It came down by heavenly grace as a permanent good for mankind. It was his to define. And he did define it in Genesis 2:24 as one mortal life fully shared between one man and one woman."[1]

Our culture has made a mess of marriage. Marriage vows are violated through adultery and divorce. The sanctity of marriage is rejected as the sexual privileges of marriage are taken without the commitment that the physical union is meant to represent. In more recent days, society has sought to redefine God's institution through mandating same-sex marriage.

1. Ray Ortlund, *Marriage and the Mystery of the Gospel* (Wheaton, IL: Crossway, 2016), 31.

Human corruption of God's gift is not something unique to our age. Biblical history portrays sexual sins of every kind and even the attempted redefinition through polygamy of God's design of marriage as one man and one woman.

This book will examine God's design for marriage and the difficulties that have arisen because of human sin. Most of what this book addresses would be unnecessary apart from the fall—polygamy, homosexuality, adultery, conflict, divorce, and remarriage.

God offers hope for fallen men and women and for the institution of marriage. Our great Bridegroom, Jesus, has come to redeem and to cleanse his bride, the church. As he transforms us inwardly by his love, we are able to reflect such love in our marriages. Thus, not only are we redeemed as individuals, but our marriages are redeemed, so that they can begin to attain the beauty and joy of God's original design. According to Ray Ortlund, "Nothing is more natural in our fallen world today than trying to build a marriage on a foundation of God-avoidance. But it cannot work. Without peace with God we inevitably shatter the peace we desire with one another."[2] He continues, "Only the gospel of Jesus can free us from this endless power struggle and restore the romance, the beauty, the joy, the harmony God intended."[3]

2. Ibid., 42.
3. Ibid., 49.

PART 1

MARRIAGE

A. THE FOUNDATIONS OF MARRIAGE

1

WHAT IS MARRIAGE?

We must begin our discussion with that which is the most crucial of all the questions. Without a correct definition of marriage, our trajectory will be flawed and all subsequent answers skewed. A proper understanding of the nature of marriage is especially crucial today as Western culture presses for the radical redefinition of marriage. This societal shift springs from the premise that marriage is a contract established by humankind, which evolves to meet the needs of a changing society. Sociologists claim that marriage originated for pragmatic and economic reasons (e.g., in an agrarian society, a man would want assurance that he is the father of the children for whom he is providing). Because marriage is perceived as nothing more than a societal invention, people are free to redefine the marriage contract to meet their evolving needs (e.g., with the availability of birth control, the ability of many women to provide for themselves, and the societal acceptance of homosexuality). Tim Keller points out that another significant shift began over a century ago as people began to think of marriage from the standpoint of personal fulfillment, with little concern for duty or the benefits of a stable marriage to the community.[1] This approach to marriage has led to no-fault divorce laws and skyrocketing divorce rates.

Once divine authority has been removed from human relationships,

---

1. Timothy Keller and Kathy Keller, *The Meaning of Marriage* (New York: Penguin, 2011), 28.

anything is permissible (Judg. 21:25). Biblical gender roles within marriage have been rejected as archaic and patriarchal. Some advocate eliminating the institution of marriage altogether. Many heterosexual couples cohabit with no intention of ever marrying. Same-sex "marriage," unthinkable only a generation ago, is today enshrined in law and widely celebrated. But Jesus reminds us that "from the beginning it has not been this way" (Matt. 19:8).

GOD DEFINES MARRIAGE AT CREATION

Marriage is a creation ordinance established and explained the sixth day when "the Lord God said, 'It is not good for the man to be alone; I will make him a helper suitable for him'" (Gen. 2:18). Then "the Lord God fashioned into a woman the rib which He had taken from the man, and brought her to the man. The man said, 'This is now bone of my bones, and flesh of my flesh; she shall be called Woman, because she was taken out of Man'" (2:22–23). Upon bringing the man and woman together, the basic elements of marriage are set forth. "For this reason a man shall leave his father and his mother, and be joined to his wife; and they shall become one flesh" (2:24). Everything else the Bible teaches about marriage flows from these foundational passages. God, as the Creator and Lord, is sovereign over humanity, including our relationships. He has revealed in his infallible, timeless, and all-sufficient Word the nature of marriage, the obligations of marriage, who may be married, and when divorce and remarriage are permissible. No one has the right to modify what God has established.

A BRIEF DEFINITION OF MARRIAGE

Marriage is a lifelong covenant of companionship between a man and a woman that has been established under God and before the community.[2]

2. Köstenberger defines marriage as "a sacred bond between a man and a woman

Marriage Is Covenantal

Marriage is a covenantal relationship, which is implied in Genesis 2 and is explicitly stated elsewhere in Scripture. Proverbs 2:17 warns that the strange woman (the adulteress) "forgets the covenant of her God." Malachi 2:14 rebukes the man who abandons his wife: "The LORD has been a witness between you and the wife of your youth, against whom you have dealt treacherously, though she is your companion and your wife by covenant."

The implications of the covenantal nature of marriage are manifold. A biblical covenant involves mutual obligations, promises of blessing upon fulfillment, and consequences for breaking the covenant. The obligations for marriage, including lifelong faithfulness and the divinely established gender roles, are revealed in Scripture and will be further explained throughout this book. The blessings that God offers in the marriage covenant are significant, including loving companionship, sexual union,[3] and children. The consequences of violating a covenant promise are severe. Covenants were typically established along with animal sacrifice, as in Genesis 15:9–21 when God made his covenant with Abraham. Those making the covenant promises in essence say, "May what happened to these sacrificial animals happen to me if I don't fulfill my obligations under this covenant." If one properly understands the seriousness of the marriage vows, he or she will not enter into them lightly.

Marriage Is under God

Another crucial aspect to a proper understanding of marriage is to recognize that a marriage union is not merely a contract between two people; a third party is involved—God himself. Many people see only

---

instituted by and publicly entered into before God (whether or not this is acknowledged by the married couple), normally consummated by sexual intercourse." Andreas J. Köstenberger with David Jones, *God, Marriage, and Family: Rebuilding the Biblical Foundation*, 2nd ed. (Wheaton, IL: Crossway, 2010), 270.

3. The mere fact that a man and a woman have had sex does not make them married. Marriage is a covenant that is ordinarily expressed in sexual union. Sexual union before the making of the covenant is a sinful distortion of God's design.

the horizontal dimension of marriage, while failing to see the vertical one. God joins every married couple; consequently, both spouses have covenant obligations to God (Prov. 2:17; Mal. 2:14), even if they don't acknowledge his place in their relationship. A properly conducted marriage ceremony emphasizes the reality that the man and woman are making their vows before God, to whom they will give account. Jesus also warns that anyone who participates in or promotes the breakup of a marriage will answer to God, who is the defender of the marriage covenant. "What therefore God has joined together, let no man separate," he declares (Matt. 19:6).

Marriage Is for Companionship

God designed marriage to provide the good gift of companionship. When Scripture initially declares the need for marriage, the focus is not on sexual gratification or the need to produce children. Rather, we are told that the man needs a companion with whom he can share life, so that he will not be lonely: "It is not good for the man to be alone" (Gen. 2:18). In context, the statement "It is not good" is especially striking, given that this was before the fall and up until then, everything God had created had been declared good (1:4, 10, 12, 18, 25). But the man alone was incomplete. Just as most of us would regard popcorn without salt as deficient, the man lacked an essential element to his humanity.

Moreover, it is significant that before creating the woman, the Lord God paraded all the other creatures before the man, but a suitable helper could not be found among them (Gen. 2:19–20).[4] Only a woman, who was his equal, could complete him. Then the Lord brings him Eve, and he senses that this is good. "This is now bone of my bones, and flesh of my flesh," he cries out. "She shall be called Woman, because she was taken out of Man" (2:23). This

---

4. Ray Ortlund puts it this way: "God bends down, touches the man and says, 'Son, you can wake up now. I have one more creature for you to name. I'm very interested to see your response to this one.'" *Marriage and the Mystery of the Gospel* (Wheaton, IL: Crossway, 2016), 26–27.

unique and intimate marriage relationship is encapsulated in the summary declaration in Genesis 2:24, in which a man leaves his parents to be united to his wife as his primary life companion. God's design is for the husband and wife to walk together as lifelong best friends.

Marriage Authorizes Sexual Intimacy

In addition to companionship, the Lord has given marriage for sexual intimacy. From creation, Scripture makes it clear that God intends sexual intimacy to take place exclusively between a man and a woman who have entered into the marriage covenant together. The two "shall become one flesh" (Gen. 2:24c). In our culture, the wedding ring is the outward sign of the marriage covenant. According to Scripture, however, the sexual union between husband and wife is the sacred sign and symbol of their covenant commitment. This one-flesh union involves far more than sex. Coming together physically is meant to be a picture of the oneness of life and relational intimacy enjoyed by a man and a woman who have committed themselves to one another for life. Every other sexual expression is against God's will and is a perversion of his wonderful design.

Marriage Is for Life

God hates divorce because it is a betrayal of the marriage covenant (Mal. 2:14–16; Matt. 19:3–9). It is he who joins man and woman in this covenantal one-flesh union, and he designed it to last until death parts the husband and wife. Jesus teaches this explicitly, warning that "they are no longer two, but one flesh. What therefore God has joined together, let no man separate" (Mark 10:8b–9). Scripture also teaches that "the married woman is bound by law to her husband while he is living; but if her husband dies, she is released from the law concerning the husband" (Rom. 7:2; see also 1 Cor. 7:39). We see from this passage that marriage ends with the death of one of the spouses. Jesus also teaches that there will be no marriage in heaven: "For in the resurrection they neither marry nor are given in marriage, but are like angels in heaven" (Matt. 22:30).

ORDINARILY THE MARRIAGE COVENANT IS MADE PUBLICLY

Marriage is not merely a private arrangement into which a man and a woman enter secretly. Marriage involves the community. Biblical marriage covenants were made in full view of the community and family. For example, Boaz went to the city gate to transact the business that was necessary to acquire Ruth as his wife (Ruth 4:1–10): "The people who were in the court, and the elders, said, 'We are witnesses'" (4:11). Other biblical weddings are celebrated with a public feast (Gen. 29:22; Matt. 22:2; John 2:1; Rev. 19:7). Weddings are public events in our culture as well. Those in the congregation are not solely spectators. Family and friends serve as witnesses to the covenant promises made by the man and the woman. If, at some time in the future, one or both parties to the covenant are tempted to abandon the marriage or to fail to keep their covenant obligations, the witnesses will hold them accountable.

Marriages are public affairs because healthy marriages are necessary for the well-being of the extended family and for the welfare of society as a whole. When marriages are strong, a culture thrives, but when marriage as an institution is weakened, the overall community is in trouble.

THE TRADITIONAL MARRIAGE VOWS SUM UP THE COVENANTAL OBLIGATIONS OF MARRIAGE

As some couples approach marriage, they don't seem to care enough about their vows. Instead, they are more concerned about the catering, the flowers, and the bridesmaids' dresses. But the vows are what will remain long after the cake has been eaten, the flowers have wilted, and the dresses are in mothballs. Many couples unthinkingly repeat the traditional vows much as they would blindly click acceptance of the terms and conditions for using a piece of software. A couple should carefully choose and study their marriage vows, which are among the most important words they will ever speak. They should also recognize that they will be in continual need of grace both from God and from each other when they fall short of God's perfect standard. We can begin to fulfill God's design for marriage only through our union with Christ, who sends us his Spirit to help us (John 15:5; Phil. 4:13).

I, *N*, take you, *N*,
to be my wife/husband,
to have and to hold
from this day forward;
for better, for worse,
for richer, for poorer,
in sickness and in health,
to love and to cherish,
till death us do part;
according to God's holy law.
In the presence of God I make this vow.[5]

SUMMARY

Marriage is not a human invention or convenience that can evolve or be discarded as society changes. At creation, God established marriage as a lifelong covenant of companionship between a man and a woman. A proper view of marriage is essential for the good of each spouse, for the proper structure of the family, for the training of children, and for the benefit of society as a whole.

— QUESTIONS FOR REFLECTION —

1. How might one's views of creation versus evolution affect one's view of marriage?
2. What are the implications of the viewpoint that the institution of marriage is evolving and can be redefined as culture changes?

5. http://www.churchofengland.org/prayer-worship/worship/texts/pastoral/marriage/marriage.aspx.

3. What are the basic elements of the marriage covenant that God established from creation?
4. How could the proper understanding of the nature of marriage help a couple to enjoy a more successful marriage?
5. What is the primary purpose of marriage?

2

WHY DID GOD CREATE THE INSTITUTION OF MARRIAGE?

People tend to view marriage in terms of what is in it for them. They get married because they anticipate that marriage will make them happy. While it is true that God created marriage for the benefit of humankind, the highest purpose in all that we do is to love and glorify God (Deut. 6:4–5). God has designed the world in such a way that we will find our greatest joy and fulfillment as we love and serve him.

GOD ESTABLISHED MARRIAGE FOR HIS OWN GLORY

Marriage Is How We Fulfill God's Command to Fill the Earth and Exercise Dominion.

Everything that God does is good and is for his own glory—which is the highest good. He created the world, fashioning mankind, both male and female, in his own image for his own glory. He then blessed them and charged them, "Be fruitful and multiply, and fill the earth, and subdue it; and rule over the fish of the sea and over the birds of the sky and over every living thing that moves on the earth" (Gen. 1:28). For the Christian, marriage is not merely about seeking self-fulfillment and personal happiness; rather, it is an opportunity to glorify God as we continue the work he entrusted to mankind at creation. We fulfill this creation mandate as we have children and build our families under God's lordship.

Marriage Is a Picture of the Relationship between God and His People

Throughout Scripture, God's covenant relationship with his people is portrayed as a marriage. The Old Testament depicts Israel as the Lord's bride, condemning her pursuit of idols as adulterous (Jer. 3:6–10, 20; Ezek. 23). The book of Hosea vividly sets forth the nature of Israel's unfaithfulness, while expressing God's willingness to restore her (Hos. 1–2). We learn from their relationship that God is a gracious husband who is ready to redeem his adulterous people: "'For your husband is your Maker, whose name is the LORD of hosts; and your Redeemer is the Holy One of Israel, who is called the God of all the earth. For the LORD has called you, like a wife forsaken and grieved in spirit, even like a wife of one's youth when she is rejected,' says your God. 'For a brief moment I forsook you, but with great compassion I will gather you. In an outburst of anger I hid My face from you for a moment, but with everlasting lovingkindness I will have compassion on you,' says the LORD your Redeemer" (Isa. 54:5–8).

In the New Testament, Jesus speaks of himself as the Bridegroom (Luke 5:34). The Old Testament echoes of God's relationship with Israel come to fullness in Christ's relationship with the church. He is the Bridegroom, and the church is his beloved bride. Paul develops this picture further when he declares, "Husbands, love your wives, just as Christ also loved the church and gave Himself up for her, so that He might sanctify her, having cleansed her by the washing of water with the word, that He might present to Himself the church in all her glory, having no spot or wrinkle or any such thing; but that she would be holy and blameless" (Eph. 5:25–27). Finally, the consummation at the end of the ages is portrayed as the joyful marriage feast of the Lamb to his bride, the church (Rev. 19:7–9).

God's design is that as we more deeply understand our relationship to him and our marriage relationships, these will enhance one another. According to Paul, this connection between marriage and our union with the Lord is a wonderful mystery (Eph. 5:32). The experience of a loving marriage helps believers to better understand God's love for us. Similarly, the ongoing experience of God's love for us in Christ provides a model for us to emulate in our marriages.

God Is Glorified When His People Honor Him in Their Marriages

There is no better goal for a marriage than that each spouse will be able to experience the love and grace with which each of them is treated and say, "This must be something of how God loves me." Surely God is glorified when Christian couples grow together in their ability to serve each other and display the fruit of the Holy Spirit. Such unions are a testimony of God's grace to their extended families, to their churches, and even to a lost world.

God is also glorified when Christians honor their marriage vows under difficult circumstances. We used to regularly attend a conference to which a certain gentleman would bring his disabled wife. He pushed her wheelchair to the meetings, brought her food at mealtimes (and helped feed her), and even assisted her in the restroom. All the while, he had a smile on his face and treated her like a queen. He wasn't enjoying all the benefits and fulfillment that many hope for in marriage, but he found joy in being faithful to the vows he had made before God many years before. Others find themselves in marriages fraught with never-ending conflict and sin. Those whose chief goal in life is personal happiness or who lack a biblical understanding of their marriage vows often abandon such marriages. In contrast, when a believer—in obedience to the Word of God and by faith—heroically seeks to show grace to a disobedient or unbelieving spouse, this brings much glory to God (1 Peter 3:1–2).

MARRIAGE IS GIVEN FOR THE GOOD OF HUMANITY

Marriage Promotes the Happiness of Both Husband and Wife

God created us to be social creatures. So for the majority of us, it is "not good . . . to be alone" (Gen. 2:18). In his kindness, God provides a suitable person with whom we can walk through the various stages of adult life. As Solomon writes, "Two are better than one because they have a good return for their labor. For if either of them falls, the one will lift up his companion. But woe to the one who falls when there is not another to lift him up. Furthermore, if two lie down together they keep warm, but how can one be warm alone? And if one can overpower him who is alone, two can resist him" (Eccl. 4:9–12). In addition to the pleasures of mutual fellowship and the blessing of mutual help, God has given the sexual union as a privilege of marriage to be enjoyed by both the husband and the wife (Deut. 24:5; Prov. 5:18–19; Song of Solomon; 1 Cor. 7:3–5). Moreover, the children God gives to a husband and wife through their union are a great blessing from God (Ps. 127).

Marriage Promotes the Holiness of Both Husband and Wife

In addition to these many and happy blessings, the Lord works through our marriages to conform us to the image of Christ. Sometimes this comes through trials. Living in such close quarters with another person is bound to expose our faults and weaknesses. You will sometimes hear a discerning newly married Christian say, "I never knew what a sinner I was until I got married." Marriage helps us learn to quickly confess our sins to God and to those whom we have hurt. Through marriage, we learn to reflect the grace and mercy that we have received from God as we show grace and forgiveness to a fellow sinner (Eph. 4:31–32). Marriage also teaches us to patiently overlook our spouse's weaknesses and learn to please others instead of ourselves (Rom. 15:1–2). Marriage offers the best opportunity that most of us will have to put the "one-another" verses of Scripture into daily practice.

The Institution of Marriage Is Beneficial to the Community

Families are the building blocks of society, forming the basis of the other social institutions of church and state. The family structure prescribed in Scripture, in which children are raised by a father and a mother who are fully committed to each other in marriage, is a blessing to both children and society at large. Children do best when, according to God's design, two parents raise them in a stable family environment.

When marriages break down and family structures are splintered, the children suffer most. This leads to burdens on the community, which often pays a price both financially (as the government steps in to care for children) and socially (as children who grow up in broken homes frequently fare worse educationally and vocationally).

SUMMARY

God's design for marriage reflects both his wisdom and his loving-kindness. Through marriage, we learn more about our relationship with him that, in turn, helps us to better understand marriage. When by his grace our marriages reflect his love for us, he is glorified. God also designed marriage to be a blessing for humanity, both as we participate in marriage and as strong marriages bring blessing to the wider community.

— QUESTIONS FOR REFLECTION —

1. How do Christians and unbelievers differ in their ideas about the purposes for marriage?
2. In what ways does God glorify himself through human marriage?
3. In what ways does marriage help us to understand our relationship with God?
4. How does marriage promote our well-being?
5. In what ways do strong families help the broader community?

3

WHAT CONSTITUTES A VALID MARRIAGE?

SEPARATION OF CHURCH AND STATE

Throughout history, some competition has existed between the institutional church and the state when it comes to regulating marriage. The Roman Catholic Church claims jurisdiction over marriage as a sacrament of the church. Those not married through the Roman Catholic Church are not considered validly married.[1] The Roman Catholic Church has also sought to regulate marriage according to its own traditions and its interpretation of Scripture. For instance, it forbids divorce, though in certain circumstances it may grant an annulment of a marriage. In countries such as the Philippines, where Roman Catholicism is dominant, the civil laws reflect Roman Catholic teachings. Other denominations, especially those that have functioned as state churches, have viewed marriage as being under their authority as well. In the past, marriages would have been registered with the church and not necessarily with the state.

In our day, the government is the primary institution regulating marriage. The state establishes who may be married (age requirements, forbidding the marriage of close relatives, outlawing bigamy, etc.), issues marriage licenses, and adjudicates divorces. Governments generally allow religious institutions a role in performing marriages

1. http://www.catholiceducation.org/en/culture/catholic-contributions/must -catholics-marry-in-a-church.html.

according to their own traditions, but with the oversight of the state. This is seen at the conclusion of a marriage ceremony, when clergymen say something like this: "Now, by the authority vested in me as a minister of the gospel in the state of California, I pronounce you husband and wife."

The Bible never explicitly grants authority over marriage to the church or the secular state. While God's law regulated marriage, divorce, and remarriage under the theocracy of the old covenant, nothing in the New Testament defines the role of the secular state in governing marriage. Nor is there any example of a marriage's being performed by a church officer or in a church building. While holding the traditional ceremony[2] a clergyman conducts in a church building is one way that a couple can formally create their marriage covenant, it is not the only valid way for such a covenant to be established. The role of the clergyman is simply to facilitate the making of the covenant by the bride and the groom. Nothing in the Bible mandates that a minister do this. Nor does the Bible teach anything about a ceremony by which the covenant should be made.[3]

SOME GOVERNMENTS ALLOW INVALID MARRIAGES AND FORBID VALID MARRIAGES

Some Islamic nations allow polygamy (see the next question). Other governments have allowed marriages between close relatives.

---

2. Numerous elements in the traditional ceremony reflect biblical principles. The bride's coming down the aisle is a picture of the church's meeting Christ, our Bridegroom, in the air when he comes for us. The bride's white dress expresses the purity that the church possesses because of the work of Christ (Rev. 19:8).

3. Recently, when performing a wedding, I saw that the groom was very dizzy and was about to faint. As I thought of how carefully the ceremony had been planned, I realized that only one thing had to be done—the vows. We could skip the Bible reading, the sermon, the songs, the unity candle, and the recessional (though these are not wrong). But the marriage would not be a marriage unless the couple made it through the vows. As it was, we helped the groom to be seated and gave him some water. While he was recuperating, I delivered a shortened meditation about marriage, and then we moved straight to the vows.

Now many governments are allowing same-sex marriage. Because such "marriages" are forbidden by Scripture, they are not valid in God's eyes.

On the other hand, some governments have wrongly forbidden marriages between people who have every right to be married—for example, when the bride and groom belong to different races. An Islamic nation would forbid a woman born into a Muslim family to marry a Christian man. Governments influenced by the Roman Catholic Church have promoted laws that keep an abandoned spouse from biblically allowable divorce and remarriage. In cases like these, is a Christian free to marry against the will of the state? While such a step should be taken with great caution, the government is not free to prevent what God's Word allows. This does not mean that believers must take a stand against the government when it oversteps its authority in this way. Yet they may do so. And they must be prepared to face any consequences that result.

MUST WE HAVE A PIECE OF PAPER?

A marriage is valid when a covenant of companionship is made between a man and a woman who present themselves forward to the community as being married. The Bible does not require that the couple obtain a license issued by the state or gain the sanction of a church. Jay Adams notes, "In biblical times a marriage did not require approval and licensure by the state . . . contracts were drawn up and executed by the parties in question with witnesses."[4]

BIBLICAL EXAMPLES

The marriages recorded in Scripture are formalized without direct involvement of church or state. In Genesis 24, Abraham sends his servant out to find a bride for his son Isaac. Rebekah willingly goes back with the servant. Her family members acknowledge the impending

4. Jay Adams, *Marriage, Divorce, and Remarriage in the Bible* (Grand Rapids: Zondervan, 1980), 18.

marriage as they bless her (Gen. 24:60). The marriage takes place when Isaac, in public view of his family/community, takes Rebekah as his wife: "Then Isaac brought her into his mother Sarah's tent, and he took Rebekah, and she became his wife, and he loved her; thus Isaac was comforted after his mother's death" (24:67). In a similar way, Jacob takes Leah (and then Rachel) as his wife in the context of the family and community as the marriage is celebrated with a feast (29:21–22). The marriage of Ruth to Boaz is most unusual to us because the bride was not even present when the covenant was formally solemnized at the city gate (Ruth 4:1–10). The community in Bethlehem witnesses the marriage covenant and calls on God to bless the marriage union (4:11–12).

CAN A COUPLE BE TRULY MARRIED IF THEY DON'T HAVE A LICENSE FROM THE GOVERNMENT?

While it may be wise and desirable to obtain a license from the government for practical reasons, such as tax advantages or certain spousal legal rights, a couple can be truly married in God's eyes without the involvement of the state. The Bible does not explicitly authorize the government to define and regulate the marriage covenant. As human governments continue to pervert their definition of marriage, some Christians may choose to make their marriage covenant before God and their community (family, friends, and church) without involving the government. One might object that as Christians, we are obligated to obey the government (Rom. 13:1–7); therefore, we should get married under the authority of the state. An answer to this objection is that there is nothing illegal in most jurisdictions about a couple's living together without a license from the government.

COMMON-LAW MARRIAGE

Some government jurisdictions recognize "common-law marriage," by which a couple, though never legally married, have been living together for a certain time and have been putting themselves forward as married.[5] They are treated, for all legal purposes, as if they are married. Other arrangements, including both formal and informal domestic partnerships and civil unions, further complicate the situation in our day.

EXCEPTIONAL SITUATIONS

In rare cases, certain extenuating circumstances can affect what constitutes a valid marriage. Jay Adams mentions these kinds of "irregular" marriages that might take place.[6] For example, if a man and a woman were stranded alone on a desert island, they might choose to make a covenant of marriage together, even though no government would recognize their marriage. Nor would there be a community to witness their vows. If they were to be rescued, they would then need to make their marriage known to their community in an appropriate way.

When I was pastoring a church in a closed Middle Eastern country, Azeb and Mo asked me to perform their marriage. Their situation, however, was complex. Azeb and Mo were impoverished refugees from an African nation with no legal standing in the country where we were living. Nor did they have the means or the ability to leave the country. This meant that there was no way for them to be legally married. After much prayer and biblical study, we concluded that Azeb and Mo could make their marriage covenant in the context of our Christian community and that such a marriage would be valid in the eyes of God.

IS GRANDMA LIVING IN SIN?

A trend in recent years has been for older widows and widowers to enter into committed marriage-like relationships, living together as husband and wife, without becoming legally married. The motivation for this is usually financial. They have concerns about the effects of

---

5. As of this writing, only nine states and the District of Colombia continue to recognize common-law marriages (http://en.wikipedia.org/wiki/Common-law _marriage).

6. Adams, *Marriage, Divorce, and Remarriage in the Bible*, 18.

marriage on their retirement income (surviving spouse), or that significant complications would arise regarding the inheritance to be left to their children. In the past, such people would probably have married anyway because of the social stigma attached to cohabitation. One option for people in this situation might be to enter into a marriage covenant, typically with the help of the church, but not to obtain a license from the government.[7] There may also be situations in which practical or financial reasons motivate younger people to marry without receiving a license from the state. These decisions should be made quite carefully, in light both of complications that might arise (in terms of spousal legal rights) and of motivations (greed).

IS A COUPLE TRULY MARRIED IF THE MARRIAGE HAS NOT BEEN CONSUMMATED?

While sexual union is ordinarily part of marriage, a couple can still be truly married without physically consummating the marriage. In the same way, having children is also ordinarily part of marriage, but is not always possible. The essence of marriage is the public vow made between a man and a woman. An elderly widow and widower who are no longer physically capable of sexual union may choose to marry because of a mutual desire for the companionship God offers in marriage. One spouse may not be able to function sexually because of a physical injury or an impairment (though the couple should openly discuss this issue before marriage). In such situations, a man and a woman can enjoy a unique level of personal intimacy, along with some special level of physical intimacy, even if it falls short of full sexual consummation. If a marriage has not been consummated because one or both spouses are not willing, there are serious problems that must be addressed from God's Word, often through godly counsel (see 1 Cor. 7:3–5 and the questions about grounds for divorce below).

7. In the United States, the Internal Revenue Service treats a couple as married only if they are considered legally married in the state in which they reside (http://www.irs.gov/publications/p17/ch02.html).

SUMMARY

Marriage is ultimately a divine institution. The Lord, through Scripture, defines which marriages are valid. Neither the church nor the state has authority to modify that which God has established. But the church may become involved in marriages through discipline of those who break their marriage covenants, and the state may be called to adjudicate legal matters pertaining to separation and divorce. When the institutions of the church and state stray from biblical principles, complications arise, and Christians will face difficult decisions about whether to comply or to exercise the freedom God gives them.

— QUESTIONS FOR REFLECTION —

1. What involvement, if any, should the government have in regulating marriage? What involvement, if any, should churches have in regulating marriage?
2. What would you say to a couple who want to be married, but don't plan to get a license from the government?
3. Would it be wrong to do this for financial reasons?
4. How should we regard people who act as if they are married, but have not formalized the relationship?
5. Is a "marriage of convenience" (e.g., to help someone obtain citizenship) a valid marriage?

4

IS POLYGAMY FORBIDDEN BY SCRIPTURE?

While polygamy is not a major issue in most Western churches, the practice of having multiple spouses still exists in many countries around the world. Furthermore, how do we explain the fact that so many men of God had multiple wives under the old covenant?

POLYGAMY IS A VIOLATION OF GOD'S ORIGINAL DESIGN FOR MARRIAGE

In the garden, the Lord could have chosen to create many women for Adam, which actually could have been more effective for fulfilling his mandate that humanity would be fruitful and multiply. Instead, the Lord created one woman for the man and set this forth as his intended design for marriage. Polygamy is a violation of this original design and compromises the exclusiveness and intimacy of the companionship God intends for a husband and wife in the covenant of marriage.

Polygamy is also frowned on in the Mosaic law, which forbids a man from marrying "a woman in addition to her sister as a rival while she is alive" (Lev. 18:18). Kings are warned, "He shall not multiply wives for himself, or else his heart will turn away" (Deut. 17:17).

Furthermore, Scripture never speaks of polygamy in a positive light and almost always portrays it as harmful. The first record of polygamy occurs in the wicked line of Cain, when Lamech—an unrighteous, vengeful man—takes two wives for himself (Gen. 4:19). Later, when Abraham, at the encouragement of his wife, Sarah, takes Hagar who bears Ishmael, rancor occurs in his own family (16:4–5; 21:8–21), and great trials result for many generations of his true offspring through Isaac (16:12). Similarly, when Jacob takes both Rachel and Leah as his wives, his household experiences conflict and jealousy (30:1–24). "So Rachel said, 'With mighty wrestlings I have wrestled with my sister, and I have indeed prevailed'" (30:8). Also, "But she [Leah] said to her [Rachel], 'Is it a small matter for you to take my husband? And would you take my son's mandrakes also?' So Rachel said, 'Therefore he may lie with you tonight in return for your son's mandrakes'" (30:15). The book of 1 Samuel opens with the distress of barren Hannah at the hands of her husband Elkanah's second wife, Peninnah: "Her rival, however, would provoke her bitterly to irritate her, because the LORD had closed her womb" (1 Sam. 1:6).

While David and other kings had multiple wives, in violation of Deuteronomy 17:17, King Solomon presented the most tragic example of the harmful effects of polygamy. Early in his life, Solomon had prayed to God for wisdom (2 Chron. 1:8–13) and was among the wisest men to ever live (1 Kings 4:29–34). During his reign, the temple was built, and Israel became a great world power. But Solomon's many wives drew his heart away from the Lord, and he began to participate in their idolatry (1 Kings 11:1–8). As a result—in the next generation—the kingdom was divided into two parts, and Israel never again reached the heights it had achieved under Solomon's reign.

POLYGAMY IS CONTRARY TO
GOD'S WILL FOR MARRIAGE

The New Testament makes it clear that polygamy is contrary to God's will for marriage. The foundational passage about marriage in Genesis 2:24 states that "*they* shall become one flesh," without stating how many are joined in marriage (though certainly only two are implied). When quoting from this text, Jesus explicitly describes that

26

"'the *two* shall become one flesh.' So they are no longer *two*, but one flesh" (Matt. 19:5b–6a).

The qualifications for a church leader expressly teach that he must be "the husband of one wife" (1 Tim. 3:2, 12), which is literally "a one-woman man." This implies that while there may have been men in the early churches with more than one wife, such a man is unfit for church leadership. Polygamy is wrong.[1]

WHY DID GOD ALLOW POLYGAMY?

The answer to why God allowed polygamy resembles the answer Jesus gives when he is asked why the law of Moses regulated divorce. "They said to Him, 'Why then did Moses command to give her a certificate of divorce and send her away?' He said to them, 'Because of your hardness of heart Moses permitted you to divorce your wives; but from the beginning it has not been this way'" (Matt. 19:7–8). Because of human sin, people abandon their marriage covenants; therefore, divorce must be regulated. The legal regulations for divorce (Deut. 24:1–4) were given to protect the vulnerable woman who was sent away, and to maintain order in the community. In the same way, laws pertaining to the regulation of polygamy served to safeguard the rights of each wife, especially a first wife when another (presumably younger and more fertile) wife was added: "If he takes to himself another woman, he may not reduce her food, her clothing, or her conjugal rights" (Ex. 21:10). Like divorce, polygamy was never part of God's design for marriage. The Lord chose to tolerate it for a time, but he never sanctioned it.[2]

---

1. Some might use Romans 7:3 ("If while her husband is living she is joined to another man, she shall be called an adulteress") to show that it is forbidden for a wife to marry a second husband. (The KJV translation says that she "married" another man, but this translation is not demanded by the verb *ginomai*.) On the other hand, "joined" could refer to joined through adultery or after an unlawful divorce.

2. Slavery would be another example of a wrong practice that God tolerates and Scripture regulates (in this case, both Old and New Testaments; see Eph. 6:5–9).

ARE POLYGAMOUS MARRIAGES VALID TODAY?

Throughout most of the world, it is illegal for a man or a woman to have multiple spouses.[3] Yet polygamy still exists in many places. Polygamy is still legal in many Islamic countries in the Middle East, North Africa, and Asia. Moreover, polygamy continues to be practiced in certain tribal situations and within some religious cults (e.g., offshoots of Mormonism).[4]

Although presumably no biblical church would sanction a polygamous marriage and a true Christian would not pursue a second spouse, complex questions arise when a polygamist (or his entire family) is converted to Christianity. Must the new Christian divorce all but his first wife? What responsibilities does he have to take care of them and their children? In these rare cases, the new believer should seek the wisdom of godly church leaders.

While the answer that we might be most comfortable with would be to say that only a first marriage is valid, there is not a decisive biblical argument for this conclusion. Though Scripture is clear that God's design for marriage is for one man to join in a covenant of companionship with one woman, we are not explicitly told that a polygamous marriage is always invalid. Just as a couple who is divorced without biblical grounds is actually divorced,[5] there may be rare cases in which a man who wrongfully takes a second wife is really married to both women. When Paul excludes a polygamist from church office (1 Tim. 3), he does not say anything about this man's being forced to get rid of all but one wife. Nor does he say that this man cannot be a Christian and a member of a local church. Such a man may find himself in a difficult position—similar to that faced by Jacob and some of the other Old Testament patriarchs.

---

3. The abandonment of biblical moorings when it comes to the definition of marriage opens the door to all kinds of other arrangements' being recognized in some jurisdictions, including polygamy, polyandry, and group marriages.

4. Typically, such groups would not attempt to have the government recognize their marriages.

5. This matter will be further explained in chapter 31.

SUMMARY

God's design for marriage is clearly that the two, one man and one woman, become one. Polygamy, like divorce, is against God's ideal. He tolerated and regulated polygamy under the old covenant, but Scripture never presents polygamy favorably. Those who practiced it suffered the consequences. Because the New Testament is even clearer than the Old Testament on this subject, Christians should not practice polygamy.

— QUESTIONS FOR REFLECTION —

1. What scriptural proof exists that polygamy is contrary to God's design for marriage?
2. Why did God tolerate polygamy among the leaders of his people in the Old Testament era?
3. How does the New Testament shed new light on the issue of polygamy?
4. What role, if any, do the church and the government have in determining whether a polygamous marriage is valid?
5. How would you advise a polygamous Muslim man who has converted to Christianity?

5

MUST MARRIAGE BE BETWEEN A MAN AND A WOMAN?

This is a question that probably would not have come up very often in previous generations, but now the issue of same-sex marriage is one of the most pressing social issues of our time. Those promoting same-sex marriage claim that the situation of homosexuals today is equivalent to that of other minorities who suffered discrimination in the past. Those who defend marriage as being exclusively between a man and a woman are frequently branded as haters who are no better than the racists who opposed equal civil rights in previous generations.

CAN WE ARGUE SUCCESSFULLY FROM NATURAL LAW?

Many oppose same-sex marriage based on arguments from nature, rather than arguing from God's revelation in Scripture. They claim that such arguments are more effective because believers can find common ground for discussion with unbelievers through natural law. Arguments of this nature include the fact that homosexual acts are unnatural and contrary to the way in which male and female bodies are designed. Paul actually makes such an assertion: "For this reason God gave them over to degrading passions; for their women exchanged the natural function for that which is unnatural, and in the same way also the men abandoned the natural function of the woman and burned in their desire toward one another, men with men committing indecent acts and receiving in their own persons the due penalty of their error" (Rom. 1:26–27). They also assert that it is best both for children and for society when children are raised by their biological mother and father. They will point to long-standing social customs and traditions as well.

While these arguments have weight, I don't think that we should argue exclusively from natural law. Advocates of homosexual marriage assert that this behavior is part of their inborn nature. They claim that just as people are born left-handed or into a certain race, they are born with same-sex attraction. While Scripture says that in some sense they know deep down that they are guilty of wrongdoing (Rom. 1:32a), few will admit this because sin corrupts their thoughts and desires (Rom. 8:5–8; 1 Cor. 2:14). They call evil good and good evil (Isa. 5:20) and give hearty approval to those who practice such things (Rom. 1:32b). With reference to the arguments about what is good for children and for society at large, the academic community has published studies claiming to show that homosexual parents are as good as or better than heterosexual couples.[1] And with reference to the argument from the traditional structure of marriage, they will respond that traditions are man-made and subject to change, and that the structure of the family has evolved over time to meet changing societal needs.

THE BIBLE HAS THE ANSWERS

We must base our arguments against same-sex marriage on Scripture. Marriage is what it is because God has revealed it to be so in his Word. Same-sex marriage is wrong because God says so, and it is wrong for the reasons God states. Once God's authority is removed, virtually anything is possible. Human laws and judges' decrees are substituted for divine revelation. People can do whatever is right in their own eyes (Judg. 21:25)—that is, whatever feels good and makes them

1. http://www.bu.edu/today/2013/gay-parents-as-good-as-straight-ones/.

happy. Why does marriage have to involve only two people; why not more? Why does marriage include only humans and not pets as well? Can one marry oneself? If someone claims to be born homosexual and believes that this justifies his or her behavior, why can't someone else claim to be born a pedophile, or a polygamist, or an adulterer, or someone wired for bestiality? The world says that you create your own gender identity and that society is free to redefine marriage. Scripture teaches that God has assigned your gender as male or female and that he defines marriage.

Advocates of homosexual marriage go to great lengths to try to reinterpret biblical texts as they attempt to prove that committed homosexual relationships between consenting adults are not forbidden in Scripture.[2] All their arguments fall by the wayside as we carefully consider what God has revealed positively about marriage and sex. God created mankind as male and female (Gen. 1:27). He ordained that marriage is a lifelong covenant of companionship between one man and one woman, and he established different roles for the man and the woman in marriage (Gen. 2:18; 1 Cor. 11:8–9). The issue of God's having assigned men and women to perform different roles in marriage is crucial in the debate over homosexual marriage. The feminist movement, which sought to eliminate the differences between the roles of men and women in marriage and in society, contends that we are all the same.[3] That has led to the argument that since we are all the same, any two of the same kind (humans) can marry each other. God made men and women to be different not just physically, but also in the part they play in marriage. A true marriage requires one of each.

In addition, God directs that sexual activity is allowed only within the marriage relationship (Gen. 2:24). No other relationship is truly a marriage, regardless of what government officials, opinion polls, and

2. For example, some claim that the sin of Sodom was a lack of hospitality or perhaps attempted rape (Gen. 19), not homosexual practice.

3. Sadly, many evangelicals have followed culture by embracing egalitarianism, which denies biblical teaching concerning the complementary roles of women and men in the home and the church.

law courts say. Any sexual expression outside the marriage covenant is forbidden, sinful, and harmful—whether that be adultery, fornication (sex between people who are not married), homosexuality, bestiality, or private lust (Matt. 5:28; Heb. 13:4). Furthermore, Scripture explicitly and repeatedly forbids sexual acts between people of the same gender: "If there is a man who lies with a male as those who lie with a woman, both of them have committed a detestable act; they shall surely be put to death. Their bloodguiltiness is upon them" (Lev. 20:13; see also Lev. 18:22; Rom. 1:26–27; 1 Cor. 6:9; 1 Tim. 1:9–10).[4] Any honest examination of these texts by a reader who affirms biblical inerrancy leaves no room for debate on the subject.

WHAT ABOUT PEOPLE WHO EXPERIENCE SAME-SEX ATTRACTION?

So how should we understand the issue of same-sex attraction? First Corinthians 10:13 declares, "No temptation has overtaken you but such as is common to man," which means that we all experience our various temptations in a similar way. A person who has never felt tempted by homosexuality may experience temptation by heterosexual lust or adultery. Another person may be tempted by anger or by sinful fear and worry. Yet another person may be tempted by substance abuse or gluttony. Though the source of temptation to sin may differ from person to person, the experience is common to all. Temptation occurs when people are carried away and enticed by their own sinful desires (James 1:14). One error of our culture is the assumption that our

---

4. The Old Testament law speaks to many of the issues pertaining to marriage, divorce, and remarriage addressed in this book. Christians hold varying opinions about how these regulations, which were originally for the theocratic nation of Israel, are to be applied under the new covenant era, in which there is no more theocracy. The position I am taking is that the moral principles set forth in commands such as Leviticus 20:13 are timeless and still apply in our era, though the sanctions (in this case, death) do not apply because there is no longer a theocratic state in which they can be carried out. Adultery and the cursing of parents were also capital crimes under the Mosaic law (Lev. 20:9–10).

desires (including homosexual desires) are valid. Some desires, however, are contrary to God's will and are harmful.

God offers hope to all those who feel tempted by sin, including those who have been enslaved by homosexual sin. The great need of the homosexual sinner is not merely to become a heterosexual sinner. Nor is his or her greatest need to merely become more outwardly moral. Former lesbian Rosaria Butterfield writes, "My new affection was not heterosexuality, but Jesus. . . . I was converted not out of homosexuality, but out of unbelief."[5] Sinners need a Savior who will forgive and transform them. The first step is to agree with God that your desires and actions are contrary to his will and then to ask him to forgive you for Jesus' sake. John explains, "If we say that we have no sin, we are deceiving ourselves and the truth is not in us. If we confess our sins, He is faithful and righteous to forgive us our sins and to cleanse us from all unrighteousness" (1 John 1:8–9). Through the atoning death of Jesus Christ, any sin can be forgiven. The New Testament actually tells us that some of the early Christian believers had been homosexuals before their conversions: "Or do you not know that the unrighteous will not inherit the kingdom of God? Do not be deceived; neither fornicators, nor idolaters, nor adulterers, nor effeminate, nor homosexuals, nor thieves, nor the covetous, nor drunkards, nor revilers, nor swindlers, will inherit the kingdom of God. Such were some of you; but you were washed, but you were sanctified, but you were justified in the name of the Lord Jesus Christ and in the Spirit of our God" (1 Cor. 6:9–11). Jesus provides not only for our forgiveness, but for our transformation as well. He gives us a new inward nature (2 Cor. 5:17) and fills us with his Spirit, who works within us to make us more like Christ.

This does not mean that it is always easy for a homosexual to abandon the old lifestyle, even after becoming a Christian. But the same could be said for any other person who has spent much of his or her

---

5. Rosaria Butterfield, *Openness Unhindered: Further Thoughts of an Unlikely Convert on Sexual Identity and Union with Christ* (Pittsburgh, PA: Crown and Covenant, 2015), 50.

life in a particular sin pattern, such as that of a liar, a thief, a substance abuser, or an adulterer. One married Christian man who admits to having been attracted to men states, "We all have part of our desires that we choose not to act on."[6] He and his wife agree that "people in any marriage must work to resist attractions from outside the relationship, whether from the same or opposite gender."[7] The one who has been saved by Jesus Christ has a new identity. Through union with Christ, his or her life is being transformed.[8]

Those of us who haven't faced this particular temptation can have compassion on those who are drawn to homosexual sin because we, too, were slaves to sin. As we have been set free by the power of the gospel, we can offer them the freedom that only Jesus Christ can give.

SUMMARY

The best argument for the fact that marriage is exclusively defined as being between a man and a woman is not from natural law or human tradition, but from God's revelation in Scripture. God brought together the first man and woman in marriage and has plainly set forth in his Word what marriage is and how it is to be practiced. No human institution has the right to change what he has established. Those who struggle with same-sex attraction can turn to Christ for forgiveness of their sin and for strength to walk in newness of life.

---

6. http://www.npr.org/2015/01/04/374857829/a-pastor-moves-past-his-attraction-to-men-and-so-does-his-wife.

7. Ibid.

8. The goal for those who have struggled with homosexuality is not merely to make them practicing heterosexuals, and certainly it is not to encourage them to lust after people of the opposite sex. The focus of their sanctification is growth in the gospel as they are being conformed to Jesus Christ. Even if there is no desire for marriage to a member of the opposite sex, there should be agreement that God's way is the right way. And inappropriate sexual desires of all kinds are to be resisted and starved.

— QUESTIONS FOR REFLECTION —

1. How effective is the use of natural law to argue against homosexual marriage?
2. Why is it necessary to use Scripture from which to derive a proper definition of marriage and the reasons that all sexual activity outside marriage is sinful?
3. What harm is caused to society when homosexual marriage is allowed or promoted?
4. May a Christian attend a homosexual marriage ceremony?
5. How should a Christian treat homosexual friends or family members? Can they come to Christmas dinner?

B. ENTERING INTO MARRIAGE

6

IS COHABITATION PERMISSIBLE APART FROM MARRIAGE?

Perhaps the most dramatic cultural shift in the past generation is the widespread practice of cohabitation, in which an unmarried man and woman live together and engage in a sexual relationship. Cohabitation in the United States has increased by more than 1,500 percent in the past half century.[1] "Two-thirds of couples married in 2012 shared a home together for more than two years before they ever waltzed down an aisle."[2] In the majority of cases, these people are considering marriage, and their initial time of living together is considered as a trial period to determine whether the relationship works.[3] After all, you wouldn't buy a car without taking it for a test drive. Others cohabit with no plans to marry. Some fully expect a sequence of such relationships during a lifetime. Others hope that their relationship will endure, but resist getting married for one reason or another. They

1. http://www.nytimes.com/2012/04/15/opinion/sunday/the-downside-of-cohabiting-before-marriage.html.

2. http://www.theatlantic.com/health/archive/2014/03/the-science-of-cohabitation-a-step-toward-marriage-not-a-rebellion/284512/.

3. "Among Americans who have ever lived with an unmarried partner, nearly two-thirds (64 percent) say they thought about it as a step toward marriage" (http://www.pewresearch.org/daily-number/cohabitation-a-step-toward-marriage/).

often give these long-term committed relationships other names, such as *partnerships*.

Another remarkable societal transformation is the widespread social acceptance of this practice, which used to be called "living in sin." A dwindling minority of Americans disapproves of couples' living together.[4] Cohabitation is also on the increase among professing Christians. I have counseled young people who profess to be Christian believers, but claim to have never been made aware that sexual activity before marriage is sinful.

This dramatic shift toward both the practice and acceptance of cohabitation has impacted society and the family in many ways. For instance, the age at which young people first get married has significantly increased—not because young people are delaying sexual activity, but rather because they are cohabiting, frequently with a sequence of partners, before marriage. Additionally, far more children are being born out of wedlock, and because cohabiting parents are much more likely to break up than are those who are married,[5] the harmful result is that fewer of these children are being raised by both parents.

SO WHAT'S THE DIFFERENCE?

Most cohabiting couples outwardly look very much like married couples. They maintain a home together and have to work through issues of shared finances, household responsibilities, and sex. They socialize together as a couple and are involved with each other's families. They have expectations of one another in terms of time commitments and sexual faithfulness. They also expect their friends and families to fully accept their relationship. They will claim that a ring and a piece of paper don't really have an impact on the strength of

4. http://www.usatoday.com/story/news/nation/2014/02/26/arizona-gay-rights-brewer-marijuana/5812997/?siteID=je6NUbpObpQ-y44ewbeey68Pat93gDN3qA.
5. http://www.dailymail.co.uk/femail/article-2516347/Most-family-break-ups-involve-unmarried-parents-Co-habiting-couples-times-likely-separate.html.

their relationship.[6] Some might even claim that they are "married in the eyes of God."

The main difference between cohabitation and marriage is in the level of commitment. The person entering into the covenant of marriage says, "I am committed to you in all the ways you will change—physically, emotionally, intellectually, and spiritually—for the rest of your life. I will love you not only for who you are, but for whatever you will become until God, by death, parts us." In the vows of marriage, both people promise that, regardless of what the future may bring (difficulties, feelings of attraction to another person, etc.), they will fight to preserve their marriage and keep their commitments.

On the other hand, the person in a cohabiting relationship is essentially saying, "I am willing to stay with you as long as neither of us changes too much. If you change in ways I don't like, I reserve the right to leave the relationship. Or if, because of changes in my life or personality, I decide that I can be happier without you, I can leave at any time." As Tim Keller puts it, "I don't love you enough to close off all my other options for life."[7] This puts a lot of pressure on each party in the relationship to perform.[8]

WHY DO SOME ARGUE FOR COHABITATION?

Many claim that living together before marriage will help to ensure that a couple will be compatible within marriage. Studies have shown, however, that marriages of couples who cohabited before marriage are much more likely to end up in divorce than are marriages of noncohabitants.[9] Various causes have been suggested for this

6. Those who cohabit might claim that the fact that they never married makes their breakups less complicated legally.

7. Timothy Keller and Kathy Keller, *The Meaning of Marriage* (New York: Penguin, 2011), 28.

8. Sadly, many married people are no more committed than those who are cohabiting, believing that if the marriage ceases to make them happy, they are free to divorce and find someone else.

9. Alfred DeMaris and K. Vaninadha Rao, "Premarital Cohabitation and Subse-

phenomenon. Perhaps the most reasonable explanation is that these relationships, which begin on a poor foundation of a reduced level of commitment, have difficulty transitioning to the higher level of commitment demanded by marriage. From a practical standpoint, responsibilities and commitments increase, but benefits remain more or less the same. From a biblical standpoint, you never win when you defy God. Sin has consequences. Paul advises, "Do not be deceived, God is not mocked; for whatever a man sows, this he will also reap" (Gal. 6:7).

COHABITATION IS WRONG BECAUSE GOD'S WORD SAYS SO

God, who alone is all-wise, has decreed that the great privileges of personal and sexual intimacy between a man and a woman be exclusively enjoyed by those who have entered into a marriage covenant. Moreover, he has decreed that all sexual activity outside marriage is sinful: "Marriage is to be held in honor among all, and the marriage bed is to be undefiled; for fornicators and adulterers God will judge" (Heb. 13:4).[10] Sex with anyone other than a marriage partner is a distortion of God's design and is essentially a lie. The cohabiting couple seeks to enjoy the privileges and benefits of marriage, while refusing to make the commitment that God requires as a prerequisite for enjoying these blessings. Their physical relationship declares a level of commitment and oneness that doesn't truly exist (1 Cor. 6:16). It is also important to emphasize that sexual sin is not merely what we do with our bodies. The root of the problem is in our hearts. According to Jesus, "For from within, out of the heart of men, proceed the evil thoughts, fornications, thefts, murders, adulteries" (Mark 7:21). We

---

quent Marital Stability in the United States: A Reassessment," *Journal of Marriage and Family* 54 (1992): 178–90. On average, researchers found that couples who cohabited before marriage had a 33 percent higher chance of divorcing than did couples who moved in together after the wedding ceremony. https://contemporary families.org/cohabitation-divorce-brief-report/.

10. *Fornication* refers to sex between an unmarried man and woman.

fall into sexual sin because we don't trust that God's way is best (Prov. 3:5–6) and instead believe that our hearts can be satisfied with what God has forbidden, rather than finding our ultimate joy in the Lord (Isa. 55:1–2).

CAN WE LIVE TOGETHER IF WE PROMISE TO BEHAVE?

I have run into several cases in which an unmarried Christian man and woman want to live as roommates or housemates without engaging in sex. In some cases, there is no romantic relationship. They simply want to share a living space, usually for economic reasons, much as two or more guys or girls would share an apartment. I have also encountered situations in which a cohabiting couple have come to faith and intend to be married, but claim that because they cannot afford two separate households, they must remain together. They agree, however, to abstain from further sexual activity until after the marriage.

While it is true that the Bible—in its prohibition of sex outside marriage—does not explicitly forbid unmarried people from living in the same home, many biblical principles speak to these arrangements. Scripture repeatedly advises us to avoid tempting situations. Paul instructs Timothy, "Flee from youthful lusts and pursue righteousness, faith, love and peace, with those who call on the Lord from a pure heart" (2 Tim. 2:22). In addition, he urges all believers to "put on the Lord Jesus Christ, and make no provision for the flesh in regard to its lusts" (Rom. 13:14). To the couple who claim that they are strong enough to resist temptation, Paul warns, "Therefore let him who thinks he stands take heed that he does not fall" (1 Cor. 10:12). Even when the man and woman claim that theirs is just a roommate situation with no romantic attraction, feelings often change and temptations arise.[11] Another reason that such living situations are inappro-

---

11. Many years ago, a woman from our church, who was in economic need, decided to rent a room from a man whom she knew. When I warned her about the dangers of such a situation, she told me that she had no romantic interest in this man. Later, she confessed that her feelings changed and that she had become quite

43

priate is the poor testimony to others, including unbelievers, who may presume that they are cohabiting, and other Christians, who may be tempted to follow their example (Eph. 5:3).

When a man and a woman claim that they are living together for economic reasons, other options should be pursued. The church may be able to help by matching up same-gender roommates. Or family members in the church may invite a woman to move out of the apartment she had been sharing with her fiancé and live with them until the wedding. Some couples delay marriage because they are saving their money for the "perfect" wedding and honeymoon. If they are otherwise ready for marriage, it would be wiser for them to get married sooner with a more modest wedding. Paul counsels, "But if they do not have self-control, let them marry; for it is better to marry than to burn with passion" (1 Cor. 7:9).

SHOULD THOSE WHO HAVE
COHABITED GET MARRIED?

While in many cases it may be wise to help a cohabiting couple enter into the marriage covenant, the Bible does not require that couples who have lived together and been sexually involved marry each other.[12] If one person is a believer and the other is not a believer, the biblical principle against a religiously mixed marriage would preclude the believer from marrying the unbeliever (see question 8). When children are involved (including a pregnancy), in many situations, it may be most wise and honorable to pursue marriage. We cannot say from Scripture, however, that the couple must marry. More than one pregnant woman, after repenting of her sin of fornication, has wisely chosen not to marry the father if he is an irresponsible and ungodly man. Even if a man does not marry the mother of his children, he

---

attracted to him. Their relationship ended very badly.

12. Exodus 22:16 requires a man who seduces an unengaged virgin to marry her, if her father agrees. This rule, however, is part of the old covenant theocratic law, and no evidence exists that it is to be strictly applied under the new covenant, by either the church or the state.

should make every effort to fulfill his financial obligations to her and his personal obligations to his children.

FOLLOWING GOD'S PLAN FOR MARRIAGE BRINGS THE GREATEST BLESSING

Although many factors contribute to a joyful, God-honoring marriage, those who honor God by keeping their relationship pure before marriage are in a position to most fully enjoy the privileges of marriage. The Lord did not make rules for the purpose of spoiling our enjoyment of life. Rather, his ways are always the best ways for the good of his people and for his own glory. There are few areas in life in which our faith will be more tested than in our approach to romance and marriage.

SUMMARY

As our culture continues to drift away from the biblical ideal for marriage, Christians will feel the pressure to follow the trend toward cohabitation before marriage. But Paul exhorts us: "And do not be conformed to this world, but be transformed by the renewing of your mind, so that you may prove what the will of God is, that which is good and acceptable and perfect" (Rom. 12:2). God's plan is that his people enjoy the great privileges of marriage, including sexual union, only after the marriage covenant has been made.

— QUESTIONS FOR REFLECTION —

1. What would you say to professing Christians who plan to live together before marriage?
2. How should the church treat cohabiting couples who want to become members?
3. Is there ever a time when a cohabiting couple should be treated as married?
4. Should Christians allow a relative and his or her partner in a

cohabiting relationship to stay in their home? May a Christian stay in the home of a cohabiting couple? Does it make a difference if those who are living together claim to be Christians?

5. Must a couple get married if they have engaged in premarital sex? What if there is a pregnancy?

7

HOW CAN YOU KNOW WHETHER IT IS GOD'S WILL FOR YOU TO GET MARRIED?

The trend in our culture is that fewer people are getting married, and that those who do marry wait until much later in life. This is not because more people are choosing to be celibate, but because they expect the privileges of marriage without the covenant commitments. Christians, however, do not conform to the world (Rom. 12:1–2); rather, they respect God's lordship over their relationships and their bodies (1 Cor. 6:20). They also trust that God's way is best and will ultimately lead to the greatest blessing and happiness (Prov. 3:5–6). Four questions remain as believers consider whether they should be married.

ARE YOU MADE FOR MARRIAGE?

In 1 Corinthians 7, the apostle Paul addresses whether his readers should pursue marriage. God has gifted certain people to remain single. As a single man, Paul appreciates the fact that his singleness gives him greater freedom to serve the Lord. "It is good for a man not to touch a woman," he says (1 Cor. 7:1b). "But I want you to be free from concern. One who is unmarried is concerned about the things of the Lord, how he may please the Lord; but one who is married is

47

concerned about the things of the world, how he may please his wife, and his interests are divided. The woman who is unmarried, and the virgin, is concerned about the things of the Lord, that she may be holy both in body and spirit; but one who is married is concerned about the things of the world, how she may please her husband" (7:32–34). Jesus speaks of some who remain unmarried for the sake of the kingdom as well (Matt. 19:12). These Scriptures do not mean that one must remain single to serve God.[1]

While Paul wishes more people had his gift of singleness, he recognizes that others are gifted to be married (1 Cor. 7:7) and that many would not be able to endure the temptations that singleness may bring: "But because of immoralities, each man is to have his own wife, and each woman is to have her own husband" (1 Cor. 7:2). He goes on to say, "But I say to the unmarried and to widows that it is good for them if they remain even as I. But if they do not have self-control, let them marry; for it is better to marry than to burn with passion" (7:8–9). Paul makes it clear that each person is free to choose whether to be married, according to his or her own gifts and desires (7:28, 35–39). For most of us, it is "not good . . . to be alone" (Gen. 2:18)—not just because of sexual urges, but also because we are incomplete without a mate with whom we can enjoy personal intimacy as we share life together. The person who is not gifted for singleness will be better suited to serve God in the context of marriage.

How, in practical terms, can people know whether they have the gift of singleness? Throughout the history of the church, many men and women, like Paul, remained single and were able to effectively serve the Lord.[2] Scripture does not claim that people who are gifted to be single have no sexual desire and no interest in the close

---

1. Peter and the other apostles were married, and Paul says that he, too, had the right to "take along a believing wife" (1 Cor. 9:5). Elsewhere, he warns against those who would wrongfully forbid marriage (1 Tim. 4:3). The requirement imposed by some churches, that their clergy members remain unmarried, is unbiblical and has resulted in much sin and scandal.

2. John Stott, who had a remarkable life of service to Christ and his church, and the missionary Amy Carmichael are more recent examples.

companionship that marriage offers. Instead, those who are gifted to be single can be content without being married and are able to keep sexual desires under control. They opt to remain single because they believe that they can best serve the Lord with the greater freedoms of a single person (1 Cor. 7:32). This is in direct contrast to the usual self-centered reasons that unbelievers remain single—avoiding commitment so that they can pursue their own selfish agenda in life. In the same way, those who choose to pursue marriage should do so because they recognize that God has made them for companionship. They believe they can best serve and glorify God in the state of marriage, rather than as single people.

Some Christians choose to delay marriage so that they can fully serve the Lord for a season without the responsibilities that marriage would bring. For example, the first fully supported missionary that our church sent out was a single man, who needed only a thousand dollars a month to carry on his work in an orphanage. While there, he met a wonderful young lady, whom he married at the end of his term. Now that he has a wife and children to support, he must spend more time taking care of them, but he still remembers the last year of his singleness with great satisfaction and thanksgiving. All believers who wind up getting married spend a season of life as single adults. Rather than following the world, which considers such a season as an opportunity to sow wild oats, Christians should take advantage of the extra opportunities for service to God, until such time as God leads them into marriage.

ARE YOU READY FOR MARRIAGE?

Just because people have determined that they are probably gifted to be married, this does not necessarily mean that they are ready for marriage. Some want to be married for the wrong reasons. Many are eager for marriage simply so that they can have their desires for companionship and sexual fulfillment met. A man who is enslaved to lust may think that marriage will solve his problem, but if he is not fighting the battle for self-control, he is not ready for marriage. If sex is his idol, his wife will not be able to fully satisfy his expectations, and terrible conflict may result. In the same way, if a woman wants to be married so that she can have a strong, romantic man worship the ground she walks on as he caters to her every wish, she, too, will be sorely disappointed. A man who is judgmental and angry is not ready to be married (Prov. 22:24). A woman who is insecure, and who seeks to find her significance through the attention of a man, is not ready to be successfully married. It takes maturity and grace to be married. The closeness experienced in marriage, which is meant to create joyful personal intimacy, can instead create friction for those who marry for the wrong reasons.

In addition to having the proper motive, one must be ready to assume the responsibilities of marriage. A married couple is to "leave father and mother" (Gen. 2:24), which implies that they need to be capable of independence. Does the young man have the job skills (Prov. 22:29) and work ethic (10:4) needed to provide for a family? Is the young lady prepared to shoulder the burdens of being a wife and a mother? Many young people live irresponsibly, failing to take advantage of opportunities to gain an education or learn a trade. Some who would like to be married will need to delay marriage until they are able to be self-sufficient. Those who long for marriage should continually work at growing in grace, in bearing the fruit of the Holy Spirit, and in preparing themselves in a practical way to take on the responsibilities of marriage.

DO YOU HAVE OPPORTUNITY
FOR A GODLY MARRIAGE?

Even if you desire to be married and believe that you are ready to be married, you should not get married until the Lord provides the right opportunity. Because we live in a painfully fallen world, some people face sorrow and disappointment. Some who yearn for children remain barren. Some who marry are widowed while still young through disease, calamity, or war. Some who would like to be married have to wait longer than they would like for a godly spouse. And some who grew up expecting to have a spouse and children never get the opportunity to be married. Jesus states, "For there are eunuchs who were born that way from their mother's womb; and there are eunuchs who were made eunuchs by men; and there are also eunuchs who made themselves eunuchs for the sake of the kingdom of heaven" (Matt. 19:12). By this he is saying that in addition to those who remain single for the sake of the kingdom, some will be unable to marry because of physical handicaps or circumstances that others imposed on them.

Some Christians can't find someone suitable who is willing to marry them. Many Christians are in churches or communities in which there are few or no viable candidates for marriage. I have been to churches in Asia where the women outnumber the men by a significant percentage. Numerous godly single women yearn for marriage, but have no prospects. Some who are very eager to be married feel the temptation to lower their expectations, especially as the years pass by. A Christian should have high standards for a potential spouse (see chapter 8). Getting married to an unbeliever or even to a weak, immature Christian will likely result in great trouble and misery, and will very likely hamper one's usefulness in God's kingdom. It is better to remain single and to wait on the Lord than to enter into a bad marriage. Those who badly want to marry often marry badly.

CAN YOU BE SURE THAT THE LORD WILL PROVIDE A SPOUSE?

While there are many happy stories of believers who found marital bliss after waiting patiently for the Lord to provide a godly marriage partner, Scripture does not promise that Prince or Princess Charming will walk through the door of your home (or your church). A single believer would be wise to use appropriate means to seek interaction with godly members of the opposite sex. Many Christian marriages have been facilitated through interaction among churches from different regions, through mutual friends, and through the Internet. Particular caution needs to be exercised when a relationship begins online or at a distance. The couple must thoroughly get to know each other's true character. It can be helpful in the early stage of such a relationship to have a family member or church leader speak to those who have known the other party well over a period of years to acquire an honest assessment. Some believers do end up remaining single, contrary to their desires. In such cases, they need to learn to be content in their unwilling singleness and to find their satisfaction in knowing and serving the Lord, who will never leave them or forsake them (Heb. 13:5).

SUMMARY

For most of us, it is not good to be alone (Gen. 2:18), but some are gifted by God to serve him in singleness. Those who feel that they are called to marriage must be sure that they are ready for marriage and then wait for the Lord to provide a suitable life partner. Some believers who yearn to be married don't ever receive that opportunity and must learn to be content, and even joyful in the Lord, while remaining single.

— QUESTIONS FOR REFLECTION —

1. What are valid and invalid reasons for remaining single?
2. What are valid and invalid reasons for pursuing marriage?
3. How can one know whether it is God's will for him or her to be married?
4. Should a person who desires to be married expect to be married? Explain your answer.
5. What means should a single person use to find a spouse?

8

HOW CAN YOU KNOW
WHOM YOU SHOULD MARRY?

There is a great deal of mysticism about finding a life partner. In the old movies, the hero and the heroine look across the room and, as their eyes meet for the first time, they immediately know that they are meant for each other. Many young people are told that "when the right one comes along, you will know." In the Disney movie, the wise owl tells Bambi and Thumper that animals suddenly get *twitterpated* in the spring. The Bible, however, warns that feelings, including romantic attraction and infatuation, can often be misleading. Hearts are deceitful (Jer. 17:9); charm and beauty are seductive (Prov. 31:30a); and in many cases, "There is a way which seems right to a man, but its end is the way of death" (Prov. 14:12). Samson thought he had found "love at first sight" (Judg. 14:1–2; 16:4). In the end, however, what he believed to be love was only his lust, which then proved to be his ruin. Single people must guard their hearts and have biblical priorities as they look for a spouse. Scripture tells them that nothing is more important in a marriage partner than possessing fear of the Lord: "But a woman who fears the LORD, she shall be praised" (Prov. 31:30b).

Many Christians have been told that they should look for the special person whom God has picked out just for them. While it is true that God in his sovereign will has determined whom we will marry, Scripture does not teach that we should expect mystical guidance in finding the perfect spouse. We are responsible to make a wise choice based on what God has revealed in his fully sufficient Word (Ps. 119:105). As in the story of Samson (with Delilah), God will not always prevent someone from making unwise or even sinful choices. I have known people who thought God had—through an impression, a fleece, or some other mystical means—told them whom to marry. In most of these cases, the objective examination of the prospective partner would have demonstrated that he or she was unsuited to be a godly spouse. Such marriages are usually very unhappy, with the believers who made the foolish choice often being tempted to blame God. In reality, they are victims of their own misguided theology.

YOU BOTH MUST BE ELIGIBLE TO MARRY

There are biblical limitations on whom you may marry. Scripture forbids marriage between close relatives (Lev. 18:8–18). Is one party still legally married to someone else? Has one of you been unlawfully divorced? Jesus says, "Whoever divorces his wife, except for immorality, and marries another woman commits adultery" (Matt. 19:9; see also questions 31–33). Are there other unresolved entanglements from the past, such as children from prior relationships, an existing relationship such as a previous engagement, etc.? Both parties must have such issues resolved in a godly way before they are free to enter into a marriage that will honor the Lord.

CHRISTIANS MUST MARRY ONLY IN THE LORD

According to Scripture, a believer should not even consider dating or courting an unbeliever. The old covenant forbade the Israelites from marrying outside the covenant community: "You shall not intermarry with them; you shall not give your daughters to their sons, nor shall you take their daughters for your sons. For they will turn your sons away from following Me to serve other gods; then the anger of the LORD will be kindled against you and He will quickly destroy you" (Deut. 7:3–4). In the New Testament, Paul issues a general warning about being "bound together" with unbelievers (2 Cor. 6:14–18).

He also explicitly mentions his right to "take along a believing wife" (1 Cor. 9:5), and likewise tells widows that they are free to remarry whom they will, "only in the Lord"—that is, only a Christian (1 Cor. 7:39). The tragic example of King Solomon, whose heart was drawn away from the Lord by foreign wives, serves as a warning for those who would disobey these commands (1 Kings 11:1–8). If the wisest man who ever lived could be turned into a fool by marrying outside the faith, how much more should we all beware of our own romantic choices?

Some Christians claim that they plan to use their dating relationship for the purpose of evangelizing their boyfriend or girlfriend. Paul says that they can't know whether they can lead another person to faith: "For how do you know, O wife, whether you will save your husband? Or how do you know, O husband, whether you will save your wife?" (1 Cor. 7:16). When a believer opts to pursue a romantic relationship with an unbeliever, it is usually the believer who is being influenced. The very fact that a believer is willing to choose this other person over his or her relationship with the Lord is a dangerous compromise. More compromises are likely to follow.

JUST CLAIMING TO BE A CHRISTIAN IS NOT ENOUGH

Nor is it enough that someone merely professes to be a believer. Scripture warns that many who claim to be followers of Jesus prove to be false (Luke 8:13–14; James 2:14–26; 1 John 2:19). I have seen several cases in which people will claim to be Christians, or will pretend to become Christians, so that they can court or marry a certain believer. In more than one case, tragedy (abuse and/or divorce) resulted. When considering marriage, you must look beyond someone's profession for evidence of a vital relationship with the Lord. According to Jesus, "You will know them by their fruits" (Matt. 7:20). Do they exhibit the fruit of the Holy Spirit (Gal. 5:22–23), or are they characterized by the deeds of the flesh (5:19–21)? Are they committed, serving members of a biblical church? Do they have a good reputation with their church leaders? These are all good indicators of a person's true spiritual state.

Even real Christians may not be prepared for marriage. Someone who is young in the faith may still need to work through some serious sin issues (e.g., lust) or may need to grow spiritually in the understanding of the grace and love of Christ, so that he or she will be able to exercise such grace and love with a spouse. Some true believers may lack the personal maturity required to take on the responsibilities of being a spouse and a parent, or may not yet have the capability to fulfill their godly role in the marriage.

YOU SHOULD BE ATTRACTED TO THE PERSON YOU WILL MARRY

Because most people rely almost solely on physical and emotional attraction, I began by emphasizing the objective aspects of choosing a spouse. It is important first to be sure that he or she is a committed believer who is ready to assume the responsibilities of marriage (Prov. 31:30). While it is true that romantic feelings can be deceptive, it does not mean that we must completely disregard them. Some might wonder, "Does it matter whether we are attracted to each other?"

From the standpoint of Scripture, it is possible for two mature believers who share a biblical view of marriage to have a successful marriage even if they were not greatly attracted to each other physically or emotionally before marriage. Throughout history, many couples have entered into marriage, often arranged through their families, before they knew each other well (for instance, Isaac and Rebekah in Genesis 24). God arranged the very first marriage, between Adam and Eve. While I am not advocating a return to arranged marriages, my point is that two people who have shared values can make a marriage work. In the play *Fiddler on the Roof*, Tevye sings the song "Do You Love Me?" to his wife, Golde, as they recall their arranged marriage twenty-five years before. They conclude that they did learn to love each other as they shared life together.

While objective qualifications are the most important (and most neglected) considerations in choosing a spouse, I do believe that it is important for one to be attracted to the person whom he or she is considering marrying. God's design is that a husband and wife find delight in each other, both physically and emotionally (Prov. 5:18; Song 1:2). Most people would not want to be married to someone who did not find them to be attractive and delightful. Leah suffered because Jacob did not love her the same way he loved Rachel (Gen. 29:30–31). It would not be fair to marry someone merely for being the logical choice.

SUMMARY

Single believers must exercise great caution when considering romantic relationships. It is all too easy to become emotionally and/or physically entangled with the wrong person (Prov. 7:21; 31:30a). Frequently, pride leads people astray: "He who trusts in his own heart is a fool" (28:26a). It is all too easy to fall in love with someone who does not measure up to biblical standards.

In addition, single believers should carefully study what the Bible says about Christian maturity in general and the marriage roles in particular. First, believers should examine themselves to ascertain how they need to grow and learn to become the kind of people that women or men of godly excellence would want to marry. Then they should study the Word of God (e.g., Prov. 31:10–31; Eph. 5:22–33) to know what qualities they should look for in a prospective spouse. I often give an assignment to single believers to make a prioritized list of the characteristics that they are looking for in a mate. Biblical requirements come first, followed by personal preferences (e.g., common interests and hobbies, physical appearance). Finally, I encourage them to pray for a future wife or husband in light of this list and to use the list to objectively evaluate any prospects who may enter their lives.

It is wise for single believers to take advantage of the wisdom of those in the body of Christ who have happy and successful marriages. While some of us grew up in homes with exemplary marriages, many of us have not had close exposure to a marriage that reflects God's design. It is beneficial for single believers to spend time with, and seek counsel from, couples whose marriages enjoy God's rich blessings. They will thus be able to determine what to seek in a spouse, as well as what they should strive for in their role as a husband or wife.

— QUESTIONS FOR REFLECTION —

1. What would you say to someone who believes that God will mystically show him or her whom to marry?
2. Why is it wrong for a believer to marry an unbeliever?
3. What are the most important qualities to look for in a husband?
4. What are the most important qualities to look for in a wife?
5. What is the place of physical and emotional attraction in choosing a spouse?

9

HOW SHOULD YOU GO ABOUT FINDING A SPOUSE?

People look for a spouse in our culture predominantly by dating. This relatively recent historical phenomenon is defined as "a part of [the] human mating process whereby two people meet socially for companionship, beyond the level of friendship, or with the aim of each assessing the other's suitability as a partner in an intimate relationship or marriage."[1] While dating seems very normal to us, arranged marriages have actually been the norm in most cultures throughout history. In recent years, many Christians, recognizing dangers in "dating" as it is practiced in our culture, have begun promoting the idea of courtship—"the period in a couple's relationship which precedes their engagement and marriage, or establishment of an agreed relationship of a more enduring kind."[2] Numerous Christians have advocated significant parental control over the courtship process, often claiming that they are following the practices found in Scripture.[3] Does Scripture actually endorse one of these practices above the other?

1. http://en.wikipedia.org/wiki/Dating.
2. http://en.wikipedia.org/wiki/Courtship.
3. I once heard an entire sermon describing the betrothal process in detail and advocating its present practice based on Matthew 1:18, which states that Mary had been betrothed to Joseph.

THE BIBLE DOES NOT EXPLICITLY
TEACH EITHER DATING OR COURTSHIP

Scripture does teach principles that single people should consider as they seek a mate, but the Bible does not explicitly prescribe a particular approach to dating or courtship. While we have examples of how marriages were made in biblical times—Isaac with Rebekah (Gen. 24), Jacob with Rachel and Leah (Gen. 29), Boaz with Ruth (Ruth 4), and Joseph with Mary (Matt. 1:18)—we are never told to imitate these examples. The provision of Rebekah for Isaac was a unique event in redemption history—the son of promise had to be married and have a son, so that the godly line could continue. God gave Abraham's servant supernatural guidance, but we are never told to expect such supernatural intervention in our day. Jacob's acquisition of Rachel and Leah was also a crucial part of Israel's history as we recognize the origins of the twelve tribes, but the deceit of Laban and the polygamy of Jacob are not examples to be imitated. Ruth and Boaz were married under a provision of the old covenant law that a near relative had the responsibility to provide offspring through the widow of a man who died, so that his name would not perish and his inheritance in the land would remain in the family. Because we are no longer under the old covenant, the provision for such marriages is no longer in force. While Joseph and Mary were betrothed, the betrothal process is neither described in detail nor mandated in Scripture. Upon examination of all these cases, it becomes clear that they were never intended to be prescriptive of how Christians ought to seek a spouse.

GENERAL PRINCIPLES

While no specific methodology for courtship or dating is mandated in Scripture, important principles are applicable as one seeks a spouse. One such principle is that sexual relations are to be enjoyed only within the covenant of marriage. Whatever approach people take to finding a spouse, they must take care to preserve the moral purity of their relationship. Fornication (sex between two unmarried people) is sin and comes under God's judgment (Heb. 13:4). Sexual sin is not limited merely to intercourse. God designed every aspect of physical intimacy between a man and a woman to be enjoyed only within marriage. Using someone's body for sexual pleasure intrudes on what God intended only for a spouse. First Corinthians 7:3–4 says that your body belongs to your spouse and that your spouse's body belongs to you. If you are not yet married, you belong to the spouse whom God will give you one day. When I was single, a wise friend told me, "When you get married, you will wish that you had never kissed anyone other than your wife." He continued, "Treat the girl you take out on a date as if one day she will be married to your best friend. Or treat her the way you hope the guy who is out with your future wife is treating her."

There are other dangers to becoming physically involved while dating or courting. Kindled sexual desire is quite difficult to control (James 1:15). I have counseled many young people who never intended to "go all the way" and claimed to have been shocked when they fell into fornication. Another problem is that premature physical involvement stirs one's emotions and desires in such a way that it is very hard to objectively evaluate whether this person has the godly character for a suitable spouse. If someone is leading you into fleshly sin, it is probably an indication that this person is not ready for marriage.

Another potential danger of dating relationships is that strong emotional attachments are formed prematurely—that is, before a couple is ready to make a commitment to marriage. This is the reason that many Christians object to dating as it is practiced in our culture. A man and a woman in a dating relationship become a couple without any plan to pursue marriage. This couple create what is, in effect, a minimarriage, in which they pull away from their families (leave) and are united emotionally (cleave), and in which there is some physical component (one flesh). God's design, in contrast, is that a man and a woman first enter into the covenant of marriage before leaving, cleaving, and uniting physically (Gen. 2:24; Matt. 19:5). Exclusive dating relationships, which are in effect minimarriages, usually end in minidivorces that cause both hurt and regret, especially for Christian young people.

It is far better to wait for romance until you are ready for marriage. Lust demands what it wants right now and is unwilling to postpone gratification. Godly love is mostly concerned about pleasing God and trusts that his ways, including reserving physical and emotional intimacy for marriage, are best. Moreover, godly love seeks what is best for others (Phil. 2:3–4) by being careful not to do what hurts the person you are dating or violates the rights of a future spouse. Love "does not seek its own" (1 Cor. 13:5).

It is wise to set standards before entering into any dating/courting relationship. Paul warns, "Flee from youthful lusts" (2 Tim. 2:22). Touching should be kept to a minimum, also realizing that what may be a friendship hug to one person may feel like sexual foreplay or an expression of undying love to the other. In the interests of maintaining moral purity, don't get into such a private situation that sin would be possible if both parties are weak. In the interest of protecting your hearts, it is vital to maintain a measure of emotional reserve. Avoid creating and expressing a strong emotional bond before you both are prepared to make a commitment to each other. Furthermore, my wise friend told me, "When you get married, you will wish that you never said 'I love you' to anyone other than your wife." Again, he was right.

WHAT PROCESS SHOULD BE USED?

Within the Christian community, many different practices and expectations exist for singles who are interested in getting to know one another. Some young women have made arrangements with their fathers that they would speak to any young men who would like to get to know them, even as friends. Other fathers might find it very strange and somewhat off-putting for a man to speak to them, unless engagement was already in view. In light of this, a friend of mine once counseled a young man to ask the question, "What are the customs in your tribe?" A young man who is interested in a young lady should seek to know what expectations she and her family have as he pursues a relationship with her.

Another scenario for young people in certain Christian communities is that they are so sheltered that they have virtually no contact with the opposite sex, other than family members, before a serious courtship begins. In such cases, I think it is best for single men and women to get to know many members of the opposite sex in informal (and safe) group settings. This allows them to learn about gender differences in general, while additionally recognizing what qualities they might desire in a spouse. It also helps them, as discussed above, to avoid pairing up in intense romantic relationships before being ready to pursue marriage. This does not mean that we can expect young people to avoid being attracted to one another before they are mature enough for marriage. The point is to constrain, rather than to prematurely unleash, these romantic desires (Song 8:4).

In contrast to worldly approaches to dating, which often have no deeper objective than to enjoy having a boyfriend or girlfriend, courtship or purposeful dating takes place when a man and woman take time to get to know each other to determine whether they would be suitable for each other in marriage. It is vital that there be honesty and openness in these situations. Both parties should understand the nature and intent of their relationship. Both must be honest about where they stand with each other. A decision to explore the possibility of marriage does not mean that the couple are, in effect, engaged (though, in some circles, courtship is unhelpfully regarded in this way). One or both parties may realize that the relationship will not be able to progress further, which should be communicated in a kind and timely manner.

WHAT ROLE DOES THE FAMILY PLAY IN CHOOSING A SPOUSE?

Our culture has swung from the extreme of marriages' being arranged by parents to the other extreme, in which parents do not have any involvement in their children's selection of a spouse. In an ideal situation, two people would explore the possibility of marriage with significant helpful involvement from each of their families. Parents typically have wisdom that may be able to identify problems in the prospective fiancée's character or difficulties in the relationship, which their children may not recognize. I have seen cases in which young adults have been spared a very hard marriage because they listened to their parents. Parents can also help to maintain accountability for the emotional and physical purity of the relationship. Many a family has a happy memory of a young man's respectfully approaching the father of the girl whom he loves to ask for her hand in marriage. Parents and children should work out well in advance their mutual expectations for the role that Mom and Dad will play during the process. The success of this involvement will largely rest on the quality of the relationship and the level of mutual trust that has been built over many years. If parents are unavailable or unwilling to offer guidance, a couple may look to church leaders to fulfill this role.

Some claim that parents have the right to choose whom their children (especially daughters) will marry, or at least to veto any prospective suitor. They base this on the requirement that children obey their parents (Ex. 20:12; Eph. 6:2) and the references to parents' giving their children in marriage (Deut. 7:3; Matt. 24:38; possibly 1 Cor. 7:36[4]). While I believe that it is very important to have the enthusiastic approval of both families, I cannot say that it is an absolute biblical requirement. A girl who has converted from Islam will never obtain approval from her Muslim father to marry a godly Christian man. I have also known of situations in which selfish parents didn't want their child to marry because the parents wanted the child to remain at home and take care of them. I have encountered a father who was completely unreasonable as he tried, without any biblical basis, to end a courtship, simply stating that he had the right to do so and that he didn't have to tell anyone his reason. Approaches like these completely

---

4. The NASB reads, "But if any man thinks that he is acting unbecomingly toward his virgin daughter, if she is past her youth, and if it must be so, let him do what he wishes, he does not sin; let her marry." This translation would imply that Paul is assuming that the father has authority to let his daughter marry or not marry. The word *daughter* does not, however, appear in the Greek text. Other translations (including the ESV and the NIV) interpret this passage to refer to one's betrothed—that is, the woman to whom one is engaged.

overlook Paul's admonition that fathers not provoke their children to anger (Eph. 6:4a).

Scripture teaches that when children reach adulthood, they come of age and become responsible for their own adult decisions (John 9:21). We have already seen that single men and women may choose to devote their lives to the Lord, which implies that they are acting as independent adults no longer under the authority of parents (1 Cor. 7:32–34). A widow is told that she is free to be married "to whom she wishes" (1 Cor. 7:39), not to whom her father or brothers tell her to marry. Any decision to pursue a relationship, become engaged, or marry apart from parental approval, however, should be taken with great caution and ideally with counsel from church leaders. Every effort should be made to make peace between children and their parents before the marriage takes place (Rom. 12:18), though, in some rare cases, peace may prove to be impossible.

WHAT ISSUES NEED TO BE RESOLVED DURING COURTSHIP?

The purpose of courtship (or intentional dating) is to explore whether a couple can be convinced that they can joyfully glorify God in a marriage together. Frequently, there are deal-breakers. He can't get over and forgive her sexual past. She can't deal with his financial irresponsibility and debt. She likes him, but does not feel physically and romantically attracted to him. He likes spending time with her, but is reluctant to make a commitment. He wonders if he is merely her Mr. Right Now, while she waits for Mr. Right. Several questions should be considered to help couples navigate through the issues that may arise during courtship.

1. Are They Both in Love with the Gospel, and Is It Impacting Their Lives?

The foundational question for each person to consider is whether the other demonstrates evidence of love for the gospel. Do they each perceive themselves as the chief of sinners, saved only by God's grace in Christ (1 Tim. 1:15)? Do they both love Christ and his free grace? Does the experience of his love and grace affect how they treat others (Eph. 5:1–2)? Is he willing to confess his own faults and sins? Is she willing to be honest about her own weaknesses and sins? Are both willing to show grace to the other in these areas?

2. Do They Each Respect the Other's Character?

In addition, both parties need to evaluate whether the other person's character measures up to what the Scripture says is desirable in a husband or wife. Is he a spiritual leader? Is he a man to whom she can submit for the rest of her life? Can she trust him to lead her and their children? Would she make a suitable helper for the vocation and ministry to which he is called? Does he have a sinful temper? Is she insecure? Does she have a quiet spirit (1 Peter 3:3–4)? Are both hardworking and responsible with money? Is she a woman of excellence who loves and fears the Lord (Ruth 3:11; Prov. 31:10)? Can he trust her (Prov. 31:11; Eph. 4:25)?

3. Do They Have Compatible Life Goals?

Any couple contemplating marriage should also take the time to discuss their goals for the future. I once had a case in which the man wanted to be an overseas missionary, and the woman was determined to live in the same town with her parents. Neither would budge, so the courtship ended. In another situation, the young lady wanted to have many children, starting immediately after they were married, while the young man strongly preferred to have one or two, and then only after they had been married at least five years. He may want to be involved in the Baptist Church, while she prefers Presbyterianism. How would they plan to work out these differences and others that will come up through the course of a marriage?

4. How Do They Function Together in Group Settings?

Another key indicator to consider is how well the couple functions when they are with other people. Do they work well together as a team in public? Does he make efforts to get along with her family and friends? Does she have godly friends who are a good influence on her? Do they like each other's families? Do they enjoy being with each other's friends? What do their families and friends think about their relationship? Any concerns should be taken seriously.

5. Have They Been Able to Work through the Past?

It is important that two people who are seriously considering marriage talk through their past romantic and sexual history, both for the sake of honesty and so that they can decide whether they can forgive the past and leave it behind. To what degree have they been involved with others in the past? Do they have any present struggles with sexual sin, such as pornography or masturbation? When the relationship is becoming serious, the other person has a right to know. We have seen cases in which, following marriage, one party feels betrayed when he or she discovers the spouse's present or past struggles with sexual sin. She might say, "I wouldn't have married him if I had known." Or, "I certainly would have delayed the marriage until this issue had been resolved."

6. Are They Able to Be Honest with Each Other about Their Sins and Faults?

Early in a dating relationship, both people typically put their best foot forward as they try to create the best possible impression to attract the other person. As a courtship progresses, conflicts may arise, and sin will be exposed. Are both parties able to admit when they are wrong? Is she a peacemaker? Is he quick to forgive? Are both of them aware of their own areas of sin as they strive to become more like Christ?

7. Can They Love and Accept Each Other as They Are?

Sometimes one or both parties unwisely enter into marriage with expectations that the other person will be different after the wedding. They need to ask themselves honestly whether they can love and accept their partners just as they are. Do they expect that the other will change after marriage? Do they think that marriage will solve all his anger and lust problems and will end her financial irresponsibility and laziness?

While they may rightfully hope that God will continue to sanctify each of them (Phil. 1:6), the marriage vows call us to be prepared to love "for better or for worse."

8. Why Do They Want to Marry Each Other?

Many couples marry for the wrong reasons. Have they honestly asked themselves whether they are attracted to each other for the right reasons? Can they express their reasons for wanting to get married in a clear and convincing way? Boaz was attracted to Ruth because of her excellent character (Ruth 3:11). There is no reference to her physical appearance. Outward beauty will fade (Prov. 31:30); godly character will grow more attractive over time.

9. What Are Their Expectations of Marriage?

It has been said that a woman gets married expecting that her husband will change and that a man gets married expecting that his wife will never change. Before entering marriage, both the husband and wife should evaluate their expectations for marriage. Are they realistic? Do they want to be married so that someone else will take care of all their wants and desires? Are they expecting their spouse to meet needs and desires that only God can satisfy (Jer. 17:5–8)? Are they prepared to stick it out through conflicts and trials that are bound to come? Are they convinced that the other person will endure in keeping the vows of marriage even when it may become very difficult?

10. How Well Do They Know Each Other and Themselves?

Some people "fall in love" without knowing nearly enough about the other person. Many people, after having been married for a short time, realize that they hardly knew their spouse before marriage. One way to get to know another person is to learn more about him or her through close friends, pastors, and family members. Wayne Mack's book *Preparing for Marriage God's Way*[5] includes some excel-

---

5. Wayne Mack, *Preparing for Marriage God's Way* (Phillipsburg, NJ: P&R Publishing, 2014).

lent diagnostic quizzes that can help couples determine how well they know each other and enable them to get to know each other better. Pre-engagement counseling can also be a means to test a budding relationship.

SUMMARY

Christians recognize that marriage is the God-ordained place for personal and physical intimacy between a man and a woman. Those who are committed to Christ will be careful in relationships with the opposite sex out of respect for God and out of concern for whomever they may marry in the future. The purpose for a single man and woman to spend intense time together, whether it be labeled courtship or purposeful dating, is to carefully explore whether God may be leading them into marriage. Honesty and openness are essential throughout the process. Ideally, one must not progress too far ahead of the other in terms of emotional attachment and commitment. The one who is more committed will have to be patient while waiting on the other person and, ultimately, on the Lord. If one party realizes that marriage is unlikely or impossible, this should be communicated honestly so that the other person will not be hurt any more than is necessary, and so that both can be free to explore other possibilities. Reasons for the breakup should be explained honestly and kindly. In such cases, the courtship/purposeful dating relationship has not failed. They set out to determine whether they were compatible for marriage, and discovered that they were not. Ideally, as they conducted themselves honorably during the courtship, they can pray God's blessing on each other.

— QUESTIONS FOR REFLECTION —

1. Does it matter whether you call your relationship *courtship*, *dating with a purpose*, or something else?
2. What biblical principles apply to the process of a man and woman's exploring whether they should marry each other?

3. Why is it important that both parties be open and honest during courtship?
4. What role should the family play in courtship? When may a couple become engaged and marry without parental approval?
5. Which issues should be worked out during courtship?

10

WHAT IS THE PURPOSE OF ENGAGEMENT?

An engagement is a promise to enter into the covenant of marriage. Ordinarily, this serves as a period during which the couple can prepare for both the wedding and the marriage.

WHEN ARE YOU READY TO BECOME ENGAGED?

Engagement is a serious commitment that is not to be entered into lightly. You should not become engaged unless you are convinced that this person meets the biblical requirements for a godly spouse, that you anticipate being able to successfully build a life together, and that you are mutually attracted to each other. Ideally, an engagement should come with the blessing of both sets of parents and should be celebrated by family and friends.

During the engagement period, both the man and the woman should take care to be circumspect in relationships with the opposite sex. Being engaged or married does not prevent someone from being attracted to someone else. Engagement is a promise to cut off all other options, which includes avoiding circumstances in which another romantic relationship might be formed.

ARE YOU PREPARING FOR A
WEDDING OR FOR A MARRIAGE?

Many people exert incredible amounts of effort and expense in planning a wedding. Every detail, from the florist to the caterer to the bridesmaids' dresses, must be perfect. This is appropriate because marriage is a gift of God to be celebrated (Prov. 18:22). Jesus himself attended at least one wedding celebration and contributed to its success (John 2:1–10). Sadly, however, some couples place far more emphasis on planning the ceremony and the reception, which last only a few hours, than they place on preparing for the marriage, which will ideally last for many decades.

The period of engagement should be a time of getting ready for marriage. One aspect of marriage preparation is practical—setting up and furnishing a place to live, planning a honeymoon, etc. The most important preparation, though, is spiritual. Now that you have chosen your love, you must learn more about how to love your choice. Engagement is a great time for a couple to perform an extensive study of what God's Word says about marriage. I strongly encourage engaged couples to receive extensive premarital counseling, which includes studying the origins of marriage, biblical roles of the husband and wife, conflict resolution and communication, sex, finances, and children. I seek to pair up the engaged couple with a godly, experienced mentor couple who can instruct and assist them as they work out any problem areas in their relationship. During the time of engagement, the couple should be preparing for their respective roles in marriage as they learn how to work together as a team.

HOW LONG SHOULD AN ENGAGEMENT LAST?

The Bible does not specify how long a couple should wait after engagement before they are married. Some couples may wait to get married until they have finished their education and acquired jobs. Some couples use the engagement period as a time to get to know each other better, so that they can be more prepared for marriage.

Many couples think they need a long engagement because of the time it takes to save for and plan the big wedding that the woman has been dreaming of all her life. Others even wait until they can afford a down payment on a house. Occasionally, marriage will be delayed because one or both partners are unsure about the relationship. In such a case, they should openly and honestly discuss and resolve this issue.

While each of these reasons may have some validity, and couples are free to choose the timing of their marriage, there can be downsides to a long engagement. Engagement can be a time of sexual temptation. Paul writes to the unmarried, "If they do not have self-control, let them marry; for it is better to marry than to burn with passion" (1 Cor. 7:9). In many cases, the benefits of entering into marriage sooner outweigh the desire that a bride or her mother (or, in some cases, the groom) may have for the perfect society wedding. With the help of family, church, and friends, a young couple can have a lovely, meaningful wedding without incurring an overwhelming expense or even going into debt.

HOW MUCH PHYSICAL AFFECTION IS APPROPRIATE FOR AN ENGAGED COUPLE?

Engaged couples need to be especially careful when it comes to physical affection. I have encountered several cases in which couples rationalized that sexual activity during engagement was permissible because they were going to be married anyway. The Bible makes it clear that sexual activity is not authorized until the vows of marriage have been made (Gen. 2:24). Couples who have "gone too far" during engagement sometimes have to deal with personal guilt and possible resentment against the other person for leading the relationship into sin. Falling into sexual sin during engagement or courtship additionally affects the couple's ability to trust each other in marriage and often negatively impacts their sexual relationship in marriage. Does he have the self-control to resist forbidden sexual experiences? If he couldn't be trusted during engagement to wait to enjoy sex in God's authorized way, she may find it hard to trust him to exercise self-control when he

73

is deployed with the military or out of town on a business trip, or when she is eight months pregnant and not fully available to him sexually. If she can't be trusted to resist his pressure to engage in sexual sin, he may have trouble trusting her to resist pressure from the guy at the gym or the friendly neighbor when he is away, or when they are in the midst of a conflict.

Some engaged couples, especially the guys, want to know "what I am allowed to do before we are married." Rather than listing what body parts are off-limits and giving them a stopwatch, I offer three general principles. First, sexual expression as an activity is reserved for marriage. It may be permissible to hold hands or to share a good-bye kiss, but ongoing kissing, fondling, and touching as activities are not appropriate before marriage. The second principle is that if what you are doing is causing your body to get ready to have sex (and you know when that is happening!), you are engaging in sexual foreplay (that is part of sex), which is not appropriate until you are married. The third principle is to avoid situations so private that you could sin sexually without the possibility of being interrupted or caught. While there is grace for those who fall short of these standards, there is great joy for those who wait until the proper time to receive God's gift of sex in marriage.

CAN AN ENGAGEMENT BE BROKEN?

Engagements should be entered into sincerely and carefully, and should be broken only for very good reason. In New Testament times, breaking an engagement or betrothal was a legal act like a divorce. Grounds would be necessary—such as when Joseph thought he would end his betrothal to Mary because she was pregnant (Matt. 1:18–19). Sometimes during an engagement, something serious comes to light, such as hidden past relationships or sexual history, ongoing besetting sins of lust or anger, etc. Engagements that were made too hastily are often broken. Perhaps the parties mistook infatuation for love. Sometimes one of them has found someone else, which may indicate a character fault that is better discovered before marriage rather than after.

If one party entertains serious doubts about going through with the marriage, that person should make every effort to work out the troubling problems and issues. The couple should seek godly counsel and take time to try to solve their problems. If one of them still wants to break the engagement, that person must be honest. It is better to release someone from a commitment than to try to force the person to marry against his or her will. The one who has caused the breakup should seek the forgiveness of those who have been affected: the former fiancée, family members, friends, etc.

THE WEDDING MATTERS

While it is most important to use the time of engagement to prepare for the marriage, the wedding itself is significant, too. The essence of a wedding is the public making of vows between the bride and the groom as they enter into the covenant of marriage. The vows should express the commitment of the bride and groom to lovingly and graciously fulfill their biblical roles in the marriage until death parts them. Many of the traditional vows do an excellent job of summarizing the biblical principles of marriage. Christian weddings also provide an excellent opportunity to proclaim how marriage is a picture of Christ's love for the church both for the encouragement of the believers and for the evangelizing of any unbelieving family and friends who are in attendance.

SUMMARY

The period of engagement is primarily a time for marriage preparation, both practically and spiritually. The practical arrangements can be a test of how the couple works together as a team, sometimes in stressful situations. The frantic busyness of preparation for a wedding should not distract a couple from preparing themselves spiritually for marriage. In addition, they should be careful not to indulge in the privileges of marriage before entering into the covenant of marriage.

— QUESTIONS FOR REFLECTION —

1. What is the purpose of engagement?
2. What are the content and the benefits of premarital counseling?
3. What should be done if one partner is getting cold feet?
4. When is it permissible to break an engagement?
5. What amount of physical affection is appropriate for an engaged couple?

C. HAVING A SUCCESSFUL MARRIAGE

11

WHAT IS THE KEY TO KEEPING A MARRIAGE STRONG?

The gospel of Jesus Christ is the key to keeping a marriage strong. After Paul offers instructions concerning the roles of the husband and wife, he writes, "This mystery is great; but I am speaking with reference to Christ and the church" (Eph. 5:32). The deeper your knowledge and experience of God's love for you in Christ, the more you will be motivated and empowered to show merciful, gracious, and sacrificial love to your spouse.

YOU MUST FIRST KNOW THE LOVE OF CHRIST

If you haven't experienced the love of Christ, you won't be able to love as he does. "We love, because He first loved us" (1 John 4:19). For this reason, Paul spends the first three chapters of Ephesians reminding the believers of Christ's love for them in the gospel. God chose us in Christ to be adopted as sons of God (Eph. 1:3–6). He has graciously redeemed and forgiven us through Christ's blood and sealed us with the Holy Spirit (1:7–14). We who were dead in our sin have been made alive together with Christ, having been justified by faith as the free gift of God (2:1–10). We have been made a part of God's household (2:11–22) and heirs of God's promise (3:1–13). Only after this extensive description of God's love for us does Paul instruct husbands to love their wives, just as Christ loved the church (5:25). A husband fails to love his wife because he has lost sight of Christ's love for him. What he needs most is not techniques or rules, but a heart awed and transformed by Christ's love for him.

If you want to have a joyful, loving marriage, pray for yourself (and your spouse) the same prayer that Paul says for the Ephesians: "For this reason I bow my knees before the Father, from whom every family in heaven and on earth derives its name, that He would grant you, according to the riches of His glory, to be strengthened with power through His Spirit in the inner man, so that Christ may dwell in your hearts through faith; and that you, being rooted and grounded in love, may be able to comprehend with all the saints what is the breadth and length and height and depth, and to know the love of Christ which surpasses knowledge, that you may be filled up to all the fullness of God" (Eph. 3:14–19). Then participate in the answer to this prayer by daily studying God's Word and meditating on the greatness of Christ's love for you. Such love will motivate and empower you to show love to your spouse.

The best thing you can do for your marriage is to grow closer to Jesus. The more you understand and appreciate God's love for you in Christ, the better your marriage will be as you reflect that love to your spouse. A strong marriage in which both partners are showing Christlike love to each other will help both of them to better appreciate God's gracious love. One reason that a Christian would never want to marry an unbeliever is that a non-Christian does not know the love of Christ and, as a result, is incapable of expressing Christlike love.

LOVE IS FOUNDED ON GRACE, NOT LAW

Most human relationships, including marriage, are implicitly governed by a kind of law that says, "I will treat you as you deserve. If you are kind to me and meet my expectations, I will be kind to you. But if you treat me badly, I will either withdraw from you or do unto you as you have done to me." To the natural man, this approach seems both just and reasonable. But when this worldly approach is applied in marriage, it can lead to strife, anger, bitterness, separation, and divorce.

In contrast, believers will recall with thanksgiving that this is not how God has dealt with us. Though we are great sinners, God has shown us mercy and grace. "He saved us, not on the basis of deeds which we have done in righteousness, but according to His mercy, by the washing of regeneration and renewing by the Holy Spirit, whom He poured out upon us richly through Jesus Christ our Savior" (Titus 3:5–6). He calls us to love one another in like manner: "Be imitators of God, as beloved children; and walk in love, just as Christ also loved you and gave Himself up for us" (Eph. 5:1–2).

An honest assessment of one's own need for this kind of love and grace is key to extending such grace to others. According to Tim Keller, "The gospel is this: We are more sinful and flawed in ourselves than we ever dared believe, yet at the very same time we are more loved and accepted in Jesus Christ than we ever dared hope."[1] A true Christian recognizes that he or she is a great sinner (1 Tim. 1:15) and is grateful for the mercy that God has shown. Awareness of personal sin helps the believer to be free from being judgmental about the sins of others. Moreover, Christians are aware that they have married a fellow sinner and are not shocked when he or she sins. Instead of reacting in anger, they can remember God's mercy to them and then seek to gently restore their spouse (Gal. 6:1), just as God graciously forgives and restores them when they sin (1 John 1:8–9). In showing such grace, they are imitators of God, whose kindness leads us to repentance (Rom. 2:4).

KEEP FIGHTING FOR LOVE

Love infused with gospel grace does not just happen. Husbands and wives must work continually to show each other this kind of love. Paul encourages us that if we walk by the Spirit, we will not carry out our fleshly desires, which include fleshly strife and anger (Gal. 5:16, 19–21). Rather, we will be characterized by the fruit of the Spirit,

---

1. Timothy Keller and Kathy Keller, *The Meaning of Marriage* (New York: Penguin, 2011), 48.

which includes love, joy, peace, patience, kindness, goodness, faithfulness, gentleness, and self-control (5:22–24). Such qualities will bring joy and harmony to any marriage. But Paul warns us that it is not easy to maintain one's walk by the Spirit: "The flesh sets its desire against the Spirit, and the Spirit against the flesh; for these are in opposition to one another, so that you may not do the things that you please" (5:17).

If you don't feel love for your spouse—or, worse, find yourself guilty of fleshly words and deeds, including jealousy, disputes, and dissensions—you will be tempted to blame your spouse. The real problem, however, is that you have stopped walking by the Spirit, and instead you have given in to the flesh. Your spouse's sin may tempt you, but it cannot make you fleshly. Paul writes elsewhere, "No temptation has overtaken you but such as is common to man; and God is faithful, who will not allow you to be tempted beyond what you are able, but with the temptation will provide the way of escape also, so that you will be able to endure it" (1 Cor. 10:13). No matter what situation in which you find yourself, you can choose to continue to walk in the Spirit. Then you will bear the Spirit's fruit and not carry out the deeds of the flesh. Rather than waiting for your spouse to change, you must get right with God, remembering your sin and his grace and mercy to you.

COVENANT LOVE ENDURES

The vows by which we enter into the marriage covenant reflect the depth of the commitment we are making: "For better and for worse, for richer and for poorer, in sickness and in health, until God by death parts us." During the course of a marriage, circumstances change. You each will change through the experiences of having and raising children, experiencing trials, aging, caring for sick parents, etc. One spouse may become physically disabled or be diagnosed with a mental illness. Your spouse may lose his job or lose the family savings in a bad investment scheme. You both may endure the trials of wayward children. People also change over the years. Some change physically by becoming obese. Others experience personality changes as they struggle with depression, anxiety, or anger. It has been said that you don't marry just one person—that is, the man or woman who stands at the altar with you—you marry several people,[2] or whom your spouse will become through the phases of your life together.

A Christian entering into marriage commits to love her spouse, not merely for what she thinks he is or hopes he will become, but for who he is and whatever he will become. This reflects the kind of eternal unchanging love with which God has loved us. He promises never to leave us or forsake us (Heb. 13:5). The world, through movies and songs, creates the false expectation that love will be easy when you find that special someone. Along with the belief that romantic love should be easy is the idea that if it isn't, then someone else must be out there for you (your true soul mate). The reality is that you are a sinful person who has been joined to a fellow sinner. Only with the help of God's Spirit, and in light of his enduring love for you, will you be able to endure in your love for your spouse.

LOVE DESCRIBED

First Corinthians 13 is Paul's famous love chapter. In it he explains love in its purest form: "Love is patient, love is kind and is not jealous; love does not brag and is not arrogant, does not act unbecomingly; it does not seek its own, is not provoked, does not take into account a wrong suffered, does not rejoice in unrighteousness, but rejoices with the truth; bears all things, believes all things, hopes all things, endures all things" (1 Cor. 13:4–7). Only one person has perfectly loved in this

---

2. Lewis Smedes: "When I married my wife, I had hardly a smidgen of sense for what I was getting into with her. How could I know how much she would change over 25 years? How could I know how much I would change? My wife has lived with at least five different men since we were wed—and each of the five has been me. The connecting link with my old self has always been the memory of the name I took on back there: 'I am he who will be there with you.' When we slough off *that* name, lose *that* identity, we can hardly find ourselves again. And the bonds that connect us to others will be frayed to breaking" (http://www.christianitytoday.com/ct/2002/decemberweb-only/12-16-56.0.html).

way. Paul is describing Christ's love for us. Go through each phrase, and think about how Jesus has loved you in this way. Then go through the passage again, and think about ways in which you can imitate Jesus' love as you care for the spouse he has given you.

SUMMARY

The one key to a successful marriage is the gospel. If your love seems to be waning, your need is not for your spouse to change, but for you to better grasp Christ's love for you. Your goal should be that your spouse would look at you and say, "How you treat me reminds me of how God loves me." When both spouses strive to love in this way, with the help of the Holy Spirit, marriage is a beautiful picture of the love between Christ and his church.

— QUESTIONS FOR REFLECTION —

1. Why is the gospel the key to a successful marriage?
2. How do non-Christians get along in marriage without the gospel?
3. What would you say to a man who says that he no longer feels love for his wife?
4. What would you say to a woman who is planning to leave her husband because they have grown apart?
5. What can one do in practical terms to better grasp Christ's love?

12

WHAT ARE THE RESPONSIBILITIES OF A HUSBAND?

A number of years ago, I received a phone call from a friend who said that he desperately needed to speak with me. When I met with him, his appearance was haggard and he was in tears. He explained that his wife was thinking of leaving him for another man. His response to this situation, though, surprised me. Rather than being angry and self-righteous, he was broken. "I know that I have failed to love my wife as I ought and that I haven't been a good spiritual leader. This is as much my fault as hers," he told me. "If I had been a better husband, this would have never happened. Teach me to be a godly husband." By God's grace, my friend repented of his own sins in the marriage and went about trying to win back his wife. By God's grace, their marriage was restored. Their story demonstrates the power that a husband's Christlike love can have to transform (change) his wife.

All of a husband's duties can be summed up in one simple command: "Love your wives, just as Christ also loved the church and gave Himself up for her" (Eph. 5:25). The best thing a man can do for his wife is to study and revel in Christ's sacrificial love for him, so that he can reflect that love in his marriage.

LOVE HER UNCONDITIONALLY

The world has cheapened the meaning of love so that it is merely an emotional feeling or a sexual passion. Such so-called love is dependent on the worthiness of the beloved, essentially saying, "I love you because of what you do for me." Many men treat their wives in a manner similar to how they think their wives are treating them. If a woman's outward appearance fades or if her performance as a wife does not meet her husband's expectations, his love falters. Christ, by contrast, loved you when you were not worthy to be loved. According to John, "In this is love, not that we loved God, but that He loved us and sent His Son to be the propitiation for our sins. Beloved, if God so loved us, we also ought to love one another" (1 John 4:10–11). Paul declares, "But God demonstrates His own love toward us, in that while we were yet sinners, Christ died for us" (Rom. 5:8). In addition, he reminds us that when we were God's enemies, we were reconciled to God through Christ's death (5:10). Gospel love treats us as if we had perfectly kept God's law, even though we are sinners. In the same way, a husband should treat his wife as if she was a perfect wife, even though she sometimes lets him down. When there is a conflict, the husband should imitate Christ by taking the initiative to bring about reconciliation, instead of waiting for his wife to come to him.

Some men might object that they often don't feel like loving in this way. Christlike love, however, is not merely a feeling, but also a commitment to the good of the other person, regardless of how one feels. We see at Gethsemane that Jesus did not feel like going to the cross. But he went anyway because of his great love for the Father and for his people. In like manner, much more than performing an outward duty, a husband should care deeply for the wife whom the Lord has given him. There is nothing that she wants more from her marriage than to know that she is loved and cherished. Few things are sadder than an unloved wife. A husband who initiates in love will help his wife to respond in love, reflecting what John says about our love for Christ, "We love, because He first loved us" (1 John 4:19).

LOVE HER SACRIFICIALLY

Many men are enthusiastic about the Bible's teachings on marriage roles because they think that they have been appointed as the boss of the family. Such men typically claim to have great expertise concerning what Paul teaches about submission in Ephesians 5:22–24, but they show little grasp of what it means for them to love in a Christlike way. As Jesus gave himself up for his bride, the church, a husband is to sacrificially give himself up in love for his earthly bride. Paul is not merely explaining that a husband should be willing to die for his wife in the unlikely event that she is tied to train tracks or someone is shooting at her. Rather, Paul's admonition is applied in the day-to-day sacrifice of getting up at three o'clock in the morning to help with the baby, giving up a Saturday golf game to assist with a project around the house, or getting up earlier on Sunday morning to help get the children ready for church. Robertson McQuilkin exemplified such sacrificial love when he resigned from his position as president of Columbia Bible College to care for his wife, who was suffering from Alzheimer's disease. He writes, "When the time came, the decision was firm. It took no great calculation. It was a matter of integrity. Had I not promised 42 years before, 'in sickness and in health, . . . till death do us part?'"[1] When a man commits to marriage, he promises to have a Christlike attitude as he humbly puts his wife's needs ahead of his own (Phil. 2:3–5).

Yes, the husband is the head, but God gives authority for the purpose of service. John tells us that this is why Jesus washed the disciples' feet: "Jesus, knowing that the Father had given all things into His hands, and that He had come forth from God and was going back to God, got up from supper, and laid aside His garments" (John 13:3–4). As Jesus contemplated his unique status and authority, he humbly served those under his authority. Elsewhere, our Lord declares his ultimate expression of humble service to his people: "The Son of Man did not come to be served, but to serve, and to give His life a ransom for many" (Mark 10:45). A husband who selfishly exercises dominion in his marriage, expecting everything to revolve around him, from how the money is spent to what the family watches on television, distorts what should be a picture of Christ's love. Jesus did not use

1. http://www.christianitytoday.com/ct/2004/februaryweb-only/2-9-11.0.html.

his authority to tell his disciples to wash his feet; instead, he humbled himself to care for them. A husband who understands this will sacrifice his desires for how he would prefer to use his time and money to ensure that his wife is well cared for. He will not try to calculate a division of labor in the home that seems fair to him, but rather will be willing to do more than his share as an expression of love for his wife. Such love will help her to respond with greater love and respect toward him.

LOVE HER WITH A PURIFYING LOVE

Some men would like to change their wives, typically for their own selfish reasons. Paul teaches us that by loving your wife in a Christlike way, you can change her in ways that will matter for eternity. Christ gave himself up for his church, "so that He might sanctify her, having cleansed her by the washing of water with the word, that He might present to Himself the church in all her glory, having no spot or wrinkle or any such thing; but that she would be holy and blameless" (Eph. 5:26–27). He additionally expresses his love for us by working in our lives to make us more holy (Titus 2:14). In the same way, a husband should strive to love his wife in a way that will make her more beautiful spiritually. He should pursue her spiritual growth by praying and reading Scripture with her, by involving the family in a sound church where she can be under the means of grace, and by encouraging her to use her spiritual gifts to serve others. In his desire to maintain her purity, he will be careful not to expose her to worldly entertainment that might pollute her mind. Moreover, he can do this in practical ways by helping with the children or household tasks, so that she has personal time for the Word, prayer, and fellowship.

A Christlike husband will also have the courage to make godly decisions, which may go against his wife's preferences. For example, if the wife wants to go deeply into debt for a non-necessity, the husband may need to have the courage to say no (Prov. 22:7). Or if the wife wants to change churches for unbiblical reasons to go to a church that is less sound, the husband must have the courage to stand firm. Both

Adam and Abraham unwisely listened to their wives when they should have held their ground (Gen. 3:6; 16:2). Since then, many men have abdicated their spiritual headship in the home to keep the peace. Most godly women will respect a husband who will not let himself be pushed around concerning matters of principle. Sadly, numerous men stand their ground when they should give in (on selfish matters) and give in when they should stand firm.

When I consider Ephesians 5:26–27, I remember how Christ entrusted me with my wife on our wedding day, realizing that one day, through death, I will have to give her back to him. My job is to work with him so that she will be more spiritually spotless, holy, and beautiful than she was when he gave her to me many years ago.

LOVE HER AS YOU LOVE YOURSELF

Husbands ought to love their wives as dearly as they love themselves. Even if a man's fleshly body is not as handsome, strong, and thin as it used to be, he feeds it and cares for it if it is sick because it is the only body he will ever have. In the same way, Paul instructs us, a man should spare no effort in caring for his one and only wife: "So husbands ought also to love their own wives as their own bodies. He who loves his own wife loves himself; for no one ever hated his own flesh, but nourishes and cherishes it, just as Christ also does the church, because we are members of His body" (Eph. 5:28–30). In this passage, Paul is not commanding us to love ourselves; rather, he is assuming that we do love ourselves unconditionally, as is demonstrated by our efforts to care for our bodies. As it is unnatural to abuse one's own body, "for no one ever hated his own flesh" (5:29a), it is unnatural and self-destructive for a man to mistreat his wife. A man should care for the needs of his wife because she is one flesh with him (Gen. 2:23–24).

LOVE HER WITH AN AFFECTIONATE LOVE

Jesus has provided richly for you with redemption and forgiveness (Eph. 1:7–9). He has raised you up and seated you with him in the heavenly places (2:5–6). He has made you a fellow heir, a member of his body, and a partaker of his promises, and has given you access to God's presence (3:6, 12). He has given you spiritual gifts and a new nature (4:11, 20–23). In the same way, a husband should try to generously meet his wife's needs.

One aspect of this is caring for her material needs by working hard to provide and being generous with her. Some husbands are poor providers because they lack drive and ambition. Others act as if their headship in the family entitles them to control the family finances and to use them primarily for personal benefit. But a godly husband will do what it takes to care for his family. A Christlike husband will make sure that his wife has what she needs in terms of clothes (including the children's wardrobe) and household items, and that she enjoys freedom (within reason) to spend money on others.

A wife needs far more than material nourishment. A husband is responsible to meet her emotional needs as well. The most common complaint I hear from women in the counseling office is that their husbands do not connect with them on a personal level. Some men have the attitude that because they work hard at providing materially for their wives, the women should be grateful and should not be upset when their husbands aren't interested in talking with them. Then, when bedtime comes, these same guys will be surprised that their wives lack enthusiasm for sexual intimacy. Obviously, they are missing the big picture.

God has designed marriage to be a covenant of companionship. Your wife wants you to be best friends. Her need for communication may be greater than yours. She needs you to listen to her with interest and open your heart to her.[2] Romance is even more important to her after the wedding than it was before the ceremony. She yearns to be cherished. She wants to be the delight of your heart and your eyes, just as God rejoiced over Israel (Isa. 62:5b) and Christ rejoices over his bride, the church.

---

2. See chapter 15 below.

LOVE HER WITH AN UNDERSTANDING LOVE

Men will often joke that they can't understand women. My observation is that many husbands don't understand their wives because they haven't tried very hard to study the subject. Peter tells husbands what God expects them to do: "Live with your wives in an understanding way, as with someone weaker, since she is a woman; and show her honor as a fellow heir of the grace of life, so that your prayers will not be hindered" (1 Peter 3:7). A man must recognize that women are different in general from men both physically and emotionally, and that his wife is different from him in her own unique ways. A husband who loves his wife will work to learn what touches, words, and gifts bring her joy. He will seek to understand what their sexual union means to her and will seek to serve her in that area. If she yearns to have children, he will sympathize and do what he can to fulfill that desire.

According to Peter, she is a weaker vessel (1 Peter 3:7). This does not mean that she is inferior, but rather that she is more delicate. To expand on Peter's illustration, we have in our kitchen some very sturdy plastic drinking vessels, which can be safely put through the dishwasher and survive some rough treatment. On the other hand, we also have some fine crystal, which is quite fragile. We must wash it by hand, and I fear that it may crack if someone in the room sneezes too loudly. The crystal is not inferior to the other vessels. Actually, it is more valuable. But it is also more delicate and should be handled with care. A husband should handle his wife with care—like crystal. He must be patient with her weaknesses and sensitive to ways in which she is different. He must be sensitive to how his anger, or even his disapproval, may tempt her to be hurt and fearful.

Furthermore, Peter states that a husband should honor his wife. While you are the head of the family, she is your equal spiritually—a fellow heir of the grace of life (see also Gal. 3:28). Treat her with respect as the husband of the virtuous woman trusts his wife (Prov. 31:11). Seek her thoughts and opinions. Don't micromanage her. Instead, give her great freedom in her realms of life, just as the husband in Proverbs 31 trusts the woman to run the household, to do works of charity, and even to run a small business (Prov. 31:16, 18, 20). Your godly treatment of your wife in all these areas is so important that Peter warns that your relationship with God will be affected by hindered prayers if you mistreat her (1 Peter 3:7b).

LOVE HER WITH AN AFFIRMING LOVE

Many husbands are very critical. They manage their homes by exception, ignoring what is done right, while carefully pointing out ways their wives fall short of their expectations. Constant criticism is like a cancer that eats away at a marriage. In contrast, the husband in Proverbs 31 praises his wife, saying, "Many daughters have done nobly, but you excel them all" (v. 29). Your wife is not perfect, but neither are you. Make every effort to affirm to her the good that God is doing for you and others through her. Ray Ortlund writes, "Deep in the heart of every wife is the self-doubt that wonders, 'Do I please him? Am I what he dreamed of and longed for? Will he love me to the end? Am I safe with this man I married? Will he cast me off? Even if we go the distance will he get tired of me?' A wise husband will understand that that uncertainty, that question, is way down deep in his wife's heart. And he will spend his life speaking into it gently and tenderly communicating it to her in many ways, 'Darling, you are the one I want. I cherish you. I rejoice over you, as no other. . . . I love the thought of growing old together with you, hand in hand all the way. I will hold you close to my heart until my dying day.'"[3]

SUMMARY

Husbands are to love their wives with a love that is unconditional, sacrificial, purifying, nurturing, cherishing, and understanding. This calling to love our wives as Christ has loved us can be overwhelming. Who is sufficient for these things? Who can live up to such

---

3. Ray Ortlund, *Marriage and the Mystery of the Gospel* (Wheaton, IL: Crossway, 2016), 101–2.

a standard? This should humble us before God and our wives. We need much grace. Moreover, we have hope that as we better know and experience Christ's love for us, we will better be able to express his love to our wives.

— QUESTIONS FOR REFLECTION —

1. In what ways is the love of a husband to resemble the love of Christ?
2. How can a husband's love purify his wife?
3. Does the responsibility of a husband to nourish his wife mean that he is to be the primary provider?
4. What would you say to a husband who claims that his wife is too hard to love?
5. How can a husband grow in his ability to love his wife?

13

WHAT ARE THE RESPONSIBILITIES OF A WIFE?

When I counsel couples, it is common for the wife to come in, hoping that I will change her husband so that he will love her and treat her the way that Jesus cares for the church (as described in the previous chapter). I will often tell such women that the Bible teaches them how they can change their husbands, but not through the means that they might expect. Just as God can use a husband to change (sanctify) his wife—not by bullying her, but by loving her in a Christlike way (Eph. 5:25–27)—God can use a wife to sanctify (change) her husband—not by nagging him, but by quietly treating him far better than he deserves (1 Peter 3:1–2).

MUST WOMEN SUBMIT TO THEIR HUSBANDS?

When reading Paul's words, "Wives, be subject to your own husbands, as to the Lord" (Eph. 5:22), some assume that he was a male chauvinist who was a product of his backward patriarchal culture. This cannot be the case, though, because this command is a part of God's Word. His design for marriage is applicable in all times and cultures because his Word is infallible and timeless: "The grass withers, the flower fades, but the word of our God stands forever" (Isa. 40:8; see also 2 Tim. 3:16–17 and 2 Peter 1:20–21). God established the marriage roles of male headship and female submission from creation when

94

he made woman to be a suitable helper for man (Gen. 2:18). Paul further explains, "For man does not originate from woman, but woman from man; for indeed man was not created for the woman's sake, but woman for the man's sake" (1 Cor. 11:8–9; see also 1 Tim. 2:13). We do not have the right to redefine marriage or the roles that God has established for men and women within marriage.[1]

Many are offended at the concept of submission because they misunderstand what the Bible actually teaches about the role of the wife. They conjure up ideas of nasty, domineering men, making women wear burkas and not allowing them to drive.[2] The primary objection raised against the submission of wives to their husbands is based on an unbiblical concept of significance. It is assumed that for wives to be equal, they must have authority at least equal to that of their husbands. Jesus addresses this in Matthew 20:25–28, as he speaks to his disciples: "You know that the rulers of the Gentiles lord it over them, and their great men exercise authority over them. It is not this way among you, but whoever wishes to become great among you shall be your servant, and whoever wishes to be first among you shall be your slave; just as the Son of Man did not come to be served, but to serve, and to give His life a ransom for many." Jesus overturns the worldly idea of greatness that one must be in charge to be significant. Christ demonstrated his greatness by being a servant.

Scripture teaches that men and women are spiritually equal (Gal. 3:28; 1 Peter 3:7), but are assigned different roles in the marriage relationship. God has established these principles of authority and order in numerous other human relationships as well—including parents with

---

1. For an excellent defense of the complementary roles of men and women in the home and in the church, and for a refutation of arguments put forward by those taking the egalitarian position, see Wayne Grudem, ed., *Biblical Foundations for Manhood and Womanhood* (Wheaton, IL: Crossway, 2002).

2. "The Quran is not structured as is the Bible. The Sura, 'women,' the fourth of 114 Suras, tells a Muslim man 'Marry such women as seems good to you, two, three, four.' And 'those (wives) you fear may be rebellious admonish; banish them to their couches and beat them.'" Ray Ortlund, *Marriage and the Mystery of the Gospel* (Wheaton, IL: Crossway, 2016), 82–83.

children, church leaders with members, employers with employees, and government with citizens (Rom. 13:1; Eph. 6:1; Heb. 13:17). Jesus himself submitted to his earthly parents, though he was superior to them (Luke 2:51). Paul makes the strongest argument proving that people can be equal while one assumes a role subordinate to that of the other. He writes, "But I want you to understand that Christ is the head of every man, and the man is the head of a woman, and God is the head of Christ" (1 Cor. 11:3).[3] God the Father and God the Son are equal, but the Father is the head of Christ. The Father sends the Son into the world, and the Son submits to the Father's will in all things (Luke 22:42; John 4:34; 5:19; 17:4). The submission of the Son is not demeaning. Instead, it is his glory. In the same way, a wife's submission does not imply that her role is less important than that of her husband. Just as the husband should be Christlike in his leadership (Eph. 5:25–30), the wife has the privilege of being Christlike in her role as a helper who willingly serves her husband.

WHAT DOES SUBMISSION LOOK LIKE?

The biblical call for wives to submit to their husbands is clear: "Wives be subject to your own husbands, as to the Lord. For the husband is the head of the wife, as Christ also is the head of the church, He Himself being the Savior of the body. But as the church is subject to Christ, so also the wives ought to be to their husbands in everything" (Eph. 5:22–24; see also Col. 3:18; 1 Peter 3:1–6). From these passages, we read that the motivation for a wife to subordinate herself to her husband's leadership is not his worthiness. Rather, it is ultimately for the Lord's sake that she submits, trusting that Christ will lead her through her husband.

A wife's submission to her husband's leadership is to be comprehensive, "in everything" (Eph. 5:24b), which includes how she manages the household, her career, the children, her physical appearance,

---

3. Grudem addresses the correct interpretation of "head" (*Biblical Foundations for Manhood and Womanhood*, 145–202).

etc. This does not mean that the husband will micromanage her in all these areas. Nor does it mean that the wife has no say in family decisions. A wise husband will seek the wise counsel of his wife. Ideally, he will trust her and give her freedom to use her God-given abilities to manage her life and the household, just as the husband in Proverbs 31 trusts the noble woman to manage her responsibilities wisely: "The heart of her husband trusts in her. . . . She opens her mouth in wisdom, and the teaching of kindness is on her tongue" (vv. 11a, 26). Biblical submission means that after a couple has discussed an issue, the husband has the responsibility under God to make the final decision. A godly wife will try to work for the success of whatever decision her husband makes, as opposed to an unsubmissive wife, who might be tempted to grumble, nag, or undermine her husband's leadership.

Submission does not only mean externally following orders. In a healthy marriage, the husband will not frequently tell his wife what to do. Rather, she will gladly seek to help and please him without being asked. A godly wife's submission will not merely be outward, but she will also have an attitude of respect toward her husband. She will love him with a gracious love (Titus 2:4). She will be loyal to him, not slandering him to those outside the home. According to Proverbs, "An excellent wife is the crown of her husband, but she who shames him is like rottenness in his bones" (Prov. 12:4).

GOD HAS CALLED THE WIFE
TO BE THE HELPER

Just as the Lord made Eve to be Adam's helper to partner with him in his calling to subdue and fill the earth (Gen. 2:18), God calls wives to help their husbands fulfill their callings in the areas of vocation, family, and ministry. As Eve was created to complete Adam, a wife is to complement her husband physically, emotionally, socially, spiritually, and intellectually. A wise wife will constantly keep in mind that an important part of her role is to help her husband to flourish in that to which he is devoting his life. This can be done through wise counsel and encouragement. She will work hard to make their home a place of joy and refuge for him, too (Titus 2:5).

A wife has a very powerful influence over her husband, which can be used either for good or for evil. Few men can refuse to do what their wives want, even when they are wrong (see Gen. 3:6; 16:2). Conversely, a wife's respect and affirmation are a powerful motivator. A godly wife "does him good and not evil all the days of her life" (Prov. 31:12). Proverbs 31 implies that the husband of this excellent wife is successful, has an excellent reputation, and sits with the elders of the city because of the kind of wife God has given him (v. 23).

SUBMISSION CAN BE HARD

Even though submission is part of God's design, it can be hard to put into practice. The Lord warned Eve, "Your desire will be for your husband, and he will rule over you" (Gen. 3:16b). The word *desire* here means a desire to take control (as it is used about sin's desire to rule Cain in Genesis 4:7). Because of the fall, wives will be tempted to usurp their husbands' headship and to take over the family. In addition, husbands will be tempted to rule over their wives in a harsh manner. It takes a great work of God in a woman's heart for her to overcome her fleshly desires and to follow her husband's lead. Some wives might suggest that submission isn't so bad if you like the way the other person is leading. The test of submission comes when a wife doesn't agree with her husband's decisions, or when she believes that he is acting selfishly. The struggle is intensified when the wife believes that the husband's bad decision may affect the children. A woman in this position must learn not to be fearful, but to trust God (1 Peter 3:6; see also 1 Cor. 7:14b).

Some wives experience the opposite struggle. They would like for the husband to lead, but he is passive. In such a case, the most important thing for the wife to do is to maintain an attitude of grace and to guard against becoming bitter and judgmental toward him. Wives can severely damage their marriages by comparing their husbands with other supposedly more godly men. They should try to learn how to help them, while resisting the temptation to fill the leadership vacuum by taking over.

Many women are married to men who are hard to respect. Some men can become lazy, selfish, or even cruel. These wives must remember that they care for their husbands and follow their leadership—not because they are worthy, but for the sake of Christ, who has placed the husband in authority.

Whatever the situation, a wife in a difficult marriage must learn to depend on the Lord for her joy and satisfaction, rather than expecting to find ultimate fulfillment from her husband. Such a woman can flourish, even though she has to endure a drought in her marriage, because she is like a tree planted by the water (Jer. 17:5–8). She trusts God to take care of her and her children and does not live in fear (1 Peter 3:6b).

DOES SUBMISSION HAVE LIMITATIONS?

Does comprehensive submission mean that there are no limitations to what a wife must do? If a husband asks his wife to sin, her first loyalty is to God, whom she cannot dishonor for the sake of her husband. For instance, a wife should not lie for her husband (e.g., sign a false tax return). Or an ungodly husband may attempt to forbid his wife to read her Bible or go to church. Scripture says that we need God's Word (Ps. 1) and that we must not forsake assembling with other believers to worship God and to receive the means of grace (Heb. 10:25). Her situation would be like that of the apostles, who, when the authorities told them to no longer preach Christ, replied, "We must obey God rather than men" (Acts 5:29b). When a wife believes that she must oppose her husband's wishes for the Lord's sake, she should do so in a way that is respectful and kind.

Scripture does not obligate a wife to endure physical abuse or sexual unfaithfulness.[4] Husbands who have been involved in such sins often try to misuse their authority to prevent their wives from telling

4. See chapters 32–35.

others or from obtaining outside help. When a husband is involved in serious sin, a godly wife has the responsibility to lovingly correct him (Matt. 18:15; Gal. 6:1).[5] Additionally, she has the right to seek outside help if her husband will not repent (Matt. 18:16–20; Rom. 13:1–7, if necessary).[6] If a wife senses that she and/or her children are in physical danger, she should do what is needed to ensure their safety.

SUBMISSION IS VOLUNTARY

Numerous immature men misuse the biblical passages regarding submission to sinfully dominate their wives. This is a horrible misrepresentation of the Christlike love that a husband is supposed to show toward his wife. These men need to realize that the biblical call to submission is addressed to wives—not to their husbands. A wife should choose to follow her husband's leadership out of respect and love for the Lord. Nowhere are husbands told to subjugate their wives. In contrast to parents, who are authorized to force their small children to obey (Prov. 22:15), a husband is not called or permitted to force his wife to submit. If she resists his leadership, he should appeal to her kindly and then, if she still refuses, must entrust her to God. In some such cases, counsel or mediation may be appropriate (see chapter 18 below).

GOD MAY USE A WIFE'S SUBMISSION
TO CHANGE HER HUSBAND

Scripture does give hope for women whose husbands are disobedient to God's Word.[7] Peter writes, "In the same way, you wives, be submissive to your own husbands, so that even if any of them are disobedient to the word, they may be won without a word by the behavior

5. See chapter 17.

6. Jesus' instruction to bring one or two more does not say, "Unless the sinner is your husband, in which case you should just let him keep on sinning."

7. My understanding is that the "disobedient" husband could be an unbeliever, or a professing Christian who is walking in disobedience/unbelief.

of their wives, as they observe your chaste and respectful behavior" (1 Peter 3:1–2). Many women are tempted to think that they can change their husbands by nagging them. While such pressure may sometimes obtain short-term results (e.g., the husband will take some action, such as a household chore, just to make the nagging stop), it does not produce the desired heart change. Peter states that God may use a wife's quiet submission as a means to win a disobedient husband to Christ. "Without a word" does not mean that a wife is never free to speak to her husband. In a good marriage, a godly husband will be eager to know what his wife thinks and will seek her counsel. The reference here is to a husband who is in a state of disobedience and has made it clear that he doesn't want to hear any more from his wife at the time.

"In the same way" (1 Peter 3:1a) is significant because it refers back to how Christ humbly suffered under unjust authority (2:21–25). Just as we have been won through Christ's righteous response to suffering, an ungodly husband may be won by a wife who, instead of returning evil for evil, treats her husband far better than he deserves. Such submission is the opposite of what the flesh will tell us to do. The flesh says, "If I am good to him when he is bad to me, he will just walk all over me. I need to show him that he can't get away with this." Faith says, "I will love him for the Lord's sake, just as Christ loved me when I was unworthy, and pray that God will work in his heart, even if it takes time." Augustine wrote concerning his mother, Monica, that through her service to her unbelieving husband, she did all she could to win him and gained him for the Lord in the end.[8]

A WORD TO SINGLE WOMEN

You are free to remain single if this is how you think that you can best serve the Lord (1 Cor. 7:34). When you want to marry, you are choosing to accept your God-given role in marriage. When you select

---

8. http://webcache.googleusercontent.com/search?q=cache:Uc8jVhv05zsJ:www .sacred-texts.com/chr/augconf/aug09.htm+&cd=2&hl=en&ct=clnk&gl=us.

a husband, you are deciding to enter into the passenger seat of the marriage, while trusting that he will drive you both safely down the right roads to the proper destination. Therefore, be very careful whom you marry.

SUMMARY

The serpent persuaded the first woman, Eve, to reject God's ways and to assume headship. In the same way, the world, the flesh, and the devil conspire together to tempt women to reject their God-given role to follow their husbands' leadership. It requires faith to follow God's ways, trusting that he has established the roles in the marriage relationship and that he will bless those who obey him.

— QUESTIONS FOR REFLECTION —

1. How would you answer someone who says that submission of wives was merely a cultural issue and that it no longer applies today because men and women are equal?
2. How is a wife's submission Christlike?
3. How can a wife be a helper to her husband? How can a godly wife change her husband?
4. How should a godly couple make major decisions?
5. When does a wife have a right to seek outside help when her husband is acting sinfully?

14

WHAT MUST BE DONE TO PROTECT A MARRIAGE?

Almost every marriage begins with joy as the newlyweds anticipate sharing life together. Sadly, not all couples live happily ever after. More than 40 percent of marriages end in divorce. Other couples remain married, but drift apart emotionally because of bitterness or mutual indifference. They share a name and a home, but not a life. What can a couple do to preserve the joyful, loving intimacy of their marriage?

DO NOT TAKE EACH OTHER FOR GRANTED

Couples who are courting or engaged typically spend every spare minute together and can't bear to be apart for long. But often, after they are married, each one becomes so caught up in career, children, hobbies, sports, and other activities that the marriage relationship is neglected. Very gradually, the couple drifts apart. While there may not be much open conflict, the spark is missing. The wife may notice that something is wrong, only to have her husband tell her that she is worried about nothing.

A new marriage, like a new car, requires regular maintenance. It may look and work great today, but without sufficient maintenance, sooner or later it will break down. A husband and wife need to spend time growing closer to each other and enjoying each other. More romance is necessary after the marriage than before the ceremony.

MAKE YOUR PERSONAL WALK
WITH THE LORD A PRIORITY

Marriage takes grace. On our own, we are selfish sinners. We can endure in love only as God's Word, through his Spirit, strengthens us. We do not have the power to keep loving in our own strength. Jesus says that if we abide in him we will bear much fruit, but that apart from him we can do nothing (John 15:5). When couples with troubled marriages come to us, I typically ask them about their prayer and devotional life. In almost every case, I have found a correlation between the lack of a vibrant personal walk with the Lord and a failing marriage. We need Scripture's constant reminders of God's grace to us that, in turn, motivates us to show grace to others. As we walk in the Spirit, we don't carry out the destructive deeds of the flesh, but instead bear the fruit of the Holy Spirit in our dealings with one another (Gal. 5:16–23). If something is not right in our spousal relationships, we should start to address it by ensuring that things are right with the Lord.

REMAIN INVOLVED IN A STRONG CHURCH

God blesses and strengthens his people through the ministry of the church, both through the public means of grace (including the preached Word) and as the individual parts of the body build one another up (Eph. 4:11–16). Neglecting to gather with the people of God is to the detriment of the soul and to family life (Heb. 10:25). It is important for a couple to be in a strong church so that they can benefit from counsel and accountability if their relationship is troubled. Families who have benefited from this kind of faithful pastoral care have said, "We don't know what we would have done if this church hadn't been here for us." I have seen many families who are in the midst of a crisis suffer because they didn't have godly church leaders caring for their souls (Heb. 13:17).

QUICKLY AND COMPLETELY
RESOLVE CONFLICTS

Many couples will periodically engage in arguments in which each speaks in anger and says hurtful things. As time passes, each person cools down, and life goes on, but the disputes are not properly resolved. As the years go by, their marriage is affected by hurts and scars that never healed. Paul vividly warns the Ephesians of the danger lurking behind unresolved conflict. He declares, "Be angry, and yet do not sin; do not let the sun go down on your anger, and do not give the devil an opportunity" (Eph. 4:26–27). To angrily leave an issue unresolved is like letting the devil into the house to wreak his havoc. Marriages fraught with unresolved conflicts are more vulnerable—not only to increasingly destructive conflicts, but also to extramarital affairs.[1] Believing couples must be determined to do whatever is required to be fully reconciled with each other. As we will see in chapters 16–18, the gospel enables us to resolve our conflicts in a God-honoring, mutually satisfying way.

BE HONEST WITH EACH OTHER

Nothing is more important in marriage than mutual trust. Nothing is more destructive to marriages than falsehood. More than once, I have heard the victim of marital infidelity explain, "I can forgive the sex, but I don't know if I can forgive the lies or if I can ever trust my spouse again." Paul tells the Ephesians, "Therefore, laying aside falsehood, speak truth each one of you with his neighbor, for we are members of one another" (Eph. 4:25). Paul speaks of believers as part of one body together. In a similar way, a married couple become one body (Gen. 2:24). If the rest of the body can't trust the eyes to see danger, then the whole body is at risk. If the rest of the body can't trust the legs to run to safety, the entire body is at risk. We must be able to trust one another.

---

1. In almost every affair, the line used is, "My husband/wife doesn't understand/ appreciate me."

People lie for selfish reasons. Some lie to gain something from others, such as not being truthful about the mechanical flaws of a car they want to sell. One spouse may lie to the other (e.g., promising that he or she will take care of a household task) just to maintain the peace. Others lie because they want to avoid the consequences of the wrong they have done. I once counseled a husband who had been going to strip clubs. As part of his repentance, he needed to tell his wife and seek her forgiveness. He replied that he didn't want to tell her because it would hurt her too much. The truth is that his sin would cause the hurt—not the confession. His sin was a betrayal of his marriage vow that his wife would have a right to know. An honest confession would be his opportunity to try to rebuild trust. It would also be a demonstration of true repentance and could help him gain the accountability he required to help him decisively cut off the sin (Matt. 5:29–30). Some people are so accustomed to lying that learning to be truthful is like learning to speak a new language. Those who tell the hard truth must put their ultimate trust in God that he will bring about the best result, instead of continuing to lie or hide the truth to avoid the consequences (Prov. 3:5–6).

Another aspect of having a truthful marriage is that each spouse must strive to make it safe for the other to honestly confess sins and failings. A wife may not want to tell her husband that she received a traffic ticket because she fears his angry reaction. The husband who had visited the strip club might be afraid of a dramatic emotional outburst from his wife. Again, we are reminded that the gospel is central in marriage. Even if it is difficult to hear the truth, we can give thanks to God for helping the other person to be honest. As sinners who have received much grace from God, we can have compassion on our fellow sinners by helping restore, rather than condemning, them.

BE CIRCUMSPECT IN YOUR
DEALINGS WITH THE OPPOSITE SEX

Few Christians plan to have an affair. Yet many wind up in an inappropriate physical or emotional relationship that threatens their marriage and even their souls. The world has a myth that people just "fall in love," even though they never meant to do so. Moreover, the world promotes the myth that a man and a woman can safely enjoy a close friendship with no danger of romantic or sexual involvement.

I have observed patterns in the cases of marital infidelity that I have counseled. A man and a woman become acquainted through work, the gym, a soccer league, children's activities, or even the church. They start talking and find that they enjoy one another's company. Over time, one or both of them experience some feelings for the other, but they at first keep it to themselves. They discover that they look forward to the next time they will see each other and begin communicating through e-mail, social media, or the phone. They also notice that they are hiding their relationship from their spouses because they might get the wrong impression. Perhaps they both realize that they feel more comfortable and alive in each other's presence than they do when they are with their spouses. At some point, a barrier is crossed. There is a touch, and then an admission of attraction. Rather than the expected shocked rejection, they find reciprocation, then a kiss. The slide into an affair continues, usually until they are caught, or sometimes when the conscience of one can't stand the guilt. Many will be hurt. Marriages may end.

Don't think that it can't happen to you. If a man as good as King David could fall into adultery, you are vulnerable, too. You must be very careful in relationships with the opposite sex—not because you think you would do something wrong, but because you are determined not to do so. Research has confirmed that "mutual vulnerability leads to closeness"[2] and that when men and women spend time openly disclosing their innermost thoughts and feelings to each other, mutual attraction is quite likely.[3] Even secular writers have recognized that we "fall in love" because of choices we make.

2. http://www.nytimes.com/2015/01/11/fashion/no-37-big-wedding-or-small .html; http://www.nytimes.com/2015/01/11/fashion/modern-love-to-fall-in-love -with-anyone-do-this.html.

3. http://www.cbsnews.com/news/experimental-generation-of-interpersonal -closeness-can-you-fall-in-love-with-36-questions/.

When people enter into marriage (or engagement), they commit to cut off all other romantic options until death separates them. It is not that they are incapable of feeling attracted to someone else. Their commitment includes a promise not to engage in activities that could lead to a forbidden attraction. Husbands and wives should talk openly about this potential danger and should concur about how each of them will protect themselves and their marriage. Problems often arise because the couple's expectations have not been made clear or do not match.

Here are some guidelines for propriety in dealing with the opposite sex to which a couple might agree: (1) Spend no time alone with a member of the opposite sex at work, in a car, at a restaurant, etc. An exceptional situation should involve prior agreement from the other partner. (2) There should be no absolute privacy in conversations with the opposite sex via e-mail, chat, text, social media, or phone. If such communication must take place, share it with your spouse. (3) Do not engage in any flirting. There is no such thing as innocent flirting. (4) Show appropriate reserve in touching/hugging. (5) Do not discuss personal matters (especially your relationship with your spouse) with someone of the opposite sex. If you need to pour out your heart to someone other than your spouse, find a godly same-gender friend.

BE GRACIOUS TO EACH OTHER

Just as the Lord does not deal with us according to what we deserve (Ps. 103:10), we are to treat our spouses better than they deserve. Their sins and failures provide opportunities for us to show grace, which resembles the grace we have received from God. In an ideal marriage, each party tries to outdo the other in showing love. As Paul tells the believers in Colossae, "So, as those who have been chosen of God, holy and beloved, put on a heart of compassion, kindness, humility, gentleness and patience; bearing with one another, and forgiving each other, whoever has a complaint against anyone; just as the Lord forgave you, so also should you. Beyond all these things put on love, which is the perfect bond of unity" (Col. 3:12–14). A marriage characterized by such grace will be well safeguarded.

SUMMARY

The second law of thermodynamics states that order naturally tends to become disorder. The same is true of marriage. A marriage that appears in the present to be "together" will drift apart if the couple don't continue to exert effort. They must be careful to protect their marriage from the threats of lies, infidelity, or just taking each other for granted. Both husband and wife must continually work to build the intimacy of their individual relationships with the Lord and their relationship with each other as well. As they do so, they can enjoy experiencing God's great and gracious love together.

— QUESTIONS FOR REFLECTION —

1. Why is it significant for the marriage that each spouse is growing spiritually?
2. Why is it vital that a married couple be in a good church?
3. How do lies harm a marriage?
4. What is the best way to protect a marriage from infidelity?
5. Why is it important that marital conflicts be quickly resolved?

15

HOW CAN COUPLES IMPROVE THEIR COMMUNICATION?

God's design is for a husband and wife to be one physically, emotionally, and spiritually. While couples usually begin marriage experiencing a great deal of closeness, those feelings can fade over time. Living together in a committed relationship puts new pressures on both husband and wife as their personal sins and the sins of their spouse are exposed. Ideally, this will result in mutual spiritual growth (sanctification) as they learn to show grace to and restore one another, but sometimes this causes couples to grow apart as bitterness and hostility take root. Some marriages die a slow death because of neglect. Couples must make an effort to lovingly communicate with regularity, depth, and love as they share life together.

Our communication with one another is rooted in God's communication with us. Our capacity for intelligent speech is a significant aspect of bearing his image. God speaks perfectly and wonderfully (Gen. 1:3, 6, 9; Pss. 19; 119; 2 Tim. 3:16–17). The devil uses speech to deceive and kill (Gen. 3:1–7; John 8:44). Because human speech has been corrupted through the fall, most human speech reflects that of the devil. James warns that it is impossible to tame the sinful tongue: "For every species of beasts and birds, of reptiles and creatures of the sea, is tamed and has been tamed by the human race. But no one can tame the tongue; it is a restless evil and full of deadly poison" (James 3:7–8). Yet the gospel transforms us into new creatures (2 Cor. 5:17), who are being conformed to the image of Christ. While Christians still wrestle with the remaining fleshliness of our old nature, we are indwelt by the Holy Spirit, who enables us to produce fruitful speech (Gal. 5:16–17, 22–23). We can learn to guard our speech by protecting our heart, as Jesus teaches, "The mouth speaks out of that which fills the heart" (Matt. 12:34b). God uses marriage to help sanctify our speech as we learn to subdue the flesh, which tears down and destroys, and grow in our ability to speak in a way that builds up.

COMMIT TO COMMUNICATE

There are numerous popular communication techniques. Some people go away on retreats and write letters to one another. Some people sit around a conference table, while following certain agreed-upon written rules. Many utilize a counselor as a mediator to help them understand each other. My belief is that virtually all communication techniques have the potential to help simply because a couple are finally devoting blocks of time to listen and to speak carefully.

THE GOAL OF COMMUNICATION IS LOVE

Just as each spouse is to be careful to meet the other's sexual needs (1 Cor. 7:3–5), he or she is responsible to ensure that the other's need for communication and personal intimacy is met. Just as a husband and wife may have different levels of sexual desire, men and women frequently have different expectations in terms of communication. The roles that husbands and wives often play can exacerbate this difference. The wife, after being at home with small children all day, is looking forward to adult company and conversation when the husband returns home. The husband, who is exhausted after twelve hours of work around demanding people, wants some alone time. Each must learn to serve the other. Every couple's goal should be to understand how much and what kind of communication each spouse desires and then to do everything possible to satisfy that requirement. As Paul writes, "Each of us is to please his neighbor for his good, to his edification. For even Christ did not please Himself" (Rom. 15:2–3a).

LEARN TO LISTEN IN LOVE

We all want others to understand us, especially our spouses. Are you more concerned about being heard or hearing? James tells us to be "quick to hear" and "slow to speak" (James 1:19). Communication is most effective when you approach a conversation with a sincere desire to carefully hear what the other person is saying. Paul commands, "Do nothing from selfishness or empty conceit, but with humility of mind regard one another as more important than yourselves; do not merely look out for your own personal interests, but also for the interests of others. Have this attitude in yourselves which was also in Christ Jesus" (Phil. 2:3–5). If you are striving for Christlikeness, you will be committed to exerting effort to understand your spouse. One practical way to try listening (as you apply Philippians 2:3–5) is to repeat back what you think your spouse means. Then give him or her a chance to clarify, so that you can better understand your spouse.

Good listening skills involve giving your full attention to the other person. Many of us like to multitask. We believe that we can carry on a conversation with a family member while also checking our e-mail and watching sports on TV. Your spouse wants your full attention. Putting down your electronic gadget, turning off the television, and establishing eye contact means, "You are worth all my attention." Good listeners will take genuine interest in what the other person is saying out of love for the speaker. For example, I don't have any natural inclination toward sewing and stamp collecting, and my wife doesn't care about sports. But because we are crazy about each other, we each show interest in what interests the other.

Sometimes all your spouse wants is for you to listen sympathetically. Suppose that as I walk into the house, I smell burning pastry and then hear my tearful wife explain that she forgot about a pie and left it in the oven too long. Perhaps the worst thing I could do would be to get angry that she wasted the ingredients and stank up the house. What most men might do would be to say, "Here is ten dollars, so go to the store to buy a new one," thinking that the new pie would fix the problem. What my wife would want, however, would be sympathetic listening and encouraging words. That pie was not just a pile of dough and a few cut-up apples. It was her expression of love for her family.

Some couples consist of one who is quieter and one who is more talkative. Sometimes the talkative one could improve the situation by talking much less, so that the other would have a chance to speak. In other cases, the spouse of a less communicative partner needs to learn the skill of lovingly drawing out his or her spouse. Wisdom declares, "A plan in the heart of a man is like deep water, but a man of understanding draws it out" (Prov. 20:5). Inquiries that demonstrate genuine interest can help draw out a quiet person. Most people will eventually open up to someone who cares about them and is really interested in what they have to say.

LEARN TO SPEAK IN LOVE

Your spouse doesn't need you to merely listen to what he or she has to say. In addition, your spouse needs you to share your inner life with him or her. I had to learn early in my marriage that my wife's need to know what goes on in my life and in my mind was much greater than was my desire to share this knowledge. After church, she would ask, "Who did you speak to this morning?" And I would not be able to remember. I finally learned to carry a notepad with me during the day, so that I could write down what to tell my wife at the end of the day.

While communication should be open and honest, not everything that comes into our minds should be said. Paul declares, "Let no unwholesome word proceed from your mouth, but only such a word as is good for edification according to the need of the moment, so that it will give grace to those who hear" (Eph. 4:29). Because we are sinners, we may have sinfully angry or unkind thoughts that would best be repented of, rather than verbally expressed. This is why James says that we should be "slow to speak" (1:19) and the book of Proverbs warns, "When there are many words, transgression is unavoidable, but he who restrains his lips is wise" (10:19).

On the positive side, use your speech to build up. Offer affirmation,

113

encouragement, and thanksgiving to your spouse whenever possible. Edify one another by conversing about God's Word and works as Paul encourages us: "Finally, brethren, whatever is true, whatever is honorable, whatever is right, whatever is pure, whatever is lovely, whatever is of good repute, if there is any excellence and if anything worthy of praise, dwell on these things" (Phil. 4:8). Share what you liked about Sunday's sermon or what you learned in your personal Bible reading. Proclaim the gospel to each other. This is the kind of profitable communication commended in Proverbs: "Pleasant words are a honeycomb, sweet to the soul and healing to the bones" (16:24).

LEARN TO COMMUNICATE
ON A DEEPER LEVEL

The conversation of some couples consists mostly of coordinating schedules and finances. While communication about these things is good and necessary, it is not nearly enough. Remember how, when you were courting, you shared your deepest thoughts, emotions, and dreams with each other? Now that you are married, such intimate conversation is all the more important. Share in making decisions together. Plan together. When necessary, exhort and gently correct each other.

Learn how your spouse receives various forms of communication. Even if you think that you were clear, don't assume that your message was understood.[1] Also, recognize that different people have varied needs and desires when it comes to communicating love. Many spouses thrive on hearing loving words of appreciation. Others are more desirous of loving actions. This is especially true when a spouse is better at talking than doing. Some yearn for romance. Some appreciate gifts.

---

1. Early in our marriage, my wife kindly asked me to put the toilet seat down when I left the restroom. Over the next twenty years, I thought I was trying, but she would occasionally offer a gentle reminder that I had left the seat up again. Then one day as she saw that I was leaving the restroom, having put the seat down, she chided me, "You left the seat up again." As I looked back, for the first time I understood that, while for twenty years I had been putting the seat down, I had never realized that she meant the lid.

For some, a loving touch is what matters most. What you most want may not be what your spouse desires. Study your spouse, and consciously make efforts to meet his or her needs.

BEWARE OF COMMUNICATION KILLERS

Words have a great potential to do good, but they can also cause great harm. Proverbs declares, "Death and life are in the power of the tongue" (18:21a). James describes that "the tongue is a fire, the very world of iniquity; the tongue is set among our members as that which defiles the entire body, and sets on fire the course of our life, and is set on fire by hell" (3:6). Words can wreak havoc in a marriage in several key ways.

Lying does terrible harm to relationships (Eph. 4:25; see also chapter 14 above). Lying can additionally take place more subtly through misleading, by leaving out important information, and by exaggeration (e.g., speaking in false absolutes: "You always" or "You never"). According to Proverbs, "A lying tongue hates those it crushes, and a flattering mouth works ruin" (26:28).

Angry, cruel words damage a marriage as well. Proverbs warns, "There is one who speaks rashly like the thrusts of a sword," and "a hot-tempered man stirs up strife" (12:18a; 15:18a). Words once spoken can never be taken back and may painfully echo in the ears of a wounded spouse for many years.

The person who continually interrupts his or her spouse expresses the attitude, "What I have to say is so much more important than what you are saying that you need to be quiet so I can talk." Proverbs reminds us that "he who gives an answer before he hears, it is folly and shame to him," and "a fool does not delight in understanding, but only in revealing his own mind" (18:13, 2).

Grumbling, nagging, and complaining are destructive speech that will discourage your spouse (1 Cor. 10:10; Phil. 2:14). When your spouse feels that he or she can do nothing to satisfy you, your spouse may be tempted to give up (Prov. 25:24). When criticism takes place in front of others, the damage is multiplied. Bitterness and bringing up past wrongs also pull a couple apart. On the other hand, love "does not take into account a wrong suffered" (1 Cor. 13:5).

Finally, silence can be as hurtful as unkind words. People clam up for various reasons. Some remain silent because they don't feel the need to communicate. Others refuse to address difficult issues because they want to avoid conflict. Many won't talk because they are bitter or angry.

Moreover, it is important to be aware of nonverbal communication. We often say as much through body language and facial expressions as we do with our words. Some people who can control their words reveal their hearts through their faces. Proverbs reads that nonverbal communication can be perverse: "Who winks with his eyes, who signals with his feet, who points with his fingers" (6:13). Many express murderous anger without saying a word. Sometimes while one spouse is talking to me, I will observe the other pulling away or shaking his or her head. On the other hand, couples who love each other will draw close physically and will look at each other with love in their eyes.[2]

PRACTICAL WAYS TO BUILD UP YOUR COMMUNICATION

Because it is easy to be caught up in the tyranny of the urgent, we encourage couples to plan times when they will be free to give their undivided attention to each other. When such plans are not made, the relationship may be neglected and thus weakened. Proverbs claims, "The plans of the diligent lead surely to advantage, but everyone who is hasty comes surely to poverty" (21:5). Early in our marriage, my wife and I agreed to sit down at least once each day to talk about our day and to raise any immediate issues that needed to be discussed. We

2. Many years ago, there was a couch in the office in which I counseled. I noticed that where one particular couple sat was indicative of their relationship status. When things were going well, they were snuggled up to each other. When they were at odds with each other, they occupied opposite ends of the couch. One night, when I walked into the room and saw the wife sitting on the lap of her husband, I realized that they were probably ready to graduate from the counseling.

decided as well to go out on dates at least every other week (weekly, if possible), during which we would get away from our home (and children) so that we could have a more extended time of communication. We would save up topics and issues for our date night. Then at least once a year (ideally, twice), we would enjoy a weekend getaway (again without kids). In addition to having fun together, we would use this time to review the past year and to set goals for our family (as a whole and for each member) in writing. Even though planning and evaluating may not sound terribly romantic, we both found that this time drew us closer together and strengthened our marriage throughout the year. And yes, we did find time for romance as well!

While there are appropriate times for planning, discussing challenging issues, and solving problems, it is important that couples have fun together, too. Sometimes it is good to set life's difficulties aside, so that you can relax and enjoy each other. Solomon writes, "Enjoy life with the woman whom you love all the days of your fleeting life which He has given to you under the sun; for this is your reward in life and in your toil in which you have labored under the sun" (Eccl. 9:9). Remember the things you enjoyed doing together when you were dating. Go to a park and fly a kite, or take a walk on the beach. Because you are committed to each other under God, you can trust that he will help you to get past any problems or differences you may have.

The manner in which we speak to one another can have just as great an impact on our communication as what we actually say. "A gentle answer turns away wrath," and "sweetness of speech increases persuasiveness" (Prov. 15:1a; 16:21b). A wise spouse will look for the right time to discuss a difficult matter. As Wisdom observes, "Like apples of gold in settings of silver is a word spoken in right circumstances" (Prov. 25:11). On the other hand, forging ahead when the other person is stressed out or exhausted not only is foolish, but can be detrimental to communication. Again, Proverbs reminds us, "Like one who takes off a garment on a cold day, or like vinegar on soda, is he who sings songs to a troubled heart" (25:20).

In addition, communication and closeness are enhanced as a couple share their spiritual life. This can include informal conversations about what each is learning from God's Word, and also more formal times of family devotions, reading Scripture, and praying together. I have observed that couples who pray and share Scripture with each other have the healthiest and happiest marriages.

SUMMARY

God intends for a husband and wife to be best friends. In order for this to happen, significant communication must take place. There are a number of ways in which we can damage our marriages through sinful words, or through failure to put forth the effort to listen well and to speak with love. Thankfully, the gospel transforms us inwardly so that, with the help of God's Spirit, we are able to exercise self-control and to build one another up with our words. We have a Savior about whom it was said, "Never has a man spoken the way this man speaks" (John 7:46). He never once sinned with his tongue, and his words give life to many. God works through marriage to sanctify our communication, making us more like our Lord.

— QUESTIONS FOR REFLECTION —

1. What are the characteristics of a good listener?
2. In what ways can speech be used to build others up?
3. In what ways can speech be employed to tear others down?
4. What can a couple do in practical terms to ensure that they are spending enough time and effort communicating with each other?
5. How does the gospel transform our communication?

D. CHALLENGES IN MARRIAGE

16

HOW CAN COUPLES RESOLVE THEIR CONFLICTS?[1]

Every human relationship, including marriage, will experience conflict because every human relationship involves sinners. The difference between Christians and unbelievers is not that we don't experience conflict, but rather that we are able to resolve our conflicts through the gospel, which gives us both the model and the power to make peace. Jesus came on a peacemaking mission and made it possible for us to be justified by faith, so that we might have peace with God (Rom. 5:1). Jesus both shows us how to make peace, through grace and personal sacrifice, and empowers us to walk in his steps.

CONFLICT IS DANGEROUS

All conflict has the potential for danger. In the midst of conflict, husbands and wives often do terrible damage to their spouses and to their marriage, primarily through hurtful words. Proverbs warns, "With his mouth the godless man destroys his neighbor" (11:9a). Such words as "I hate you! I wish I had never married you!" once spoken can never be taken back and may cause lasting damage. Jesus also explains that

---

1. I am indebted to Ken Sande and Peacemaker Ministries, who have done an outstanding job of systematizing what Scripture teaches about peacemaking. For further study, see Ken Sande and Kevin Johnson, *Resolving Everyday Conflict* (Grand Rapids: Baker, 2011).

God takes our words very seriously—as seriously as murder: "You have heard that the ancients were told, 'You shall not commit murder' and 'Whoever commits murder shall be liable to the court.' But I say to you that everyone who is angry with his brother shall be guilty before the court; and whoever says to his brother, 'You good-for-nothing,' shall be guilty before the supreme court; and whoever says, 'You fool,' shall be guilty enough to go into the fiery hell" (Matt. 5:21–22). Though conflict is dangerous, conflict also brings opportunity to glorify God as we resolve our differences in a Christlike way.

DON'T BE QUARRELSOME

Some people seem to enjoy arguing. They are quick to correct others, even regarding minor issues. Whatever anyone else says, they will present an opposing viewpoint. Proverbs again reads, "An angry man stirs up strife" (29:22a), and "keeping away from strife is an honor for a man, but any fool will quarrel" (20:3). While there is a proper place for lovingly correcting one's spouse (see below), bickering and quarreling will tear a marriage apart. I have known men who hated coming home at the end of the day because they feared the conflicts that would ensue when they walked in the door. As it is written, "It is better to live in a corner of the roof than in a house shared with a contentious woman" (Prov. 25:24).

We must learn to control our speech. James exhorts, "Everyone must be quick to hear, slow to speak and slow to anger" (1:19). While outward self-control (bridling the tongue, James 1:26) is necessary, the most important issue that needs to be addressed is our heart motives (Luke 6:45; see also Matt. 15:18–19). James tells us that we sinfully engage in destructive conflict because we want something too much: "What is the source of quarrels and conflicts among you? Is not the source your pleasures that wage war in your members? You lust and do not have; so you commit murder. You are envious and cannot obtain; so you fight and quarrel. You do not have because you do not ask" (4:1–2). The object of our desire may appear to us to be perfectly reasonable—the wife wants her husband to help more with the children, or the husband wants his wife to be more affectionate. But when we don't receive what we expect, we often react in anger—with words, actions, or the silent treatment. We then continue fighting for what we think is right, and we won't give up until we get it. Another way to put it is that we quarrel because each one of us wants control and is willing to pay a steep price to gain it.

The gospel must transform the quarrelsome heart. Paul exhorts the Philippians: "Have this attitude in yourselves which was also in Christ Jesus, who, although He existed in the form of God, did not regard equality with God a thing to be grasped, but emptied Himself, taking the form of a bond-servant, and being made in the likeness of men. Being found in appearance as a man, He humbled Himself by becoming obedient to the point of death, even death on a cross" (Phil. 2:5–8). Jesus did not cling to his rights as God, but rather humbled himself, so that we could be saved. Jesus' humble submission to the Father is in contrast to the flesh, which says, "I must have, and I must control." The only answer to a quarrelsome heart is walking in the Spirit, which produces Christlike, humble, peace-loving character.

We often tell quarrelsome couples that they need to continually recall that their relationship is almost always more important than whatever they are arguing about. Paul was concerned that the Galatians would "bite and devour one another" (Gal. 5:15) if they continued to walk in the flesh, which produces "enmities, strife, jealousy, outbursts of anger, disputes, dissensions," etc. (5:19–21). If one or both of them is walking in the flesh, damage is going to be done if the strife continues. Each needs to seek the Lord and walk in the Spirit. If even one partner will do this, the quarrel can end. Proverbs instructs us, "The beginning of strife is like letting out water, so abandon the quarrel before it breaks out" (17:14).

FIRST, GET THE LOG OUT OF YOUR OWN EYE

Typically, when a couple is in the midst of a conflict, they each think that they can clearly see the sins of the other party. When quarreling couples seek counseling, each person will ordinarily start by implying that the other is primarily at fault and that if he or she would just be reasonable, problems would be quickly solved. Their interaction consists primarily of attacking the other person and of defending themselves. Jesus directs us that we should first deal with our own sins before addressing the faults of the other party: "Why do you look at the speck that is in your brother's eye, but do not notice the log that is in your own eye? Or how can you say to your brother, 'Let me take the speck out of your eye,' and behold, the log is in your own eye? You hypocrite, first take the log out of your own eye, and then you will see clearly to take the speck out of your brother's eye" (Matt. 7:3–5).

Even if you believe that your spouse is 90 percent in the wrong,[2] seek forgiveness when you have sinned. Ask God to help you to see how you have sinned. As the psalmist pleads, "Search me, O God, and know my heart; try me and know my anxious thoughts; and see if there be any hurtful way in me, and lead me in the everlasting way" (Ps. 139:23–24). It would be extremely rare for the entire fault to be on one side. Usually, when others sin against us, we are guilty of reacting sinfully or of not being sufficiently sensitive to their concerns. Before seeking the forgiveness of your spouse, confess your sin to God (1 John 1:8–10). Then quickly confess your sin, and pursue reconciliation. Numerous marriages are damaged when one or both spouses delay seeking forgiveness from the other. Jesus teaches that, as important as worship is, you should even delay worship to pursue personal reconciliation. He states, "Therefore if you are presenting your offering at the altar, and there remember that your brother has something against you, leave your offering there before the altar and go; first be reconciled to your brother, and then come and present your offering" (Matt. 5:23–24; see also Prov. 28:13).

PULL THOSE WEEDS

Just as it is impossible to make flowers grow in a garden that is infested with weeds, a marriage may be so infested with bitterness and

2. He or she probably also believes you are mostly in the wrong.

resentment, arising from years of unresolved conflicts, that the flowers of joyful marital intimacy cannot survive. Before we can grow flowers, the weeds must be pulled. If my garden were infested with weeds, I could mow them down to be short, so that my garden would look better, but the weeds would just grow back. When trying to resolve conflicts, some couples only mow the weeds, so that the roots remain and the weeds come back up, making it impossible for the flowers to flourish. Poor confessions are like mowing the weeds. For instance, saying "I'm sorry for whatever I did that offended you" never actually addresses the root issue. Ken Sande has outlined what he calls "The Seven A's of Confession," by which the weeds of sinful conflict can be effectively uprooted.[3]

1. *Address everyone involved*. For example, if a husband yelled at his wife in front of their children, he needs to ask their forgiveness, along with his wife's.

2. *Avoid if, but, and maybe*. When seeking forgiveness, take full responsibility for your sin without making any excuse (see 1 Cor. 10:13) or putting blame on the other person. Excuses nullify the effectiveness of the confession. Later, after you have successfully removed the log from your eye, you may want to help your spouse with a splinter.

3. *Admit specifically*. Don't merely say, "I'm sorry," or "I apologize for what I did." The person who is being asked to forgive needs to know that you understand exactly what you did wrong. Seek to use biblical words for sin in your confession—e.g., "I was sinfully angry," or "I lied to you."

4. *Acknowledge the hurt*. It will be much easier for your spouse to forgive you if he or she is convinced that you have sought to understand how your sin has affected your mate—e.g., "I realize that my lying

3. Sande and Johnson, *Resolving Everyday Conflict*, 63–67.

breaks your heart and makes you question whether you can ever trust me," or "I know that my careless words crushed you, and I genuinely regret having caused you such pain."

5. *Accept the consequences.* True repentance is willing to go to great lengths to make things right (2 Cor. 7:10–11). For example, if you bought something that wasn't in the budget, the consequence would be to take it back.

6. *Alter your behavior.* The person who is truly repentant is willing to take drastic measures to ensure that his or her spouse won't continue to be hurt. For example, the husband who is caught using pornography could choose to put himself under accountability to a church leader or limit his access to the Internet. Jesus says, "If your right eye makes you stumble, tear it out and throw it from you" (Matt. 5:29).

7. *Ask for forgiveness.* Don't merely say, "I am sorry," which might not be clear enough. Perhaps you are just sorry that you got caught or that your spouse is so sensitive. Instead ask your spouse, "Will you please forgive me?" You are asking him or her to graciously forgive you as God has forgiven you (1 John 1:8–9).

FORGIVE AS GOD HAS FORGIVEN YOU

Forgiveness can be very hard, but it is of utmost importance. Jesus taught us to pray: "Forgive us our debts, as we also have forgiven our debtors" (Matt. 6:12). Paul instructs us, "Let all bitterness and wrath and anger and clamor and slander be put away from you, along with all malice. Be kind to one another, tender-hearted, forgiving each other, just as God in Christ also has forgiven you" (Eph. 4:31–32). It is as we remember that God forgave us an infinite debt of our sins, which we could have never repaid, that we are motivated and enabled to forgive others. Jesus illustrates how God's grace compels us to forgive by telling a parable of a servant who had been forgiven a debt of ten thousand talents (the equivalent of billions of dollars to us), who was unwilling to forgive a debt of one hundred denarii (about a third of a year's wages) that another servant owed him (Matt. 18:23–35). Like this servant, when others wrong us, it is easy to focus on what we have lost, which will lead to anger and bitterness. When we take our eyes off the hundred denarii owed to us and remember the ten thousand talents that we have been forgiven, we are able to let go of our desire for judgment for the sake of him who died that we might be released from our debt.[4] Forgiveness is not a feeling. Forgiveness is a decision made in faith to emulate God's forgiveness as we choose to no longer remember the sins of our spouse (Jer. 31:34).

According to Ken Sande, when we forgive others as God has forgiven us, we are essentially making four promises.[5]

1. I will not dwell on this incident.
2. I will not bring this incident up and use it against you.
3. I will not talk to others about this incident.
4. I will not allow this incident to stand between us or hinder our personal relationship.

Forgiveness does not involve merely withholding punishment. God calls us to show love to those whom we forgive. When Joseph forgave his brothers, he did not merely refrain from judging them. He showed affection to them and cared for their material needs (Gen. 45:5, 11, 14–15; 50:21). In the same way, Jesus not only removes the debt of our sin; he also enriches us with his righteousness: "For you know the grace of our Lord Jesus Christ, that though He was rich, yet for your sake He became poor, so that you through His poverty might become rich" (2 Cor. 8:9).

---

4. It is important to note that the debt of one hundred denarii (each denarii would be a day's wage) is not a trifling amount when considered on its own, but compared with the huge debt forgiven, it is minuscule.

5. Sande and Johnson, *Resolving Everyday Conflict*, 94.

SUMMARY

Every marriage will experience conflict. God's Word provides the tools by which we can learn to speak gently and avoid quarrels. God's Word also transforms our hearts, so that we can be like Christ in no longer being angry and controlling when things don't go our way. When conflict takes place, we will remember to first remove the log from our own eye by seeking forgiveness in a thoroughly biblical way (pulling the weeds). Furthermore, we will be eager to forgive as God has forgiven us in Christ. Seeking and granting forgiveness will be frequent in a strong marriage.

— QUESTIONS FOR REFLECTION —

1. Why do people experience conflicts in marriage? Why do conflicts sometimes increase after marriage?
2. Why is merely controlling what comes out of your mouth not enough? Why must the heart be addressed?
3. What does a good biblical confession sound like? Contrast a confession that merely mows the weeds to one that pulls the weeds.
4. What are the characteristics of biblical forgiveness? How is such forgiveness possible?
5. What should someone do if the person is not sure that an apology is sincere?

17

HOW SHOULD YOU CORRECT YOUR SPOUSE?

The process of peacemaking begins with confessing your own sins and faults. Jesus teaches that after you have removed the log from your eye, "you will see clearly to take the speck out of your brother's eye" (Matt. 7:5)—that is, to confront your brother about his sin. It is significant that Jesus likens correcting others to eye surgery. Just as most of us are quite sensitive about having someone poke around in our eyes, we also find it very hard to receive correction. Thus, correcting others, like eye surgery, must be done very carefully. A person with a splinter in his or her eye would be inclined to run if the alleged physician was going to try to remove the splinter with rusty garden shears. Unfortunately, much of the correction that takes place in many marriages is done with the rusty garden shears of anger and bitterness instead of with the sterilized tweezers of grace and love.

WHY MUST YOU CORRECT YOUR SPOUSE?

In the previous chapter, I wrote about people who almost seem to enjoy arguments and confrontation. Others have the opposite problem. They try to avoid confrontation at all costs. These patterns of conflict avoidance can harm a marriage as much as quarreling can because important issues never get resolved. Those who constantly avoid confrontation can become embittered over time by the issues that they have been internalizing. Some conflict-avoiders ultimately choose divorce, rather than working through tough issues to reach resolution.

The Bible teaches that love sometimes requires you to do the hard work of removing the splinter from your brother's eye. The Law states, "You shall not hate your fellow countryman in your heart; you may surely reprove your neighbor, but shall not incur sin because of him. . . . You shall love your neighbor as yourself" (Lev. 19:17a, 18b). Proverbs teaches that a true friend is willing to bring reproof, even if it hurts: "Faithful are the wounds of a friend" (27:6a).

Because no one knows you better than your spouse does, no one is better suited to correct your faults. In a strong marriage, each partner is willing to bring loving correction when necessary, assuming that the other wants to be godly and will welcome help. A husband who gently removes the splinters from his wife's eye is fulfilling his call to make her more holy and blameless (Eph. 5:26–27). A wife who respectfully points out sins that her husband may be unaware of is the best kind of helper—doing him good (Gen. 2:18; Prov. 31:12). Such correction can be successful only in a relationship in which each partner trusts that the other is on his or her side, as Proverbs describes, "The heart of her husband trusts in her" (31:11a).

HAVE YOU AFFIRMED YOUR SPOUSE LATELY?

In his excellent book *Practicing Affirmation*,[1] Sam Crabtree explains that we listen best to the people who affirm us the most. He likens affirmation to making a deposit in the bank of a relationship, while correction is like making a withdrawal.[2] When correction outweighs

1. Sam Crabtree, *Practicing Affirmation: God-Centered Praise of Those Who Are Not God* (Wheaton, IL: Crossway, 2011), 50.
2. Ibid., 52. He also states that it takes several affirmation deposits to equal one withdrawal.

affirmation, relationships become overdrawn, and people become unreceptive to rebuke. In addition, Crabtree observes that most romantic relationships begin with a great deal of affirmation and very little correction (during the courtship, engagement, and honeymoon). Then, over time, more correction and less affirmation lead to the deterioration of the marriage relationship.[3]

Some of us find ourselves in this exact situation. As the years have gone by, it seems more and more difficult to affirm our spouse. Many wives, having read books and attended seminars about marriage, have very high expectations of their husbands. When they compare their husbands' love to that of Jesus, their husbands come up quite short. Husbands often fail to affirm because they tend to "manage by exception," meaning that if things are going well they say nothing, but when things are wrong they bring correction. Both spouses can become discouraged in this kind of relationship because they feel that they can never measure up to the other's expectations. Learning to practice biblical affirmation is one of the most effective ways I have seen to break this cycle.

Affirmation is very powerful. In counseling, I have asked a couple in the midst of conflict to state three things they admire about each other. I have witnessed the entire tone of the conversation change as she says something like, "I didn't know that you thought I was a good cook. That makes me feel great."

Affirmation is modeled throughout the Scriptures. The family members of the Proverbs 31 woman richly affirm her: "Her children rise up and bless her; her husband also, and he praises her, saying: 'Many daughters have done nobly, but you excel them all'" (vv. 28–29). Scripture even affirms flawed people. Though the Corinthian church fell short in many ways, Paul found some things he could affirm about it (1 Cor. 1:4–8). In Revelation 2–3, most of Jesus' letters to the churches in Asia Minor begin with affirmation before rebuke is offered (see 2:2–6). Rather than focusing on ways that your spouse falls short of Christlike perfection, you should look for

3. Ibid., 44.

and verbally praise any evidences of grace and effort on his or her part. Given that your spouse is by nature a sinner (like you), you should recognize and appreciate any evidence of selfless love. I sometimes tell my counselees that even a blade of grass on the moon would be a big deal. Even a small amount of progress in the life of a weak sinner should be affirmed.

Some might object that such affirmation would puff up the pride of spouses who already think that they are much better than they are. Crabtree answers by defining affirmation as acknowledging the good work that God is doing in others: "God-centered praise of those who are not God."[4] This is how Paul affirms the various churches, thanking God for his work in them (Col. 1:3–8; 1 Thess. 1:2–10). God receives the glory for any good work we do (1 Cor. 1:30–31; Eph. 2:10).

When you know that someone cares about you and affirms you, it is easier to receive correction from that person. According to Proverbs, "Sweetness of speech increases persuasiveness" (16:21b). A word of warning is in order, however. If the only time you affirm your spouse is right before you bring correction, the affirmation will become meaningless. Reproof is best received in the context of a relationship that is characterized by grace and affirmation.

WHICH ISSUES ARE WORTH CORRECTING?

Not all issues warrant correction. If every selfish or insensitive act in a marriage resulted in a confrontation, husbands and wives would have little time for anything else. Your spouse will do something that annoys you countless times (such as when he or she leaves the toothbrush on the bathroom counter or walks right past you without a greeting). You can choose to make the conscious decision to forgive and overlook this transgression without saying anything. Peter proclaims, "Above all, keep fervent in your love for one another, because love covers a multitude of sins" (1 Peter 4:8). Proverbs reminds us, "A man's

4. Ibid., 3.

discretion makes him slow to anger, and it is his glory to overlook a transgression" (19:11). It is a privilege to show grace to others as God continually shows grace to you. Aren't you thankful that he doesn't discipline you for every sin you commit?

There will also be times when love demands that you confront your spouse. If he or she is involved in a sin that is spiritually dangerous, you must attempt to rescue your spouse (James 5:19–20). For example, the man who learns that his wife has been shoplifting or the woman who discovers that her husband is looking at pornography is obligated by God to lovingly confront for the purpose of rescue. It may also be necessary to correct a spouse for doing something that could hurt others (e.g., child abuse) or could seriously affect the marriage relationship. For instance, it would be better for a wife who believes that her husband is not investing enough time and energy into their relationship or for a husband who is struggling because his wife is rarely available to him sexually to humbly raise these concerns for the sake of their marriage. Remaining silent might lead to bitterness and a larger conflict in the future.

SCRIPTURE TEACHES YOU HOW TO GENTLY RESTORE YOUR SPOUSE

How you confront your spouse is crucial. Before you speak with him or her, pray for God's help, and plan what you will say and the way you will say it. Proverbs tells us that the timing of what we say can be very important: "Like apples of gold in settings of silver is a word spoken in right circumstances. Like an earring of gold and an ornament of fine gold is a wise reprover to a listening ear" (25:11–12).

Perhaps the best summary in Scripture about how to approach correction is found in Galatians 6:1: "Brethren, even if anyone is caught in any trespass, you who are spiritual, restore such a one in a spirit of gentleness; each one looking to yourself, so that you too will not be tempted." It is vital that you recognize that your spouse's transgression is primarily against God—not you. This verse describes someone who is in sin as being "caught," like an animal in a trap. As a fellow transgressor, you know what it is like to be ensnared, and you should be sympathetic. Paul also makes it clear that your purpose in bringing correction is restoration (not judgment). Elsewhere, "restore" is used for fishermen mending or restoring their nets (Matt. 4:21). Many people don't try correction until they are so angry, they can't hold back. Then the reproof is anything but gentle. It is actually more for the sake of the offended party, who feels that he or she must express (vent) anger. The Lord wants you to confront your spouse—not to release your pent-up anger or to give your partner what the person deserves, but to help him or her be restored to God, in order to be holy and useful in God's service. When you attempt this kind of godly correction, you are lovingly and gently bearing your spouse's burdens for Christ's sake (Gal. 6:2).

Another key point in Galatians 6:1 is that those who bring correction should be "spiritual." The immediately preceding context explains what Paul means as he exhorts us to walk in the Spirit, so that we will not carry out the desires of the flesh (Gal. 5:16–24). Much marital confrontation is fleshly and is characterized by destructive "outbursts of anger" (5:20), frequently resulting in mutual biting and devouring (5:15) as husbands and wives defend themselves and attack each other. Those who are spiritual, by contrast, are characterized by "love, joy, peace, patience, kindness, goodness, faithfulness, gentleness, self-control" (5:22–23).

These spiritual attitudes are essential when doing the eye surgery of confrontation. If you are in the flesh (sinfully angry), do not confront your spouse until your relationship with the Lord is restored and you are walking in the Spirit.[5] You may be tempted to blame your spouse for your anger, but while your spouse's sin may tempt you, he or she cannot make you fleshly or prevent you from walking in the Spirit (1 Cor. 10:13; Gal. 5:16). If, in the midst of confrontation, one or both of you are speaking or acting in a fleshly way, it would be better for each of you to spend time alone with the Lord, confessing your sins and praying for grace, before you resume your conversation. We

5. It can be extraordinarily difficult to walk away when you are angry.

advise numerous couples to agree in advance that if they sense their interaction becoming hostile, they will take a break to each spend time with the Lord before coming back together.

HOW WELL DO YOU RECEIVE CORRECTION?

Since we are discussing correction, this is a good time to inquire, "How well do you receive correction?" Proverbs 9:8 instructs us, "Do not reprove a scoffer, or he will hate you, reprove a wise man and he will love you." This is a good verse to memorize and to recite to yourself when someone is correcting you. Are you going to be like a scoffer as you defend yourself and point out that the person rebuking you has plenty of his or her own faults? Or are you going to be wise as you humbly receive correction and show appreciation to the person who is willing to do the hard work of correcting you (even if he or she doesn't do it perfectly)? It is also good for us to receive correction, so that we will remember how challenging it is to be confronted and how much easier it is to accept when it is done in a spirit of gentleness.

SUMMARY

A husband and wife are meant to be best friends. While friends overlook many faults and slights, sometimes love requires them to confront each other. Correction is most effective in a relationship that is characterized by affirmation. When bringing correction, we must be careful to do so in a spiritual and not a fleshly way, or the rebuke may do more harm than good. One way to think about this is that, rather than approaching our spouse as a judge to condemn him or her, we should come to our spouse as a doctor, seeking to furnish restoration and healing. In addition, we should be willing to humbly receive correction from others.

— QUESTIONS FOR REFLECTION —

1. Which issues should be overlooked and which must be confronted?
2. Why is affirmation important and biblical?
3. How can your spouse learn to be more affirming?
4. What is the right way to reprove your spouse?
5. What should you do if your spouse reproves you in a fleshly way?

18

WHEN DOES A COUPLE NEED HELP RESOLVING THEIR CONFLICTS?

Most conflicts can be resolved through personal peacemaking as each partner removes the log from his or her own eye and gently restores and grants forgiveness to the other. Sometimes, however, couples get stuck and can benefit from outside counsel as they seek to resolve conflicts and improve their marriage.

SPEAK PRIVATELY WITH YOUR SPOUSE BEFORE INVOLVING OTHERS

Many marriage relationships have been harmed when one spouse tells family and friends about the other's wrongdoings. This can result in feelings of betrayal by the spouse who feels that he or she was unjustly slandered. It can also damage other relationships if family members and friends take sides. The one whose sin was exposed may additionally be tempted to avoid being with them out of shame or anger. Jesus teaches, "If your brother sins, go and show him his fault in private; if he listens to you, you have won your brother" (Matt. 18:15). Ordinarily, issues should be raised privately. Spousal abuse is an exceptional situation, which others may have to become immediately involved in for the purpose of safety.

YOU MAY NEED OUTSIDE HELP

Outside help may be required in at least two circumstances. The first is that if your spouse is involved in serious sin and will not repent, you have the duty to involve others. Jesus says: "But if he does not listen to you, take one or two more with you, so that by the mouth of two or three witnesses every fact may be confirmed" (Matt. 18:16). For example, a husband may have tried to confront his wife about drinking too much alcohol, but her behavior continues to deteriorate. Or a wife may have sought to correct her husband's use of pornography, but he won't repent and tells her to back off. In such cases, Scripture teaches that the wronged spouse has a right to bring in one or two others to join him or her in admonishing the wayward spouse to repent. The wronged spouse should involve only people who themselves are spiritually mature (Gal. 6:1). Ideally, the confronting spouse will choose those whom the wayward spouse trusts and respects. The purpose at this stage is restoration. The hope is for repentance, in which case all can rejoice. Jesus instructs us, though, that if the wayward spouse will not repent, the issue will become a matter for church discipline (Matt. 18:17–20).[1]

The other situation in which help is needed occurs when there is a dispute in which each spouse is blaming the other. When two women in Philippi were experiencing a serious conflict, Paul encouraged them to live in harmony. He encouraged someone that he called a "true companion" to help these women be reconciled (Phil. 4:2–3). For instance, a couple may reach an impasse because the husband is a careful saver, while his wife tends to overspend. Counselors can serve as peacemaking mediators who help a couple in the midst of conflict to each confess his or her own sins and then to gently restore and forgive each other. Such counselors can often help each of them to better understand the other's perspective (Phil. 2:3–4; 1 Peter 3:7) and encourage them in practical ways to graciously show Christlike love to each other (1 Cor. 13:4–7). A mature godly couple can be an ideal choice to serve as mediators and mentors to a couple with a troubled marriage. That way, both the

---

1. This situation assumes that the guilty spouse is a professing Christian.

138

male and female perspectives are represented, and neither spouse being counseled feels ganged up on. This has been known to happen when a man counsels a couple alone.

YOU HAVE THE RIGHT TO SEEK HELP

Frequently, one spouse resists involving others in marriage problems. Abusive men typically want to hide their sin and try to use intimidation to keep their wives from telling anyone else. Some people are exceedingly private and would rather suffer in silence than let others know about their failings. Many men are in denial, claiming that everything is all right when their wives try to persuade them to receive counseling. During premarriage counseling, we encourage couples to agree that if either of them thinks that their marriage is in trouble, both will go together to seek counsel. Even if one spouse resists obtaining counsel, the other spouse has the right to seek godly advice.

I was upset with my wife on an occasion many years ago (I can't remember why), and for a long time, I (shamefully) refused to speak with her or to even make eye contact. Finally, after two days of this, she said, "I want us to be reconciled. If you don't start talking to me, I am going to phone one of the other church elders to come over here and talk to us." I quickly decided to get out of my funk and to work things out. On another occasion, we had a somewhat sharp disagreement about the course of action to take with one of our young-adult sons. When we sensed that we were stuck, we contacted another church leader and his wife to help us better understand each other and to come to a mutually agreeable solution.

WHERE SHOULD YOU LOOK FOR HELP?

Numerous counselors offer varied approaches to marriage counseling. It is important for Christians to seek counsel that is based on Scripture. In 2 Timothy 3:16–17, Paul tells us that Scripture is not only inerrant and infallible—"God-breathed"—but also fully sufficient, "so that the man of God may be adequate, equipped for every good work." The Bible defines the covenant of marriage and explains God's design for the roles of husband and wife. Moreover, the Bible explains that our love for one another is founded on God's gracious love to us (1 John 4:19) and reveals how, through the gospel, we can be reconciled to one another just as God has reconciled us to himself (Eph. 4:31–32). Counsel that is not rooted in God's Word will be both flawed and ineffective.

In addition to finding a counselor whose advice will be thoroughly biblical, it is important that you identify someone who is qualified to help you. Start by seeking help from the elders/pastors of your church, who are called to meet a high standard of spiritual maturity (1 Tim. 3:1–7) and are charged with shepherding (which includes counseling) God's flock (1 Peter 5:1–5). The Bible explains that each church needs older godly women who set a good example and are equipped to help younger women love their husbands and children (Titus 2:3–5). While ideally you will find qualified counselors through your local church, you may also choose to seek godly counsel through organizations such as the Biblical Counseling Coalition (BCC), the Christian Counseling and Educational Foundation (CCEF), and the Association of Certified Biblical Counselors (ACBC).

PEACE IS NOT ALWAYS POSSIBLE

Paul exhorts, "If possible, so far as it depends on you, be at peace with all men" (Rom. 12:18), which implies that sometimes peace is not attainable. One spouse may do all that is within his or her power to pursue reconciliation, while the other completely refuses to engage in the process. Paul speaks of a situation in which an unbelieving spouse may depart, in spite of the efforts of the believing spouse to save the marriage: "Yet if the unbelieving one leaves, let him leave; the brother or the sister is not under bondage in such cases, but God has called us to peace" (1 Cor. 7:15). If your marriage is failing, you may not be able to save it single-handedly, but you want to be able to say that you did all that you could to be a peacemaker for the sake of him who made peace with God for you.

SUMMARY

While most couples can solve most of their conflicts through individual peacemaking, God has also made provision for getting outside help when individual peacemaking fails. Almost every couple will need outside counsel from time to time. It is important to have the support structure of a strong biblical church whose leaders are committed to shepherding God's flock, so that when the need for help arises, the best help is available.

— QUESTIONS FOR REFLECTION —

1. Why is it important for a couple to try to resolve a problem together before seeking outside help?
2. In what situations is it necessary for a couple to seek outside help or counsel?
3. What should be done if one spouse resists seeking counsel?
4. Where should one look when outside counsel is needed?
5. Can one spouse make peace alone? Why or why not?

19

HOW CAN COUPLES RESOLVE SEXUAL PROBLEMS?

God created sex to be a blessing for both husband and wife to enjoy within marriage, but as Ecclesiastes 7:29 says, "God made men upright, but they have sought out many devices." Mankind has misused and perverted God's gift, turning it into an idol. In spite of that, the sexual union in marriage can be redeemed by God's grace.

WHY DID GOD CREATE SEX?

Sex is part of God's perfect creation. He made us as sexual beings—male and female.[1] From the beginning, he designed marriage, including the sexual union, as a picture of his holy covenant relationship with his people (Eph. 5:32). Scripture reveals three purposes for the sexual union in marriage.

1. Sexual union between husband and wife expresses and enhances the oneness of the marriage covenant. While our culture uses a ring as a sign of the marriage bond, God designed the sexual union as the sign of a husband and wife's unique commitment to each other. Genesis 2:24 declares that as a man covenants with his wife, "they shall become one flesh." This physical oneness is a picture of the personal union

---

1. The fall was not a sexual awakening, for God had encouraged mankind to be fruitful and multiply before the fall. It did, however, lead to sexual sins and difficulties.

between husband and wife as they each, under God, fulfill the commitment to lovingly perform their roles in their marriage partnership. Tim Keller writes, "Sex is perhaps the most powerful God-created way to help you give your entire self to another human being. Sex is God's appointed way for two people to reciprocally say to one another, 'I belong completely, permanently and exclusively to you.' You must not use sex to say anything less."[2] The yearning for personal and physical intimacy drives people to make the commitment of marriage as the only place where such intimacy can be legitimately experienced. As the years of marriage go on, the personal union grows, which makes the sexual union more joyful and meaningful.

2. The sexual union between a husband and wife produces children. In the garden, God spoke to Adam and Eve, saying, "Be fruitful and multiply, and fill the earth" (Gen. 1:28). God's design is that children be conceived as the product of their parents' love for each other and that they be raised in a home in which both mother and father are committed to their marriage for life. As our culture has decoupled sex from marriage, more children are born out of wedlock. Such children are more likely to experience poverty and to become involved in crime. Another way in which our culture has changed is that many people see children as a burden, rather than as a blessing. It has not always been this way. Throughout history, godly husbands and wives have honored God's design as they have delighted in the children he has given them. Scripture teaches, "Behold, children are a gift of the LORD, the fruit of the womb is a reward. Like arrows in the hand of a warrior, so are the children of one's youth. How blessed is the man whose quiver is full of them" (Ps. 127:3–5a).

3. The sexual union in marriage is designed by God to bring enjoyment to both husband and wife. This is the one aspect of God's design for sex that the world acknowledges. Sex is pleasurable. But God has

2. Timothy Keller and Kathy Keller, *The Meaning of Marriage* (New York: Penguin, 2011), 224.

intended that the pleasure be experienced exclusively in the context of a lifelong covenant commitment and in the hope that God will bless the union of husband and wife with children. As the wise father warns his son to avoid sexual immorality, he tells him to enjoy his marriage instead: "Drink water from your own cistern and fresh water from your own well. . . . Let your fountain be blessed, and rejoice in the wife of your youth. As a loving hind and a graceful doe, let her breasts satisfy you at all times; be exhilarated always with her love" (Prov. 5:15, 18–19).[3] While loss of control is usually frowned on in Scripture, the exhilaration of married love is a happy exception. The sexual union is designed by God for the physical and emotional delight of both husband and wife, as the Song of Solomon vividly portrays: "May he kiss me with the kisses of his mouth! For your love is better than wine" (Song 1:2). Each partner is to find pleasure in the body of the other (4:12–15) as all God-given physical senses are heightened (1:2; 2:3, 6, 14; 4:9, 14; 5:1).

ANY SEXUAL EXPRESSION OUTSIDE MARRIAGE IS SIN

God intends that sexual activity take place solely between a husband and wife within marriage. The author of Hebrews declares, "Marriage is to be held in honor among all, and the marriage bed is to be undefiled; for fornicators and adulterers God will judge" (13:4). Any sexual expression outside the marriage covenant sinfully misrepresents what the sexual union is meant to express and robs both oneself and others of the joys of sexual union in marriage. The Bible warns against the sins of adultery (marital unfaithfulness, Ex. 20:14), fornication (sex before marriage, 1 Cor. 6:9; Heb. 13:4), homosexuality (Lev. 18:22; Rom. 1:26–27), lust (including pornography and self-gratification,[4]

---

3. Ray Ortlund writes, "Sex is like fire. In the fireplace it keeps us warm. Outside the fireplace it burns the house down. . . . Proverbs 5 is saying, 'Keep the fire within the marital fireplace and stoke that fire as hot as you can.'" *Marriage and the Mystery of the Gospel* (Wheaton, IL: Crossway, 2016), 65.

4. First Corinthians 7:3–5 teaches that one's sexuality has been given by God for

Matt. 5:27–28; 2 Tim. 2:22), and any other sexual expression outside marriage (Lev. 18:23; 20:15–16). God judges sexual sins, both in the final judgment and through present consequences: "Do not be deceived, God is not mocked; for whatever a man sows, this he will also reap. For the one who sows to his own flesh will from the flesh reap corruption" (Gal. 6:7–8a).

THE PROBLEM IS IDOLATRY
RATHER THAN ADULTERY

Sexual sin is primarily a theological problem. People sin sexually because they turn sexual gratification into an idol, which is anything that one values and serves above God himself. As Paul exhorts the Thessalonians, "For this is the will of God, your sanctification; that is, that you abstain from sexual immorality; that each of you know how to possess his own vessel in sanctification and honor, not in lustful passion, like the Gentiles who do not know God" (1 Thess. 4:3–5). Even that which is good, such as sex or food, can become sinfully idolatrous when we desire it more than we desire God. You can know that a desire has become idolatrous when you find that you are willing to sin in order to get it, or when you react sinfully when you don't get it. Idolatry is both enslaving and destructive. As Peter writes, "They entice by fleshly desires, by sensuality, those who barely escape from the ones who live in error, promising them freedom while they themselves are slaves of corruption; for by what a man is overcome, by this he is enslaved" (2 Peter 2:18–19). Idolatrous yearnings can never be ultimately satisfied and often result in the complete loss of that which was desired.

Sexual idolatry can occur even within marriage. One is being idolatrous by saying in his or her heart, "I must have a thrilling sexual

---

the purpose of serving and fulfilling one's spouse (or future spouse); therefore, using sex for self-gratification (masturbation) is contrary to God's design (thus, a misuse of sexuality) and is harmful to marriage (present or future). Men and women should become skilled at pleasing their spouses—not in pleasing themselves.

relationship with my spouse"; or "I must have sex whenever I want to have sex"; or "My spouse must maintain a certain fit physical appearance"; or "My spouse must be as interested in sex as I am"; or "My spouse must do certain things for me sexually (and like it)"; or "Every sexual experience must be amazing"; or "My spouse must let me sleep without making sexual demands"; etc. If you are obsessed with your personal sexual desires and if you become angry when you don't get what you think you need, you have become a sexual idolater.

Sexual idolatry creates quarrels and conflicts in marriage (see James 4:1–2) when one expects his or her spouse, rather than God, to meet one's deepest needs. The wife of the sexual idolater becomes frustrated because she comes to realize that there is nothing she can do to fully satisfy him. She may also be tempted to feel that he is just using her body to please himself, instead of expressing love and commitment. When sexual idolaters see that they aren't fully satisfied in marriage, they will often turn to sexual sin (adultery, pornography, or even homosexuality) in the vain hope that they can find happiness.

Scripture teaches that if you seek ultimate fulfillment through sex or any other idol (food, drink, money, or possessions), you will remain unsatisfied. C. S. Lewis describes this process as an "ever increasing craving for ever diminishing pleasure."[5] Solid joys and lasting pleasures can be found only in the Lord. Through the prophet Isaiah, the Lord invites us: "Ho! Every one who thirsts, come to the waters; and you who have no money come, buy and eat. Come, buy wine and milk without money and without cost. Why do you spend money for what is not bread, and your wages for what does not satisfy? Listen carefully to Me, and eat what is good, and delight yourself in abundance" (Isa. 55:1–2). Isaiah offers hope for all kinds of idolaters: "Seek the LORD while He may be found; call upon Him while He is near. Let the wicked forsake his way and the unrighteous man his thoughts; and let him return to the LORD, and He will have compassion on him, and to our God, for He will abundantly pardon" (55:6–7). As one turns in repentance to the Lord, he offers free, gracious pardon.

5. C. S. Lewis, *The Screwtape Letters* (New York: Macmillan, 1944), 112.

You must learn to find your ultimate satisfaction in Christ, who is to us living water and the Bread of Life. If you place all your hope in what man can do for you, you will be like the bush in the desert because people will fail you (Jer. 17:5–6). But if you place your trust in the Lord, you will be like a tree that is planted by the water and does not wilt in the year of drought (17:7–8). Even when your spouse fails to fulfill your sexual desires, you have the Lord. When you acknowledge God in his proper place of lordship over your life, you realize that, as Tim Keller writes, "Marriage, therefore, is penultimate. It points to the Real Marriage that our souls need . . . . Even the best marriage cannot by itself fill the void in our souls left by God."[6] Then, with this perspective, sexual union in marriage can be experienced with joy and to the glory of the Giver of every good gift. Ray Ortlund observes that "the promises of God can outperform the amusements and even the therapies of this world in keeping our souls and our marriages alive. The key to lasting romance is not endless sex but believing hearts."[7]

MOST SEXUAL PROBLEMS ARE RELATIONSHIP PROBLEMS

Most marriage problems are the result of spiritual weakness in one or both spouses. The best thing you can do for your sex life is to first pursue intimacy in your relationship with God. As you find your greatest delight in him, you will not be looking to your spouse to meet needs that only the Lord can satisfy. As your mind is continually renewed by God's Word (Rom. 12:1–2) and your heart is filled with the gospel, you will be better able to reflect God's grace toward your spouse. Tim Keller calls this "love economics."[8] As your account is filled by God's love, you are able to give yourself away to others (1 John 4:10).

The second key to building sexual intimacy is to build the personal intimacy in your marriage relationship. An experienced counselor once

6. Keller and Keller, *The Meaning of Marriage*, 198.
7. Ortlund, *Marriage and the Mystery of the Gospel*, 53–54.
8. Keller and Keller, *The Meaning of Marriage*, 58.

told me that a couple's sex life invariably reveals the quality of their personal relationship. When there is a long-term, giving, mutually satisfying physical relationship, there is a healthy personal relationship. "The quality of our relational intimacy will shape our sexual intimacy," writes Winston Smith.[9] He continues, "When we don't connect well on the inside we aren't likely to connect well on the outside."[10] Paul Tripp has also observed this correlation. He explains, "What diverts and destroys physical sexuality is a lack of love . . . . If your spouse hasn't loved you outside the marriage bed, why would you think that she would love you when you are in the marriage bed?"[11]

It takes ongoing effort to maintain personal and sexual intimacy. Sex is exciting when it is new, which is why sexual sin, including affairs, can be alluring (see Prov. 7). But it takes commitment and grace to sustain a flourishing relationship, which is why affairs usually fizzle over time.[12] God intends sex to be enjoyed in the secure context of a deep commitment to a lifelong covenant of companionship, in which each partner serves and honors the other as each seeks to fulfill a God-given role. In this type of relationship, there is not the worldly pressure to perform to earn the devotion of the other. As a couple share life together and build an ever-deepening friendship, the sexual union comes to mean more and more. We see this beautifully described by the woman in the Song of Solomon, who relates her sexual desire for her husband to the friendship they enjoy: "His mouth is full of sweetness. And he is wholly desirable. This is my beloved and this is my

9. Winston Smith, *Marriage Matters* (Greensboro, NC: New Growth Press, 2010), 221.

10. Ibid.

11. Paul David Tripp, *What Did You Expect? Redeeming the Realities of Marriage* (Wheaton, IL: Crossway, 2010), 173.

12. In one of my early counseling cases, I met with a woman who had had an affair and left her dull Christian husband for the exciting guy she met at work. Once she and her lover married, however, the relationship began to fall apart in every way. She said, "I can't understand how, when we were having the affair, we couldn't keep our hands off each other; we were like a wild man and woman. But now that we are married, we can't stand each other." She wanted to know whether she could go back to her "dull" former husband.

friend" (Song 5:16). Even sharing hardship has the potential to draw a couple closer together. As Proverbs reads, "A friend loves at all times, and a brother is born for adversity" (17:17). Some husbands overlook or neglect cultivating such a friendship with their wives. As a result, the sexual union becomes more difficult because she is tempted to feel that he is merely using her body, while not really caring for her personally. I have also been grieved to counsel couples who almost never come together sexually because of unresolved conflicts that have led to bitterness and relational distance.

A final aspect to highlight is continuing to cultivate romance in your marriage. Many couples become so busy with career and children that they neglect each other. Some become lazy, as they spend their free time with television, hobbies, or the Internet, while neglecting communication and romance. Some become sexually lazy as they wait until they are exhausted to go to bed and then don't want to put forth the effort to bring sexual happiness to each other. One wife realized that she would spend hours preparing healthy meals for her husband and would never dream of serving a peanut-butter-and-jelly sandwich for dinner; but she was convicted that she was often offering peanut-butter-and-jelly sex. She resolved, by God's grace, to begin putting the same effort into their sexual relationship that she put into their meals.

GRACE SEX

Many couples live in the realm of law, using sex as reward or punishment according to what they think their spouse deserves. The wife may think that if her husband helps around the house and treats her with respect, then she will make herself available sexually. If he doesn't meet her expectations, she turns her back to him and tells him that she must sleep. Angry husbands withhold sexual affection as a way of punishing their wives, too. Such is a graceless approach to sex.

The alternative is to practice grace sex, with each giving the other better than he or she deserves, just as God has freely and graciously shown grace. One should also deal kindly with a spouse's weaknesses if he or she has physical imperfections or personal shortcomings (awkward habits, grumpiness, not being communicative enough). Whether your spouse struggles with too much interest in sex (sexual idolatry) or a lack of interest in sex, strive to help, instead of judge, your spouse.

Another aspect of grace sex is that one must be willing to receive grace. Some spouses, because of pride or guilt, may desire sex, but are reluctant to receive sexual blessing because they feel unworthy. Just as the gospel forces us to humble ourselves to receive God's gifts that we cannot earn, marriage gives us the opportunity not only to give grace, but to humbly receive grace. In a good marriage, each spouse will marvel that the other loves him or her in spite of sinful unworthiness. Receiving such love helps us to understand how the mystery of marriage reflects the mystery of the gospel (Eph. 5:32).

FROM IDOL TO BLESSING

Grace teaches you to first think of how to bring sexual refreshment and satisfaction to your spouse, rather than merely seeking personal gratification. Paul instructs the Corinthians, "The husband must fulfill his duty to his wife, and likewise also the wife to her husband. The wife does not have authority over her own body, but the husband does; and likewise also the husband does not have authority over his own body, but the wife does" (1 Cor. 7:3–4). Because your sexuality belongs to your spouse, your objective is to learn what will bring him or her the greatest delight and then to make every effort to make your spouse as happy as possible in this area. Godly love finds great pleasure in giving pleasure to the beloved. When each is trying to outdo the other in service and love, there is great joy and God's ideal for sexual union is realized.

SUMMARY

God designed sex to be a blessing for humankind as an expression of the marriage covenant, for procreation, and for mutual pleasure. Many have turned God's gift of sex into an idol. Sexual idolatry is self-destructive and does great harm to marriages in terms of both loss of trust/unity and unrealistic expectations. The gospel of grace sets us free from idolatry, so that we can find our ultimate fulfillment in knowing God. Then we are able to enjoy God's gifts in their proper place. The sexual union in marriage gives each spouse an opportunity to graciously serve the other with a love that reflects God's love for us.

— QUESTIONS FOR REFLECTION —

1. Why does God restrict sex to marriage?
2. What is the harm in sexual idolatry?
3. How can sex be redeemed by the gospel?
4. What is the harm of law (or graceless) sex in marriage?
5. What should grace sex look like?

20

HOW DOES THE BIBLE ADDRESS THE TOUGH QUESTIONS ABOUT SEX?

Sex can be complicated. Many couples face hard questions. Thankfully, the all-sufficient Word of God gives answers and guidelines, so that we can live in joy and freedom.

HOW DO MEN AND WOMEN VIEW SEX DIFFERENTLY?

There is truth to the common saying that men tend to be more visual and women tend to be more focused on the relationship. It is not unusual for a man who hasn't had a significant conversation with his wife all day to suddenly become interested in sex as he sees her undressing for bed, while she might respond, "How could you even suggest this?" A woman yearns for a man who is interested in her in every way. I have observed that women tend to fall into extramarital affairs not because of sexual lust, but because they feel personally neglected or mistreated by their husbands. A wife may feel constantly judged and criticized by a husband whom she can never please. When another man comes along who is attentive, accepting, and affirming, she is vulnerable. On the other hand, a man who has an extramarital affair will often lie about making a commitment to the other woman (and leaving his wife), so that he can experience the sex.

A wise husband will strive to understand his wife in every way (1 Peter 3:7), including sexually, rather than being self-focused or just assuming that she is like him. Most will learn that the greatest sexual need of his wife is to be the delight of her husband in every way. She finds great joy in knowing that he still finds her attractive, even after many years (and childbirth), and that she is able to please him. Men will learn that most wives are less sexually driven than their husbands. This will require patience on his part. Many wives are more sensitive to issues of hygiene and privacy/noise. Mothers of young children desperately need more sleep. In addition, a caring husband will make efforts to learn what brings his wife joy and satisfaction sexually and will be patient when not every sexual experience involves fireworks and cannons. He will also seek to understand how issues of her cycle, pregnancy, and menopause affect her.

A wife should strive to understand her husband's perspective on sex. This is an area in which she can greatly help her husband (Gen. 2:18), and most husbands need a lot of help here. Husbands tend to think more about sex than their wives do.[1] We live in a highly sexualized culture, which can increase the level of temptation a man experiences. Proverbs 5 acknowledges that a man will experience sexual thirst, but warns him to drink only from his own well (v. 15). A wife should be glad when her husband seeks to find refreshment exclusively from her. While it is appropriate for a wife to initiate sexual relations, God's general design in marriage is for a husband to lead and a wife to respond. At times, she may be surprised by his initiative ("I thought it was going to be tomorrow night"). Her response in those moments should reflect her love for and commitment to him. A wife should also understand that many husbands will take rejection, or even a lack of interest, from their wives very personally. Husbands may be tempted to wrongfully react by becoming angry or withdrawing. A loving wife can show grace, especially when her husband is struggling in this area. In addition, a wife should realize that sex is not merely a physical act

---

1. When working on this material, I remember coming home and turning on the television to watch a miniseries we had previously begun about British monarchs from Alfred the Great until the present. My wife commented, "I've been thinking about this and looking forward to it all day." I gently informed her that it wasn't what I had been thinking about, especially in light of what I had been studying.

for her husband. He, too, yearns for the personal closeness that God has designed the sexual union to express.

HOW OFTEN SHOULD A MARRIED COUPLE HAVE SEX?

Some couples worry too much about whether they are normal, above average, or below average in sexual frequency. In general, Scripture teaches that married couples should engage in sexual union regularly. Paul writes, "Stop depriving one another, except by agreement for a time, so that you may devote yourselves to prayer, and come together again so that Satan will not tempt you because of your lack of self-control" (1 Cor. 7:5). In light of the fact that one's body (sexuality) belongs to his or her spouse, both husband and wife should try to be sure that the other is fully satisfied sexually. Even if one spouse is not experiencing sexual desire, he or she should be mindful of the spouse's desires and the need, for the sake of their marriage, to express their love to each other in this way regularly.[2]

Neither spouse should use his or her sexual rights selfishly or coercively. Sometimes the most loving, self-sacrificing thing a husband can do is to let his wife sleep after she has had an exhausting day. Sex should never be obtained under duress. If a couple cannot come to agreement about how often they come together, they would be wise to seek counsel from a mature godly couple.

WHAT IF ONE SPOUSE DOESN'T LIKE SEX?

It is common for couples to have differing sex drives.[3] It may be that one spouse's lack of sexual interest is a relationship problem and could

---

2. It has been said that if couples made love only when everything was perfect and both were full of passion, many wouldn't have sex very often (which would be bad).

3. As I have been counseling Christian couples over many years, we have found more wives than husbands who were concerned about infrequency in sexual union. The reasons that one spouse may desire sex more than the other may vary. For

be addressed by more communication,[4] romance, and help around the house. Sometimes there are issues of physical pain or discomfort. Some of these issues can be addressed as a couple speak openly about sex, and each learns what pleases or hurts the other. Some of these problems may require medical solutions. Don't wait. Get help. I have encountered situations in which one spouse has decided that there will be no sex. This is a failure to live up to the marriage covenant. Outside help and counsel will probably be necessary.

The spouse who is not as sexually driven can learn to view sex as an opportunity to lovingly serve and refresh his or her partner. Love takes great pleasure in giving pleasure to the beloved. Even if you are concerned that your spouse is making sex an idol, you should realize that it is not your job to straighten the person out by judging him or her or withholding sex. Instead, while realizing that only the Lord can fully satisfy your spouse, you will do your best to refresh him or her, thus reflecting God's grace and hoping that Christlike kindness will lead to repentance (Rom. 2:4).

IS BIRTH CONTROL PERMITTED FOR CHRISTIANS?

Scripture reveals that God's general design for marriage includes having children (Gen. 1:27–28).[5] A godly couple will recognize that an important part of God's design for sex is procreation, and they will look upon children as a blessing (Ps. 127). The Bible, however, does not require us to have as many children as is physically possible. A couple has the freedom, through certain forms of birth

---

example, a wife may want more frequent sex because she desires personal closeness with her husband, and she yearns to know that he is fully satisfied with her.

4. It has been said that foreplay begins early in the morning and goes on all day. One wife writes, "I love it when my husband gives me compliments. Also, when he helps me out during the day, it makes me feel more loving toward him." Another says, "I love it when my husband listens to me while making eye contact."

5. Some couples are providentially hindered from having children, which in no way detracts from the value of their marriage.

(conception) control, to try to time when they have their children or to limit the number of children they have. Those who make such attempts must realize, though, that God is sovereign over the womb. A couple may not be able to conceive when they planned. Some couples conceive in spite of their efforts to avoid conception. Proverbs reminds us, "The mind of man plans his way, but the LORD directs his steps" (16:9).

Some argue that couples should not practice birth control, but should simply embrace the number of children the Lord gives them. While this approach sounds pious, the Bible does not forbid a couple from taking legitimate steps to prevent conception under certain circumstances, such as if the wife's health would be endangered by another pregnancy, or if the couple determines that their physical or financial capacity has been reached with their present number of children. One argument against birth control comes from the example of Onan, who was struck dead because he spilled his seed on the ground so that Tamar would not conceive (Gen. 38:6–10). But Onan's situation is unique. The purpose of his sexual union with Tamar was to fulfill his duty under the old covenant order to provide offspring for his deceased brother. By spilling his seed on the ground, he was taking the pleasures of the sexual union while refusing to fulfill his responsibility. This case was all the more important because Onan was the son of Judah, through whom the Messiah was to come. Onan's gross dereliction of duty was an assault on the messianic line, rather than a commentary on the use of contraception.

Not every method of birth control is allowed. Because the Bible teaches that human life, which is in God's image and under his protection, begins at conception (Pss. 51:5; 139:13), any abortive method of birth control is forbidden to Christians.[6] Methods that seek to prevent conception are in the realm of Christian freedom. While some of these methods (e.g., condoms) are temporary, others are designed to be permanent (e.g., vasectomy). The decision for one partner to be sterilized

---

6. Some methods of birth control are actually abortifacients; they don't prevent conception, but just prevent a fertilized egg from developing.

should be made very carefully.[7] Since your body belongs to your spouse (1 Cor. 7:3–4), he or she should have a say. Some have lived to regret being sterilized because they later desired children.[8]

Sometimes a couple cannot agree about how many children to have.[9] One spouse may resist having children for selfish reasons. In such cases, they should seek to understand each other, putting the interests of the other party first (Phil. 2:3–4), and to apply biblical principles of conflict resolution. In many cases, a husband needs to better realize how much having babies means to his wife and that it is a large part of her identity (see 1 Tim. 2:15). Outside counsel may be required if they reach an impasse.

WHAT SEXUAL BEHAVIOR IS PERMISSIBLE FOR HUSBAND AND WIFE?

Couples have a great deal of freedom to explore and please each other sexually. On the other hand, because a husband and wife are called to serve each other sexually, one of them should never ask the other to do anything that is unpleasant or painful. Paul states, "Whatever is not from faith is sin" (Rom. 14:23), which tells us that any sexual act that goes against the conscience of either spouse is wrong. Some inappropriate sexual interests have been fueled by pornography and sexual idolatry.[10] Unnatural, harmful, or immodest sex acts are wrong.

---

7. In one case, a man chose to have a vasectomy to safeguard the health of his wife. She had been diagnosed with a heart condition, which would be life-threatening if she became pregnant. This was a Christlike act of self-sacrifice (Eph. 5:25).

8. For instance, this could be the case if a child dies or if one spouse remarries after being widowed and wants to have children with the new spouse.

9. This is one of the issues that should be settled during courtship.

10. My wife and I received a late-night phone call from a tearful young wife, whose husband was pressuring her to do something sexually that she found to be painful and unpleasant. The husband's desire had been spurred by something he had seen in pornography, and in his selfish, idolatrous lust, he thought that he couldn't be sexually satisfied unless his wife would engage in this particular activity. Needless to say, I strongly admonished him for his selfish attitude and told him that he should be very grateful that God had given him a wife and that she was willing

WHAT MEDICAL MEASURES MAY CHRISTIANS EMPLOY TO ENHANCE THE SEXUAL RELATIONSHIP IN MARRIAGE?

Just as the Bible gives us freedom in using birth control, the use of medications to help with sexual dysfunction is a matter of liberty. The crucial issue is motive. Does someone want to take this drug so that he can fulfill his loving marital duty to his wife and meet her needs? Or is this an expression of sexual idolatry by which he wants to enhance his sexual performance merely for his own pleasure?

In a similar way, a spouse may want to take other measures to be more attractive, including losing weight, straightening teeth, having cosmetic surgery, etc. Again, motive is the key issue. I have known men who have pressured their wives to undergo breast-enhancement surgery when the real problem was that they were looking at too many female breasts that didn't belong to them. If a husband would have eyes only for his wife, he would be more than content with what God has given him. I have also known of women who wanted cosmetic surgery—not so that they could be more attractive to their husbands, but so that they could feel better about themselves and, in some cases, be attractive to other men.

HOW SHOULD CHILDREN BE TAUGHT ABOUT SEX?

No matter how much we try to shelter them, our children receive a lot of bad sexual information from outside sources. In the book of Proverbs, sex education takes place in the home (5:1–4; 6:20–24; 7:1–5). Parents should train their children from a young age to see sex as God sees it—as a wonderful gift for a husband and wife to enjoy in marriage. Parents should also prepare their children to resist sexual temptation (see 5:8; 7:6–27) and to cry out if someone acts inappropriately toward them (Deut. 22:23–27). One of the best lessons that

---

to share physical intimacy with him in other ways.

parents can model for their children is to convey a true sense that they still find great delight in each other sexually.[11] The world says that the best sex takes place between attractive unmarried people. Scripture says that God's gift of sex is most fully enjoyed in marriage. You want to have a marriage affirming that truth, while building a desire in your children that they could one day enjoy what their parents have, and affirming that God's best is worth waiting for.

SUMMARY

While Scripture does not address every sexual question explicitly, general principles helpfully apply to the issues that Christian couples face. They are to lovingly serve each other sexually, with each striving to understand and fulfill the desires of the other. While we have liberty in many areas, we want to use our freedom in a way that considers both the needs and the conscience of others.

— QUESTIONS FOR REFLECTION —

1. How should a married couple decide how often to have sex?
2. How should a married couple determine how many children they should try to have and when they should try to have them?
3. What should be done if a husband and wife can't agree on having children?
4. Which sexual activities is it not proper for Christian couples to engage in?
5. How should children be taught about sex?

11. I am not at all saying that a married couple should do anything immodest in front of their children. But the children should be able to tell by the way their parents act (their touches, kisses, looks) that there is plenty of electricity left in this marriage.

PART 2

DIVORCE AND REMARRIAGE

A. THE FOUNDATIONS OF DIVORCE AND REMARRIAGE

21

WHY ARE MOST QUESTIONS ABOUT DIVORCE AND REMARRIAGE EASY TO ANSWER FROM SCRIPTURE?

When Christians think about the issues of divorce and remarriage, their minds are typically drawn to the most difficult interpretive questions that many believers disagree on and that will, of necessity, occupy much of the rest of this book. The reality is, however, that most Bible-believing Christians are in complete agreement about both the biblical ideal that the marriage covenant is to end only by death and how to apply scriptural principles in the vast majority of cases.

GOD'S DESIGN IS LIFELONG MARRIAGE

When the Pharisees tested Jesus by trying to pull him into their disputes over the grounds for divorce, he reminded them of God's design for marriage from creation. "Some Pharisees came to Jesus, testing Him and asking, 'Is it lawful for a man to divorce his wife for any reason at all?' And He answered and said, 'Have you not read that He who created them from the beginning *made them male and female, and said, "For this reason a man shall leave his father and mother and be joined to his wife, and the two shall become one flesh"*? So they are no longer two, but one flesh. What therefore God has joined together, let no man separate'" (Matt. 19:3–6).

All Bible-believing Christians agree that divorce is contrary to God's design for marriage. We affirm that both husband and wife are responsible to make every effort to remain faithful to the marriage covenant, which God designed as a picture of his covenant relationship with us, his people. We also acknowledge that all divorce is due to sin, though the blame may not be equally apportioned between the two parties.

Furthermore, we are grieved about how the marriage covenant is taken far too lightly in our culture as a thing easily disposed of through "no-fault divorce." Some people even hold celebrations when their marriages end. Even more, we are troubled by the extent to which professing Christians are being influenced by worldly ideas (Rom. 12:2). We see the negative impact on individuals and families as members of evangelical churches divorce and remarry for what we all would agree are unbiblical grounds. We deplore cases in which people selfishly and sinfully break covenant vows with a faithful spouse, as in Malachi 2:14–16 when the men of Judah abandoned their Jewish spouses to marry younger pagan women. We are brokenhearted when people give up when marriage becomes hard, rather than enduring in the power of the Spirit and seeking help from God and the church. We are troubled that many professing Christians affirm that divorce is wrong until it affects them personally or people with whom they are close, at which time they compromise biblical principles.

INVALID GROUNDS FOR DIVORCE

While there is some disagreement among biblical scholars about whether sexual unfaithfulness or abandonment by an unbeliever gives the innocent spouse grounds for divorce, we concur that numerous commonly used reasons for divorce are unbiblical, including:

1. "My spouse isn't a Christian," or "I wasn't a Christian when I married my spouse." Some of the believers in Corinth faced this same situation, and Paul commanded them to remain in the marriage if the spouse was willing (1 Cor. 7:12–13). God

may use you to bring your husband or wife to faith (1 Peter 3:1–2).

2. "We weren't married in a church." Nothing in the Bible directs that you must be married in a church building or that a Christian minister must officiate at the wedding. If you have made a covenant of marriage in any context, you are joined together in marriage by God, who expects you to keep your promise (Matt. 19:6).

3. "I need to get out of this marriage for the sake of my kids." It is reasonable to be concerned about the influence of an unbelieving spouse on your children, but Paul says that even if your spouse is an unbeliever, you should remain married and trust that your spouse and your children will in some sense be sanctified through your presence in the marriage (1 Cor. 7:14). Your testimony of enduring in a hard marriage may have a profoundly positive influence on your children. If your spouse presents a risk of physical or sexual abuse, though, you need to ensure that you and your children are safe.

4. "My spouse is a huge disappointment." "He is a loser (poor provider)." "She hasn't taken care of herself physically." "I would have never married this person if I had known what I was getting myself into." "I deserve better." The traditional marriage vows, which read "for better or for worse, for richer or for poorer," are profound. When you were married, you promised to remain faithful to this person even if he or she were to change in ways you wouldn't like. There is no denying that some marriages are very hard. Many believers remain married—not because they think that they are getting a great deal, but because they seek to honor God and trust that his way is best (Prov. 3:5–6). To graciously love and serve a spouse who is hard to love gives one the opportunity to reflect the love Christ has shown to undeserving sinners like us (Rom. 5:8). The reward for such a faithful spouse may not come in this life, but in the life to come (Matt. 25:23).

5. "We are no longer in love." Being "in love" is not among the

167

biblical criteria for remaining married. An unhappy wife told me, "There is nothing left in our marriage. There is no point in trying anymore." I answered, "Yes, there is. You made a covenant before God. He wants you to try." In Scripture, love is not merely a romantic or passionate feeling. Love involves a deliberate commitment to the good of another person. Paul tells the Ephesians, "Walk in love, just as Christ also loved you and gave Himself up for us, an offering and a sacrifice to God as a fragrant aroma" (Eph. 5:2). You can choose to love another person by acting in the best interests of and praying for him or her. If you can't feel romantic love or even the love of friendship, remember that Jesus calls you to "love your enemies" (Matt. 5:44). As you begin to love your spouse out of love for and obedience to Christ, God can help you to love your spouse from the heart—even romantically.

6. "I married the wrong person," or "We were too young." Some people look back and realize that they made an unwise choice when they got married. They may realize that they weren't ready for marriage, or that the person they married did not meet biblical criteria for a godly spouse. Some even wonder whether, by marrying the "wrong person," they missed out on their "soul mate" (or, in other words, the one whom God truly wanted them to marry). First, it is appropriate to confess to God any sin committed by marrying sinfully or unwisely (1 John 1:8–9). But don't compound that sin with more sin. Now that you are married, it is God's will that you do everything within your power to make your marriage work. There is no biblical basis for saying that by marrying your spouse, you missed out on your "soul mate" or the "right one" God intended for you. Such thinking is worldly mysticism with no scriptural foundation. The one you have is God's plan for you. Trust God that he will work even your unwise or sinful choice for your good and his glory (Rom. 8:28).

7. "I owe it to myself to be happy. God wouldn't want me to be unhappy." The desire to be happy, or the fear of unhappiness,

is probably the leading cause of divorce among unbelievers. Sadly, many marriages among professing Christians break up simply because one or both spouses are unhappy and have given up hope of ever being happy with the other. It is as if they have decided that the answer to the first question of the Westminster Shorter Catechism, "What is the chief end of man?," is "to be happy," rather than "man's chief end is to glorify God and to enjoy Him forever."[1] Just as our Lord Jesus glorified God through his suffering, sometimes we will be called to follow in his steps as we suffer to the glory of God (1 Peter 2:21). Some will suffer persecution at the hands of hostile human government. Some may suffer within hard marriages. Some marriages may be difficult because a spouse is incapacitated in such a way physically or mentally that one receives few or none of the benefits of marriage, such as companionship, provision, and physical affection. Yet there is no option to seek these benefits elsewhere because the marriage covenant is still in force. Others may suffer in marriages that are hard because their spouses are selfish and immature. They don't share the joy that they see others experiencing in marriage.

8. Yet in any of these cases, believers can continue to be faithful to the vows that they made before the Lord, in whom they can find joy (Phil. 4:4), even if their marriage is a struggle. They can persevere in hope that God can work by his Word and through the gospel to renew love and joy in their marriage. They also recognize that the idea that one can achieve greater happiness by defying God's commands (e.g., divorcing and/or remarrying against God's will as revealed in his Word) challenges both God's wisdom (that he knows what is best for you—Prov. 3:5–6) and his sovereignty (that he will bless obedience and bring consequences for disobedience). "Do not be deceived, God is not mocked; for whatever a man sows,

1. http://www.shortercatechism.com/resources/wsc/wsc_001.html.

this he will also reap" (Gal. 6:7). Do you really think that you can fight against God and win?

9. "All my friends say that I ought to leave him (her)." It is common for worldly friends and family to offer marital advice based on the unbiblical reasons listed above. Family and friends often think that it is their job to take our side and to tell us what we want to hear. But Scripture says that this kind of flattery does not actually profit in the end: "He who rebukes a man will afterward find more favor than he who flatters with the tongue" (Prov. 28:23). Their errors are often compounded by the fact that they are usually not fully informed about both sides of the conflict. "The first to plead his case seems right, until another comes and examines him" (Prov. 18:17). Those who counsel people to abandon their marriage are in grave danger of coming under God's judgment for contributing to the separation of what God has joined (Matt. 19:9). All of us need to be careful to choose wise, godly counselors (Ps. 1:1; 1 Cor. 15:33).

10. "God will forgive me." On more than one occasion, I have heard professing Christians remark, "I know that it is wrong for me to divorce my spouse and that I don't have any biblical grounds, but I know that Jesus' blood will cover my sin, and life will go on." Sometimes this was so that they could be with someone they thought would make them happier. In other cases, they just wanted to get away from a hard marriage. While it is true that God's grace is very great, a true believer will not presume upon it. As Paul says in Romans 6:1–2, "What shall we say then? Are we to continue in sin so that grace may increase? May it never be! How shall we who died to sin still live in it?" The apostle goes on to explain that Jesus did not die so that we could go on sinning. Rather, he died so that we would no longer be slaves to sin (see also Titus 2:14). Scripture tells us to question the conversion of a professing Christian who willfully defies God's Word. According to Jesus, "If you love Me, you will keep My commandments"

(John 14:15). John writes, "By this we know that we have come to know Him, if we keep His commandments. The one who says, 'I have come to know Him,' and does not keep His commandments, is a liar, and the truth is not in him" (1 John 2:3–4). While only God knows the true state of this person's soul, he or she is subject to church discipline (see Matt. 18:15–20) and at risk of being put out of the church as an unbeliever.

THERE IS WIDESPREAD AGREEMENT ABOUT OTHER BASIC ISSUES

1. Bible-believing scholars affirm that, ordinarily, the marriage covenant ends with the death of one spouse, at which time the surviving spouse is free to remarry (Rom. 7:2–3; 1 Cor. 7:39; 1 Tim. 5:14).
2. Those who have divorced without proper biblical grounds sin if they remarry someone else (Matt. 19:9).
3. If a believer divorces a fellow believer without proper biblical grounds, he or she is not free to remarry someone else (1 Cor. 7:10–11).

SUMMARY

While there is much controversy and disagreement among Bible-believing Christians regarding some of the fine points about divorce and remarriage, there is widespread agreement pertaining to the biblical ideal from creation that the marriage covenant is designed by God to be lifelong. In the overwhelming majority of actual cases, there is agreement that divorce is not a biblical option (you aren't permitted to divorce just because you are unhappy) and that every effort should be made to hold together what God has joined.

— QUESTIONS FOR REFLECTION —

1. When Jesus is asked about divorce, to which passage does He first turn? Why?
2. What are the most common reasons that people get divorced, and why are these reasons invalid?
3. What effect has "no-fault divorce" had on our culture?
4. What effect has "no-fault divorce" had on the church?
5. What would you say to someone who is in a very hard marriage and is thinking of getting out?

22

WHY ARE SOME QUESTIONS ABOUT DIVORCE AND REMARRIAGE SO DIFFICULT?

God's people have been debating the issues surrounding divorce and remarriage for thousands of years. In the first century, the Pharisees tried to get Jesus embroiled in the debate between the followers of Shammai and Hillel about what constitutes legitimate grounds for divorce (Matt. 19:3). Throughout church history, different views have been promoted and enforced by different branches of Christendom. In our day, scholars who are in agreement about most other crucial issues of the faith sometimes differ sharply concerning the biblical grounds (if any) for divorce and remarriage. The importance of getting these issues right is heightened by the practical impact they have on the lives of ordinary Christians in each of our churches.

BIBLE-BELIEVING SCHOLARS
SHARPLY DISAGREE

Good, godly, Bible-believing men and women who are careful scholars have reached different conclusions about biblical grounds for divorce and remarriage. As in Jesus' day, the interpretations vary widely, from the most strict to the more permissive. Solid pastors and

173

theologians, including John Piper and James Montgomery Boice, take the position that Scripture never allows divorce or remarriage under any circumstance. Other scholars make some allowance for divorce, but not for remarriage. Most others—including John MacArthur, John Murray, and the majority of Reformed theologians—make allowance for divorce and remarriage on limited grounds (sexual sin and abandonment by an unbeliever), but differ among themselves about exactly how to define these grounds. Books and articles have been published by people on all sides, examining the biblical texts along with historical and cultural data. There have also been helpful volumes in which people holding the different views interact with one another.[1] It can be overwhelming to sift through the opposing interpretations of the various biblical texts and the argumentation put forth. Perhaps as an example of how challenging these issues are, William Heth wrote in 1990 in favor of the "Divorce, but No Remarriage Position," only to change his view and then to be invited to write for the "Remarriage for Adultery or Desertion Position" in 2006.[2]

THE PRACTICAL IMPLICATIONS ARE EXTREMELY SIGNIFICANT

Is all this debate really necessary? Let us take the example of Stephanie, who is twenty-three years old; has been married for two years to her husband, Chris; and has a sixteen-month-old toddler, Bradley.[3] While Chris had professed to be a Christian before they were married, he seemed to lose interest in Stephanie and in church attendance after Bradley was born. Finally, it came out that Chris was having an affair with a female coworker. When Stephanie confronted Chris, he became angry and violent with her and threatened to hurt both her and Bradley. She called the police, who forced Chris to move out. He then

---

1. See H. Wayne House, ed., *Divorce and Remarriage: Four Christian Views* (Downers Grove, IL: InterVarsity Press, 1990); Mark L. Strauss, ed., *Remarriage after Divorce in Today's Church: 3 Views* (Grand Rapids: Zondervan, 2006).
2. Ibid.
3. This example is a compilation of multiple actual cases that I have dealt with.

moved in with his female coworker. Chris refuses to speak to anyone from the church and no longer claims to be a Christian.

How do you advise Stephanie about her options? May she initiate divorce proceedings against Chris? Or must she wait for him to divorce her? If they divorce, is she free to remarry? Or must she wait until Chris marries (which may never happen if he chooses simply to go on cohabiting with his girlfriend)? Or must she wait until Chris dies before she can remarry? What does Scripture really have to say for her situation?

A situation like this makes one think of James's warning, "Let not many of you become teachers, my brethren, knowing that as such we will incur a stricter judgment" (James 3:1), and that of Jesus, "Whoever causes one of these little ones who believe in Me to stumble, it would be better for him to have a heavy millstone hung around his neck, and to be drowned in the depth of the sea" (Matt. 18:6). We do not want to encourage people to do that which God forbids, remembering Jesus' warning not to unlawfully separate that which God has joined (Matt. 19:6). Those taking the strictest (permanence) view of divorce and remarriage would say that Stephanie may not initiate divorce or remarry until Chris dies. If they are right and if we were to encourage Stephanie to divorce and remarry, then we would be encouraging her to sin and would share responsibility for an adulterous divorce and remarriage (Mark 10:12). Some would argue against the permanence view by saying that it would be too hard for a young woman to spend the rest of her life alone without a husband to help her. But we cannot allow ourselves to be swayed merely by emotional arguments or by people's stories, or we will find ourselves allowing for divorce and remarriage for almost any cause.[4] As Proverbs warns, "There is a way which seems right to a man, but its end is the way of death" (14:12). We must follow what God's Word says and trust him to take care of those who are faithful to him.

---

4. The rapid change in attitude toward accepting homosexuality, even among evangelicals, has largely been the result of people's being swayed by emotional stories of friends and family members. We must assert, however, that God's Word has authority over our feelings and experiences.

On the other hand, we don't want to forbid people from doing that which God allows. For instance, if the Bible teaches that Stephanie is free to divorce her unfaithful and violent spouse and to remarry if she chooses, it would be wrong to forbid her to do so. She could be harmed by church leaders who would forbid a remarriage that could be a great blessing and help for both Stephanie and her young son, Bradley. Again, these matters must be determined biblically—not pragmatically.

SIN COMPLICATES LIFE

The saying that "God made men upright, but they have sought out many devices" (Eccl. 7:29) is certainly true in the case of marriage. As Jesus reminds the Pharisees, marriage as designed by God in the garden is very simple—one man with one woman for life (Matt. 19:4–6). The entrance of sin into the world has produced broken relationships between people and God and in all other interpersonal relationships, including marriage. After more than thirty years of pastoral and counseling ministry, I never cease to be amazed at the messes that people get themselves into and the complexity of the questions that arise in situations involving divorce and remarriage. It is virtually impossible to address every conceivable scenario, or even every situation I have ever seen personally, in the space allotted in this book. I can assert with confidence, though, that God's Word is sufficient to address any problem you may face (2 Tim. 3:16–17) and can offer principles from Scripture that will help you to face the real counseling crises you will encounter.

WE MUST BE HUMBLE,
AND WE MUST BE REDEMPTIVE

Tackling a subject as difficult as this is—and that so many good, wise, and godly men and women disagree on—should keep one humble. In spite of our best efforts, it is possible that each of us is wrong about something. There may be particular issues that people must admit to remaining unsure about or situations that they reach a tentative conclusion about, but must remain open to the possibility that they will later be forced to reconsider. There may be circumstances in a church context in which leaders have views on some of the most difficult questions about the grounds for divorce and remarriage that they agree not to impose on church members who come to different conclusions.[5] There may also be situations in which leaders within the same denomination or local church differ on certain points, but choose to work together in spite of their differences. Each should assume that the other loves the Lord, respects the Scriptures, seeks to honor marriage, and is doing his or her best to be biblical with regard to the position. Love "hopes all things" (1 Cor. 13:7).[6] Köstenberger writes, "In light of the disagreement among orthodox believers over this subject, we encourage all to hold their views of divorce and remarriage charitably, yet with conviction, being open to honest dialogue with those who espouse differing positions."[7]

We want to keep our focus on the hope that the gospel brings to broken marriages and to broken individuals as well. Many give up on their marriages because they have lost sight of God's power to reconcile people who have been living in conflict and to transform those who have been enslaved to sin. While we should labor to understand what the Bible says about whether or when a marriage may end in divorce and whether or when a divorced person may remarry, it is most important to strive to learn how the gospel can enable shattered relationships to heal. Jay Adams writes that "divorce is never desirable, and (among Christians) it is never inevitable."[8]

---

5. I am not saying that church members can choose to divorce and remarry for any grounds they choose—see the previous question for a list of grounds that are widely identified as invalid. I am saying that there are some exceptionally difficult situations, many of which will be covered in subsequent questions.

6. I appreciate how several authors have written humbly in support of their own positions and respectfully and kindly in response to those with whom they disagree.

7. Andreas J. Köstenberger with David Jones, *God, Marriage, and Family: Rebuilding the Biblical Foundation*, 2nd ed. (Wheaton, IL: Crossway, 2010), 232.

8. Jay Adams, *Marriage, Divorce, and Remarriage in the Bible* (Grand Rapids: Zondervan, 1980), 31.

SUMMARY

The questions on whether or when divorce and remarriage are allowed have been debated for centuries and are complicated on both a theoretical and a practical level. While we should sympathize with the pain that people in broken relationships experience, we must not let sympathy for particular situations determine our position. Nor can we lean on a particular church tradition or merely follow our theological heroes. Rather, we must base our conclusions solely on Scripture.

— QUESTIONS FOR REFLECTION —

1. Why do Bible-believing scholars have such a hard time agreeing on their views about the grounds, if any, for divorce and remarriage?
2. Why are these issues so difficult on a practical level?
3. Could there be situations in which you aren't sure whether the Bible allows for divorce and/or remarriage? What should be done in such situations?
4. What freedom should be given for differences of opinion concerning grounds for divorce and remarriage within a church or denomination?
5. What is the hardest question you have faced regarding the grounds for divorce and remarriage?

23

WHAT IS DIVORCE?

Divorce is the dissolution of a marriage covenant. It typically involves both the suspension of spousal rights and responsibilities and the freedom to marry someone else.

PUT IT IN WRITING

Under the Mosaic covenant, the husband who initiated the divorce would give his wife a certificate releasing her from obligation to him and thus making her available to another man. This procedure is described in the Pentateuch: "When a man takes a wife and marries her, and it happens that she finds no favor in his eyes because he has found some indecency in her, and he writes her a certificate of divorce and puts it in her hand and sends her out from his house, and she leaves his house and goes and becomes another man's wife" (Deut. 24:1–2). This is what is spoken of when the Lord, through Jeremiah, describes his divorce of adulterous Israel, saying that he gave her a "writ of divorce" (Jer. 3:8; see also Isa. 50:1).

REMARRIAGE IS EXPECTED AFTER DIVORCE

In the case in Deuteronomy 24, it is assumed that the divorced woman will remarry. Gordon Wenham tells us, "All Jews in the first century permitted divorce in certain cases, and a Jewish divorce always entailed the right to remarry."[1] Jewish writings from the first century and before include bills of divorce that contain the statement, "You are free to marry any (Jewish) man."[2] When Jesus discusses divorce, he assumes that the divorced wife will remarry: "It was said, 'Whoever sends his wife away, let him give her a certificate of divorce'; but I say to you that everyone who divorces his wife, except for the reason of unchastity, makes her commit adultery; and whoever marries a divorced woman commits adultery" (Matt. 5:31–32). The New Testament, however, contains one clear example of a situation in which marital rights and obligations are suspended, most likely through divorce, without the freedom to remarry. Paul writes, "But to the married I give instructions, not I, but the Lord, that the wife should not leave her husband (but if she does leave, she must remain unmarried, or else be reconciled to her husband), and that the husband should not divorce his wife" (1 Cor. 7:10–11).

IS DIVORCE ALWAYS INITIATED BY THE MAN?

While most examples in the Bible speak from the perspective of the man's divorcing his wife and giving her a certificate of divorce (Deut. 24:1–4; Jer. 3:8; Matt. 5:31–32; 19:3, 7–9; Mark 10:2; Luke 16:18), there are also cases in which the divorce is initiated by the woman. Under the Mosaic law, a woman is free to leave the marriage if her husband, after taking another wife, fails to meet his basic spousal obligations: "If he takes to himself another woman, he may not reduce her food, her clothing, or her conjugal rights. If he will not do these three things for her, then she shall go out for nothing, without payment of money" (Ex. 21:10–11). Jesus also addresses the wife who divorces her husband: "And He said to them, 'Whoever divorces his wife and marries another woman commits adultery against her; and

1. Gordon J. Wenham, "No Remarriage after Divorce," in *Remarriage after Divorce in Today's Church: 3 Views*, ed. Mark L. Strauss (Grand Rapids: Zondervan, 2006), 33.

2. Andreas J. Köstenberger with David Jones, *God, Marriage, and Family: Rebuilding the Biblical Foundation*, 2nd ed. (Wheaton, IL: Crossway, 2010), 287.

if she herself divorces her husband and marries another man, she is committing adultery'" (Mark 10:11–12). Finally, Paul addresses the possibility that a wife will be the one to break the marriage bond: "And a woman who has an unbelieving husband, and he consents to live with her, she must not send her husband away" (1 Cor. 7:13; see also 1 Cor. 7:10).

WHAT IS THE DIFFERENCE BETWEEN DIVORCE AND A LEGAL SEPARATION?

Some couples who are in conflict choose to become legally separated instead of divorcing. Many file for legal separation to protect their rights (e.g., not being obligated for future debts incurred by their spouse, spousal and child support, visitation rights) because these issues cannot be worked out without legal intervention. Some file for legal separation, rather than divorce, because they hold out hope that over time the marriage can be restored. Others hold out little hope for the marriage relationship to be renewed, but choose to file for legal separation because they do not want the stigma that comes with being divorced, or they have no interest in remarriage.

The Bible does not explicitly address the issue of legal separation, which seems to be in effect like a partial divorce in that it suspends most of the rights and obligations of the marriage, while not freeing either party to remarry. In addition to the obvious problem of separating what God has joined (Matt. 19:6), there likely is also a violation of the prohibition of believers' going to court against each other (1 Cor. 6:1–8) when professing Christians separate legally.

WHAT IS THE DIFFERENCE BETWEEN DIVORCE AND ANNULMENT?

As is the case with legal separation, the concept of annulment is not explicitly taught in the Bible, but there are principles that would apply. Whereas a divorce ends a marriage, an annulment declares that the marriage never existed. While I am not aware of a biblical example of an annulment, there are several situations throughout history in which annulments have been granted by certain civil or ecclesiastical jurisdictions. These circumstances would include a bigamous marriage (because one party was already married, the second marriage was not legal or valid); an incestuous marriage; a marriage in which one party did not freely consent (e.g., mental incompetence, forced against the person's will through threats); underage marriage; misrepresentation (e.g., the other person claimed to be a woman, but was a man); or willful failure to consummate the marriage. There are other disputed grounds for annulment, including sexual sins or diseases before marriage that were deceitfully concealed and unwillingness to have children.

The Roman Catholic Church regards marriage to be a sacrament of the church and holds that a sacramental marriage cannot properly end in divorce. Those who would divorce and remarry would be considered guilty of a mortal sin. The Roman Catholics do, though, grant annulments for various reasons, including the claim by one or both parties that they did not fully grasp the commitment they were making when they entered into the marriage union.[3] When a marriage is annulled, the couple is considered by the church to have never been truly married, even if they have been together as husband and wife for many years and had several children together.[4] Experience shows that grounds for annulment, like the grounds that some people use for divorce, can be stretched to meet various situations.[5] Such annulments, like many legal separations, are in effect divorces even if the word is not used. This is despite the claims of the Roman Catholic Church that marriage is indissoluble and that annulled marriages were never truly valid.

3. It could be argued that none of us fully grasps what we are getting into on our wedding day.

4. http://www.catholicbible101.com/annulments.htm; http://www.vatican.va /archive/ccc_css/archive/catechism/p2s2c3a7.htm.

5. In 2012, 90 percent of petitions for annulment were granted by the Roman Catholic Church. http://www.washingtontimes.com/news/2014/oct/15/annulments -plummet-among-us-catholics-amid-fewer-m/.

SUMMARY

Divorce is contrary to God's original design for marriage and has come into the world because of human sin. Divorce typically involves both the suspension of marital rights and duties and the legal right to enter into marriage with someone else.[6] Other arrangements, including legal separation and annulment, have similar effects.[7]

— QUESTIONS FOR REFLECTION —

1. What is the earliest biblical reference to divorce?
2. What rights in Scripture do women have regarding divorce?
3. What is the difference between legal separation and divorce?
4. What is an annulment?
5. Is there any situation in which annulment would be preferable to divorce?

6. As we will see in the following questions, however, many divorces and remarriages are sinful.

7. Typically, legal separation would involve the suspension of marital rights and duties, but not the legal right to remarry.

24

WHY DOES GOD HATE DIVORCE?

"'I hate divorce,' says the LORD, the God of Israel" (Mal 2:16).[1] In this particular situation, the men of Judah appear to be divorcing their Israelite wives to marry younger pagan women. In so doing, they invite God's wrath. As we study this text, we recognize that God has good reason for disapproving of divorce because wrongful divorce is an assault both on his lordship and on the innocent.

DIVORCE BREAKS A COVENANT
MADE BEFORE GOD

Malachi reminds the Jewish men, "The LORD has been a witness between you and the wife of your youth, against whom you have dealt treacherously, though she is your companion and your wife by covenant" (Mal. 2:14). This is a reminder that marriage is a covenant between a man and a woman, with God as witness. This is why Jesus refers to a man and a wife as being joined together in marriage by God (Matt. 19:6). Just as human witnesses to a covenant or contract are expected to hold the parties accountable to keep their promises, God holds men and women accountable to their marriage vows (see also Eccl. 5:4–5). A willful breach of the marriage covenant is a sin not just

---

1. Some translations, such as the ESV, HCSB, and NIV, translate Malachi 2:16 to refer to "the man who hates and divorces," but the idea that God hates divorce is still plainly in the text, since it describes the man who divorces as treacherous.

against one's spouse, but against God, who serves as the enforcer of the covenant. Thus, a covenant-breaker invites his wrath.

The heinous nature of divorce is compounded by the fact that earthly marriages are designed by God to reflect his covenant relationship with his people. A husband is to portray the faithful self-sacrificing love of Christ for his bride, the church (Eph. 5:25–30). Jesus showed covenant love to us at great cost, sacrificing himself that we might be saved. A husband who would abandon his covenant promise to his wife misrepresents the Lord's covenant commitment to his people.

Those considering divorce need to realize that their decision is not merely between them and their spouse. God himself was involved as a party to their marriage when it began, and he is the defender of every marriage as well. You cannot willfully defy him and come out ahead in the long run. On the other hand, if you turn to him, he will help you to keep your covenant promises and to rebuild what seems to be hopelessly broken.

DIVORCE HARMS THE INNOCENT SPOUSE

God, who is the protector of the innocent and weak (Ps. 82:3), hates divorce because it hurts the spouse who has sought to keep his or her side of the marriage covenant. The treachery described in Malachi 2:14–16 is both treachery against God and treachery against a faithful wife. In this case, she gave her best years to her husband, cared for his needs, and bore him children. She anticipated that they would grow old together as companions and friends, enjoying their grandchildren and sharing life. Instead, he has decided to cast aside the wife of his youth for a younger woman who offers the prospect of greater sensual delights and more offspring. To add insult to injury, he is marrying a pagan girl (Mal. 2:11) in defiance of God's law (Deut. 7:3). God still hates it today when one spouse divorces the other simply because the person thinks he or she can do better by finding someone younger, more attractive, or wealthier, leaving the innocent spouse alone and forsaken. "Take heed to your spirit, that you do not deal treacherously" (Mal. 2:16b).

Divorce also harms one's spouse by potentially leading him or her to an adulterous or defiling marriage. According to Deuteronomy 24:4, a woman who has been divorced from her husband and remarried has in some sense been defiled. Jesus says, "Everyone who divorces his wife, except for the reason of unchastity, makes her commit adultery" (Matt. 5:32). Jesus' assumption is that the wrongfully divorced wife will remarry, perhaps out of economic necessity, in which case she will be in an adulterous marriage. John Frame writes, "Divorce and remarriage typically lead to adultery by four people."[2]

DIVORCE HARMS THE CHILDREN

In Malachi, the Lord expresses his concern that sinful divorces and remarriages would affect the ability of the Israelites to produce godly offspring (Mal. 2:15). Deuteronomy 7:4 warns that if the Israelites intermarried, "they will turn your sons away from following Me to serve other gods; then the anger of the LORD will be kindled against you and He will quickly destroy you." God still hates the devastating effects of divorce on children. God's design is that children be raised by a mother and father who are committed to each other in lifelong love. When professing Christians divorce for unbiblical reasons, they set a terrible example to their children by choosing to defy the plain teaching of Scripture and saying by implication that the gospel wasn't enough to solve their family's problems.

Children's hearts are broken as they see their parents split up. They feel pressure to take sides when their parents are in conflict. Sometimes they wonder whether their parents' breakup was somehow their fault. Life with broken and blended families becomes quite complicated and painful for children as they are passed back and forth between their parents. They must adjust to new stepparents (and stepbrothers and stepsisters), with whom they may not get along, and they face the temptation to play their parents off each other

2. John M. Frame, *The Doctrine of the Christian Life* (Phillipsburg, NJ: P&R Publishing, 2008), 773–74.

(a temptation that they may not be mature enough to handle wisely). Research shows that children whose parents have divorced are more likely to experience abuse, to do poorly academically, to become involved in crime and drugs, and to struggle financially as adults.[3] While being the child of divorced parents does not definitively produce such results, divorce is a very negative influence that most children would do best without.

DIVORCE ALSO HARMS THE COMMUNITY

As the marriage covenant is taken more lightly and divorce becomes easier and more common, the wider community is affected. Divorce has an effect on other family members, including parents and siblings, who suffer through the breakup with their loved one and experience loss of relationship with the former spouse whom they had grown to love. The indirect effects of divorce impact the civil sphere as well with the rise of abuse, crime, drug use, and poverty (increasing dependence on social welfare).[4] A society that lacks stable marriages will be under God's judgment and will deteriorate over time.

SUMMARY

God hates divorce because it violates the two great commandments—love God and love your neighbor. Divorce is a defiant sin against the love we should have for God, who joins husband and wife in the marriage covenant and calls them to remain committed and faithful until death parts them. Divorce is also a sin against our neighbor, whom we are to love as ourselves. To unlawfully divorce one's spouse is treacherous. It harms not only that person, but children and the wider community, all of whom are under God's care and protection.

---

3. http://peacemaker.net/project/the-effects-of-divorce-on-america/.
4. http://www.heritage.org/research/reports/2000/06/the-effects-of-divorce-on
-america.

— Questions for Reflection —

1. In what sense is divorce a sin against God?
2. How were the divorces that Malachi spoke about particularly treacherous?
3. How are many divorces in our day equally harmful?
4. How does divorce affect other family members?
5. How does divorce impact the community?

25

WHY DOES GOD PERMIT DIVORCE?

We have seen that God's ideal is for a man and a woman to remain faithful to their marriage covenant until death parts them. This leads to the question that if God so hates divorce, why did he permit and regulate divorce under the Old Testament?[1] And why would he permit divorce today?

BECAUSE OF YOUR HARDNESS OF HEART

When Jesus was asked why Moses commanded a man to give his wife a certificate of divorce and send her away, "He said to them, 'Because of your hardness of heart Moses permitted you to divorce your wives; but from the beginning it has not been this way'" (Matt. 19:8). In the sinless world before the fall, human hearts were not yet hard. There was no need to have rules to deal with murder, theft, or divorce. But when sin entered into the world, God determined that social order must be maintained through the establishment and enforcement of various civil laws, which serve to restrain sin and its effects. For example, murder is contrary to God's moral will because it destroys a life made in his image, and God regulates what should

---

1. In Ezra 9–10, the men of Judah put away the foreign wives whom they had married in contradiction to God's law. It appears that the evil of divorcing the pagan women was preferable to their ongoing influence on God's people.

happen when hard-hearted men wrongfully take human life (see Gen. 9:5–6). The punishment for murder reflects the seriousness of the crime. In the same way that God's moral law regarding human life can be broken, his laws concerning marriage can and will be broken. Sinful men and women will break the marriage covenant through adultery and abandonment. Thus, biblical regulations for divorce and remarriage are given—both to discourage the sinful violation of God's design for marriage and to minimize the harmful effects on the innocent parties.

John Frame explains it this way: "God determined that a prohibition of all divorce would be, for fallen people, unbearable, and therefore counterproductive for good social order. Sin would certainly lead to divorce; the law could not be expected to prevent that. The best thing that the law could accomplish would be to regulate divorce, to mitigate its oppressiveness and maintain the rights of those cast aside."[2]

NOT ALLOWING FOR VALID DIVORCE CAN HARM THE INNOCENT

When I was working as a tent-making pastor in an underground English-speaking church in the Middle East, many of our members were from the Philippines (a nation whose laws have been greatly influenced by the Roman Catholic Church), which does not allow for divorce. We encountered several cases in which Christian men and women had been abandoned by their spouses. Even though these spouses were often cohabiting with someone new (and in some cases having children together), the innocent spouses were still not able to obtain divorces.[3] They were not free to remarry. The laws against

2. John M. Frame, *The Doctrine of the Christian Life* (Phillipsburg, NJ: P&R Publishing, 2008), 770.

3. The law of the Philippines does allow for legal separation and annulment. Many Christians, however, would have a problem with annulment. It says, in effect, that the couple's marriage was never valid. Furthermore, the official legal grounds for annulment (fraud, lack of mental competency at the time of marriage, etc.) are very limited and may not legitimately apply.

divorce, which were intended to protect marriage, actually had the effect of failing to protect the innocent party, while leaving the guilty party unpunished for abandoning the marriage covenant.

DIVORCE CAN PROTECT THE RIGHTS OF THE INNOCENT

Biblical standards for divorce are actually designed to protect the innocent party. For instance, the Mosaic law made provision for a wife whose husband refused to fulfill his responsibilities to her. Rather than being left destitute—but still in legal bondage to her covenant-breaking husband—she could be set free, presumably to find another man who would take proper care of her (Ex. 21:11).

In the case of a wife sent away by her husband (Deut. 24:1–2), her certificate of divorce would make it clear to all concerned that her former husband had no more claim on her. Instead of leaving her in a state of marital limbo with possible obligations to the first husband if he chose to return, she was free to be remarried to another man. The fact that the first husband could never remarry his former wife (even if the second husband died or they were divorced) might also serve to protect her. It would make him take his decision to send her away very seriously, knowing that if he acted rashly, he most likely could never have her back again (Deut. 24:3–4).

The New Testament provisions for divorce, in the case of unrepentant spousal adultery (Matt. 19:9) or abandonment by an unbelieving spouse (1 Cor. 7:15), protect the innocent party as well. If, as I will argue in questions 28–29, the person is free to remarry, he or she can be blessed by the opportunity to enter into a new marriage with a faithful, believing spouse. The situation of a young woman who has been abandoned by an unfaithful husband would be like that of a younger widow, who would do well to remarry and have children (1 Cor. 7:39; 1 Tim. 5:14). Remarriage to a godly husband can be God's way of providing and caring for her.

SOME DIVORCES AND
REMARRIAGES WERE FORBIDDEN

Under the law of Moses, some divorces and remarriages were absolutely prohibited. For example, a man who falsely charged that his wife was not a virgin when he married her was to be fined for defaming her, and he was never allowed to divorce her (Deut. 22:13–19). In the same way, when a man was compelled to marry a virgin whom he had seduced, he had no right to divorce her (22:28–29). Additionally, the man in Deuteronomy 24:1–4, who had divorced his wife, was not free to remarry her after she had remarried another man even after the second husband died or divorced her.[4] Priests were forbidden to marry a divorced woman (Lev. 21:7, 14; Ezek. 44:22).

SUMMARY

Every divorce involves a sinful violation of God's design for marriage, but not every divorced person is responsible for the divorce.

4. There is much discussion and debate about Deuteronomy 24:1–4. Some interpreters make much of the first husband's sending her away for "indecency" while the other "turns against her" ("hates her"), implying that the first may have divorced with cause while the other had no cause. According to a study by Raymond Westbrook, this would then have a financial impact. She would have lost her dowry for having been sent away for cause in the first marriage, but would have kept her dowry after being sent away without cause in the second marriage. Thus, this would potentially expose an evil financial motive for the first husband to take his wife back. See William A. Heth, "Remarriage for Adultery or Desertion," in *Remarriage after Divorce in Today's Church: 3 Views*, ed. Mark L. Strauss (Grand Rapids: Zondervan, 2006), 64, for a discussion of this view. I agree with John Murray that "it is exceedingly difficult if not precarious to be certain as to what the 'unseemly thing' really was," in *Divorce* (Philadelphia: Presbyterian and Reformed, 1961), 9. In addition, Köstenberger writes, "Perhaps dowry-related issues were involved as well, but this is uncertain" (Andreas J. Köstenberger with David W. Jones, *God, Marriage, and Family: Rebuilding the Biblical Foundation*, 2nd ed. [Wheaton, IL: Crossway, 2010], 224). I also believe, in light of the death penalty prescribed under the Law for adultery (Lev. 20:10; Deut. 22:22), it is unlikely that "indecency" refers to sexual immorality. I do not think there is sufficient proof that the reasons for the two divorces are significantly different, or that the motive for taking the wife back would be financial.

Because sinful people will break the marriage covenant, God regulates divorce in a way that seeks to restrain further sin and to protect the innocent.

— QUESTIONS FOR REFLECTION —

1. Did Jesus teach that no man can separate what God has joined? Explain.
2. Why is divorce inevitable in a fallen world?
3. How does God's regulation of divorce protect the innocent?
4. Are divorced people still married in God's eyes?
5. What good could come from a divorce?

B. DIVORCE AND REMARRIAGE CONTROVERSIES

26

DOES JESUS TEACH THAT THERE ARE NO VALID GROUNDS FOR DIVORCE AND REMARRIAGE?

In a day when the world has moved toward easy no-fault divorce, and most evangelical Christians allow for divorce and remarriage under certain limited circumstances, a surprising number of respected evangelical scholars take the position that the Bible never allows a Christian to initiate divorce under any circumstances or to remarry so long as the person's spouse is living. This perspective is often referred to as the permanence view.

One prominent advocate of the permanence view, J. Carl Laney, defines marriage as "God's act of joining a man and a woman in a permanent, covenanted, one-flesh relationship."[1] He also states, "I believe Scripture teaches that marriage was designed by God to be permanent unto death, and that divorce and remarriage constitute the sin of adultery."[2] John Piper additionally reaches the conclusion of "a New Testament prohibition of all remarriage except in the case where a spouse has died."[3] According to Wingerd et al., "In the Bible, the

1. J. Carl Laney, "No Divorce and No Remarriage," in *Divorce and Remarriage: Four Christian Views*, ed. H. Wayne House (Downers Grove, IL: InterVarsity Press, 1990), 20.
2. Ibid., 16.
3. John Piper, *Divorce and Remarriage: A Position Paper* (http://www.desiringgod

remarriage of a divorced person is consistently said to be an act of adultery, indicating that the one flesh union created by God when a marriage begins is not ended by divorce. Only death dissolves this union."[4] They share an understanding in common with that of the Roman Catholic Church—that no human power can dissolve the marriage union, though their reasons for holding this position differ.

DIVORCE IN THE OLD TESTAMENT

Those arguing that the marriage covenant is an unbreakable bond find support in various Old Testament passages. Appealing to Genesis 2:24 and Jesus' reference to it when questioned about divorce in Matthew 19, they argue that when marriage makes a couple one flesh, they become close relatives (kin), or a relationship that "endures whatever changes occur to the related individuals."[5] Furthermore, a stigma is attached to divorce throughout the Old Testament. The Law forbids a priest from marrying a divorcée (Lev. 21:7), and the prophet Malachi tells us that God hates those who act treacherously in divorce (Mal. 2:13–17). The divorced and remarried wife is said to be defiled by her remarriage (Deut. 24:4). Piper asserts that this "teaches that the one-flesh relationship established by marriage is not obliterated by divorce or even by remarriage."[6]

THE TEACHING OF JESUS

Proponents of the permanence view find biblical warrant in the teachings of Jesus as well. They begin with the texts in which Jesus calls divorce and remarriage adulterous without mentioning any exceptions: "Everyone who divorces his wife and marries another commits

---

.org/articles/divorce-remarriage-a-position-paper).

4. Daryl Wingerd et al., *Divorce & Remarriage: A Permanence View* (Kansas City: Christian Communicators Worldwide, 2009), 9.

5. Gordon J. Wenham, "No Remarriage after Divorce," in *Remarriage after Divorce in Today's Church: 3 Views*, ed. Mark L. Strauss (Grand Rapids: Zondervan, 2006), 20.

6. Piper, *Divorce and Remarriage*, 8.

adultery, and he who marries one who is divorced from a husband commits adultery" (Luke 16:18; see also Mark 10:11–12). Piper attests, "Since there are no exceptions mentioned in the verse, and since Jesus is clearly rejecting the common cultural conception of divorce as including the right of remarriage, the first readers of this gospel would have been hard-put to argue for any exceptions on the basis that Jesus shared the cultural assumption that divorce for unfaithfulness or desertion freed a spouse for remarriage."[7] Also, when Jesus declares, "Everyone who divorces his wife, except for the reason of unchastity, makes her commit adultery" (Matt. 5:32), Piper affirms that in this statement, our Lord "plainly says that the remarriage of a wife who has been innocently put away is nevertheless adultery."[8] Consequently, both the innocent and the guilty spouses are prohibited from remarriage.

When the Pharisees challenge Jesus, trying to get him to take a side in their debates over the grounds of divorce and remarriage, he reminds them that divorce has no part in God's original design (Matt. 19:3–6).[9] Piper mentions that "the implication is that Jesus rejects the Pharisees' use of Deuteronomy 24:1 and raises the standard of marriage for his disciples to God's original intention in creation."[10] In other words, this is the New Testament standard: "What therefore God has joined together, let no man separate" (Matt. 19:6). Wenham writes, "It is because God joins a couple together in marriage that the human declaration (in the typical divorce decree), 'You are free to marry any man' has no legal effect in God's eyes. He looks on remarriage after divorce as adultery."[11] According to them, Jesus is not taking sides in the debates among the Pharisees.[12] He is setting a standard higher than anything they could have imagined.

7. Ibid., 1.3.
8. Ibid., 4.2.
9. Laney, "No Divorce and No Remarriage," 32.
10. Piper, *Divorce and Remarriage*, 3.5.
11. Wenham, "No Remarriage after Divorce," 26–27.
12. Wingerd et al. argue in *Divorce & Remarriage*, "If the exception clause in Matthew 5:32 permits divorce in cases of adultery, Jesus' divorce doctrine would not have differed substantially from that of the Shammai Pharisees," 57.

WHAT ABOUT THE EXCEPTION CLAUSE?

Those who hold to the permanence view contend that the plain teaching of the texts stating that divorce and remarriage are forbidden should govern the interpretation of the more difficult texts (such as Matthew 5:32), which some take to allow for exceptions.[13] In Matthew 19:9, Jesus states, "And I say to you, whoever divorces his wife, except for immorality, and marries another woman commits adultery." Permanence proponents insist that an interpretation must be found that will be consistent with their understanding that divorce and remarriage are prohibited by clearer texts. They note, "Unless there are compelling exegetical reasons to take Jesus' prohibition of divorce as less than absolute, we must interpret Matthew 19:9 in a way that preserves the categorical nature of His original answer to the Pharisees' question,"[14] which is an absolute prohibition of divorce.

In this text, the Greek word translated as "immorality" is *porneia*. The meaning of *porneia* is central to the case for those holding to the permanence view because it appears to be making an exception to the general rule against divorce and remarriage. Most of those who maintain this position, including Piper and Wingerd et al.,[15] claim that *porneia* refers to sexual sin during the betrothal or engagement period. They assert that this was what Joseph planned to use as grounds to break his engagement to Mary when he learned that she was pregnant before their marriage, assuming that this could have happened only through fornication (Matt. 1:19). Many view an implicit accusation by Jesus' opponents based on rumors of such premarital fornication on Mary's part. "They said to Him, 'We were not born of fornication; we have one Father: God'" (John 8:41). They claim that if Jesus had meant that adultery is grounds for divorce, he would have used the more precise Greek word for adultery, which is *moicheia* (and that

---

13. Ibid., 30.
14. Ibid., 21.
15. Piper, *Divorce and Remarriage*, 11.1; Wingerd et al., *Divorce & Remarriage*, 33.

occurs in the context of Matt. 5:32; 19:9). Hence, he must have meant something other than adultery.

Others, including Laney, limit *porneia* to the prohibited (incestuous) sexual or marriage relationships with near relatives described in Leviticus 18:6–18, thus saying that these illicit marriages cannot be regarded as genuine.[16] This closely resembles what is now referred to as an annulment, which treats a marriage as if it had never taken place. Laney offers the case of the man involved in an incestuous (*porneia*) relationship with his father's wife (1 Cor. 5:1) and suggests that the Jerusalem Council refers to such relationships in its letter to the Gentile churches (Acts 15:20, 29). Laney also implies that a reference to incestuous marriage would fit with the circumstances of Matthew 19, in which the Pharisees may have been trying to draw Jesus into the controversy over the illicit relationship of Herod Antipas with his brother's wife.[17] John the Baptist's statements on this subject led to his beheading (Matt. 14:1–12).

Both those who assume the position that *porneia* means fornication before marriage and those who believe it refers to an incestuous marriage think it is significant that the exception clause appears only in Matthew's Gospel, which was written primarily for a Jewish audience that would have been accustomed to the practice of divorce for immorality during betrothal.

Some interpreters, including Wenham, acknowledge that *porneia* may refer to adultery and take a view that permanent separation may be allowed after adultery, but there would be no right to remarry in such cases. They seek to argue grammatically that the exception in Matthew 19:9 refers only to the divorce for *porneia*, but not to remarriage.[18] Moreover, they propose that the surprised exclamation from the disciples, "If the relationship of the man with his wife is like this, it is better not to marry" (Matt. 19:10), makes the most sense if Jesus had shocked them with the teaching that divorce and remarriage are

---

16. Laney, "No Divorce and No Remarriage," 35.
17. Ibid., 37.
18. Wenham, "No Remarriage after Divorce," 34.

never allowed and that his answer implies that the man whose wife has been put away is like others who, in God's providence, are destined to remain single.

SUMMARY

Those who think Scripture teaches that a believer should not initiate divorce and should not remarry after divorce feel that marriage, as designed by God at creation, forms an indissoluble union that man cannot break. They believe that Jesus plainly teaches that all divorce and all remarriage are adulterous.

— QUESTIONS FOR REFLECTION —

1. What is the permanence view of marriage?
2. How do those who maintain the permanence view argue from the origins of marriage at creation?
3. Which of Jesus' statements appear to support the "no divorce and no remarriage" position? How would you explain these statements?
4. How do those who believe that there are no valid grounds for remarriage after divorce explain the apparent exceptions in Matthew 5:32 and 19:9?
5. How does the permanence view of marriage compare to the position on divorce held by the Roman Catholic Church?

27

DOES PAUL TEACH THAT THERE ARE NO VALID GROUNDS FOR DIVORCE AND REMARRIAGE?

Those who hold the permanence view believe that Paul's teaching is consistent with that of Jesus in that it does not allow for a believer to initiate a divorce or to remarry after divorce. They also assert that their view has strong support throughout the history of the church and that more permissive views were not widely taught until the sixteenth century.

PAUL'S INSTRUCTION REGARDING DIVORCE AND REMARRIAGE

Paul clearly explains and amplifies Jesus' teaching that married people should not divorce and that divorced people should not remarry. He writes, "But to the married I give instructions, not I, but the Lord, that the wife should not leave her husband (but if she does leave, she must remain unmarried, or else be reconciled to her husband), and that the husband should not divorce his wife" (1 Cor. 7:10–11). No other option or exceptions are contemplated.[1] In these verses, it appears

---

1. John Piper, *Divorce and Remarriage: A Position Paper* (http://www.desiringgod .org/articles/divorce-remarriage-a-position-paper), 5.3.

that the divorced person has only two options: either to be reconciled to his or her spouse or to remain permanently single (at least until the spouse dies). When Paul addresses the situation of a mixed marriage (between a believer and an unbeliever), he again forbids the believer from initiating divorce (7:12–14).

But what about the case in which the unbelieving partner departs from the marriage? Paul adds, "Yet if the unbelieving one leaves, let him leave; the brother or the sister is not under bondage in such cases, but God has called us to peace" (1 Cor. 7:15). Those holding to the permanence position state that the believer has no choice but to go along with what is inevitable, but that remarriage is still not an option. They argue that "not bound" means that the believer is not bound by Christ's prohibition of divorce, or that one is no longer obligated to cling to the marriage when the unbeliever insists on departing,[2] but it does not mean that the person is released to marry another (which is consistent with Jesus' teaching that remarriage is prohibited after divorce in Matthew 5:32).[3] The believer is now free to find peace in his or her single state.[4]

UNTIL DEATH DO YOU PART

Those holding to the permanence view would additionally contend that Paul definitively states that only death sets a person free from the marriage covenant, thus allowing for remarriage, and that any remarriage while one's spouse is still living is adulterous. He instructs

2. Daryl Wingerd et al., *Divorce & Remarriage: A Permanence View* (Kansas City: Christian Communicators Worldwide, 2009), 72.

3. Those holding the permanence position point out that the Greek word translated "not bound" (*douloō*) in 1 Corinthians 7:15 is not used elsewhere to describe being bound in marriage and is different from the Greek word used in 1 Corinthians 7:39 (which explains a woman is "bound" [*deō*] to her husband while he lives, but is free to remarry after he dies), and assert these words are not interchangeable. See Piper, *Divorce and Remarriage*, 9.12; Wingerd et al., *Divorce & Remarriage*, 72.

4. J. Carl Laney, "No Divorce and No Remarriage," in *Divorce and Remarriage: Four Christian Views*, ed. H. Wayne House (Downers Grove, IL: InterVarsity Press, 1990), 45.

the Corinthians, "A wife is bound as long as her husband lives; but if her husband is dead, she is free to be married to whom she wishes, only in the Lord" (1 Cor. 7:39). Elsewhere he states, "For the married woman is bound by law to her husband while he is living; but if her husband dies, she is released from the law concerning her husband. So then, if while her husband is living she is joined to another man, she shall be called an adulteress; but if her husband dies, she is free from the law, so that she is not an adulteress though she is joined to another man" (Rom. 7:2–3). In this passage, no exceptions are given to the rule that only death sets a spouse free from the marriage covenant. In essence, those taking the permanence position are saying that man cannot end the one-flesh relationship. Only God can do so by the death of one spouse.

ARGUMENT FROM HISTORY

Those who hold the "no divorce and no remarriage" position maintain that theirs was the position of the church from the early fathers up until the time of the Reformation as well.[5] Wenham writes, "Early Christian writers—often referred to as the church fathers—almost universally rejected remarriage after divorce."[6] It is argued that because they were "much closer in time, place, language and presuppositions,"[7] they would have a clearer understanding of the meaning of the teaching of Jesus and the apostles. In addition, Wenham contends that in light of the more permissive rules for divorce and remarriage in both Jewish and Roman culture, it is very improbable that second-century Christians would have taken such a strict view against remarriage unless this was the apostolic tradition.[8]

5. Ibid., 38.
6. Gordon J. Wenham, "No Remarriage after Divorce," in *Remarriage after Divorce in Today's Church: 3 Views*, ed. Mark L. Strauss (Grand Rapids: Zondervan, 2006), 23.
7. Ibid., 24.
8. Ibid., 36. Those taking the position adopted after the Reformation would argue that the early church fathers were wrong about a great number of things.

HOW DOES THIS WORK OUT PRACTICALLY?

Those who promote the permanence view of divorce and remarriage are faced with challenging practical questions. For example, critics of this position might ask, "Isn't it unreasonable to suggest that the innocent spouse spend the rest of his or her life alone?" To their credit, those holding the permanence view seek to answer these questions with integrity and compassion. They point out that people with less restrictive views regarding divorce and remarriage also acknowledge situations in which obedience to God and his Word produces hardship in this life and would acknowledge that it is often God's will for a believer to stay in a very difficult marriage[9] or to forgo marriage because no suitable opportunity to marry a believer is available. In each case, we must trust the Lord to give the godly person grace to endure and to faithfully serve God, who will help him or her to overcome loneliness.

Another inquiry posed to those holding the permanence view is, "Should those who have wrongfully remarried divorce or separate from their new spouses?" Laney mentions the possibility that a wrongfully remarried couple might choose to end their marriage because it was wrongfully consummated, but leaves room for people to work out these situations according to their own consciences.[10] According to Piper, the prohibition of a divorced and remarried woman from going back to her first husband in Deuteronomy 24:1–4 "suggests very strongly that today no second marriage should be broken up in order to restore a first one."[11] He also recommends that past sins be confessed to God and others who were affected and goes on to acknowledge, "While not the ideal state, staying in a second marriage is God's will for a couple and their ongoing relationship should not be looked on as adulterous."[12]

---

9. For example, being married to an unbeliever who mocks your faith and is cold; or being married to someone who is physically or mentally incapacitated, thereby leading to the loss of ordinary marital benefits of affection and companionship.

10. Laney, "No Divorce and No Remarriage," 40.

11. Piper, *Divorce and Remarriage*, 8.2.

12. Ibid., "Conclusions and Applications." See also Wingerd et al., *Divorce & Remarriage*, 7.

Moreover, there is the issue of how this works itself out in the life of the church. Some who hold the permanence view choose to work within churches and other organizations that allow for different views and practices among their members and leadership, allowing each to follow his or her own conscience. For instance, John Piper served in a church whose official position differed from his own, yet he respected the church's position as a guide in matters of membership and discipline. Other churches whose leaders hold to the permanence view practice church discipline against those who divorce or remarry against the counsel of leadership.[13]

SUMMARY

Those holding to the permanence view believe that divorce is always contrary to God's moral will as seen in his design from creation and that remarriage is allowed solely after the death of one's spouse. They argue that clear, unqualified statements in the New Testament that forbid divorce and remarriage provide the framework around which we must reach our conclusions.[14] Christians may be forced into a legal divorce because we live in a fallen world, and others may decide to abandon the marriage covenant, but the Christian spouse should never be the one to cause or initiate the divorce. The person who is divorced must remain single or else be reconciled to his or her spouse. Remarriage is always adulterous if one's first spouse is still living.

Piper makes his position clear:

"In the New Testament the question about remarriage after divorce is not determined by:

1. The guilt or innocence of either spouse,
2. Nor by whether either spouse is a believer or not,

13. Wingerd et al., *Divorce & Remarriage*, 5–6.
14. Ibid., 27–28.

3. Nor by whether the divorce happened before or after either spouse's conversion,
4. Nor by the ease or difficulty of living as a single parent for the rest of life on earth,
5. Nor by whether there is adultery or desertion involved,
6. Nor by the ongoing reality of the hardness of the human heart,
7. Nor by the cultural permissiveness of the surrounding society."[15]

— Questions for Reflection —

1. How do those who hold the permanence view explain the fact that the abandoned spouse is no longer under bondage in 1 Corinthians 7:15?
2. How do those who believe in the permanence view seek to argue for their position from church history?
3. How do those who maintain the permanence view address those who think that it would be too hard for a young divorced person, who is the innocent party, to remain unmarried for the rest of his or her life?
4. What is the one circumstance under which those holding to the permanence position think Paul taught that remarriage is allowed?
5. How do those who hold to the permanence view treat those who remarry after divorce?

15. Piper, *Divorce and Remarriage*, "Conclusions and Applications."

28

DOES SCRIPTURE TEACH THAT SEXUAL SIN IS A VALID GROUND FOR DIVORCE AND REMARRIAGE?

While all divorce is due to sin, not every divorced spouse bears responsibility for separating what God has joined. Many conservative evangelicals, myself included, believe that Scripture teaches that sexual sin is such a severe violation of the marriage covenant that it gives the innocent spouse grounds for divorce. The innocent spouse would then be free to remarry a believer and would not be in sin for doing so. This has been the majority view of Protestants since the Reformation and is the position taught in the Westminster Confession of Faith (24.5–24.6). This position is known by some as the Erasmian view, for Erasmus of Rotterdam, who was among the first to promote this interpretation in the sixteenth century.

THE MARRIAGE COVENANT
IS NOT UNBREAKABLE

The marriage covenant makes the two into one, but it is possible for sin to break them apart. In Matthew 19:6, Jesus says, "So they are no longer two, but one flesh. What therefore God has joined together, let no man separate." Jesus does not state that no man can separate what God has joined. Instead, he teaches that it should not happen. In the following verses, our Lord acknowledges the possibility that the covenant will be sinfully broken because of the hardness of human hearts (Matt. 19:8).

Furthermore, "one-flesh" relationships are not always regarded as permanent—for example, the case of a man who is joined as one flesh to a prostitute. Paul explains, "Or do you not know that the one who joins himself to a prostitute is one body with her? For He says, 'The two shall become one flesh'" (1 Cor. 6:16). It is significant that Paul here quotes Genesis 2:24 to describe a temporary one-flesh relationship between a man and a prostitute. This is the same verse that those holding the permanence view rely on to assert that the marriage bond is humanly indissoluble.

Moreover, the fact that a person who has been divorced may be tainted (Deut. 24:4) does not mean that she is still married to, or in union with, the first husband.[1] When Jesus cites sinful divorces and remarriages, he refers to the parties as being truly divorced (severed) and truly remarried (Matt. 19:9; Mark 10:11–12; Luke 16:18). They are no longer married to their former spouses.[2]

GOD HIMSELF DIVORCED ISRAEL FOR ADULTERY

One of the greatest weaknesses of the permanence view is the fact that the Lord himself is divorced: "And I saw that for all the adulteries of faithless Israel, I had sent her away and given her a writ of divorce, yet her treacherous sister Judah did not fear; but she went

---

1. If people were still "married in God's eyes" or "one flesh" after divorce, why couldn't the woman in Deuteronomy 24:1–4 go back to her first husband?

2. Some who promote the permanence position recognize the possible consequences of their idea that the marriage bond cannot be severed. Would this mean that upon remarriage one would be married to two people simultaneously? "When a marriage ends in divorce, the union that remains intact is no longer correctly identified as a marriage," according to Daryl Wingerd et al., *Divorce & Remarriage: A Permanence View* (Kansas City: Christian Communicators Worldwide, 2009), 112.

and was a harlot also" (Jer. 3:8; see also Isa. 50:1).[3] The twofold pattern of the Lord's divorce is the same as in valid human divorces. The guilty party was guilty of gross covenant-breaking acts, and the innocent party chose to use those grounds to formalize the dissolution of the marriage (in this context, through a writ of divorce). Jay Adams writes, "If God Himself becomes involved in divorce proceedings with Israel, it is surely wrong to condemn any and all divorce out of hand."[4]

JESUS TEACHES DIVORCE AND REMARRIAGE AS ORDINARILY ADULTEROUS

In Jesus' day, as it is today, divorce was far too common. Jewish rabbis would debate the grounds for divorce. Many held that a man could divorce his wife "for any reason." Others were somewhat more restrictive.[5] In Matthew 19, the Pharisees attempt to draw Jesus into their debate (19:3). He first answers by reminding them of God's ideal from creation that the two become one and that they never separate (19:4–6). The Pharisees then ask Jesus about the instructions concerning divorce in Deuteronomy 24:1–4 (Matt. 19:7). Jesus' initial answer points out an error within their question. Moses did not

---

3. Those advocating the permanence position try to answer by pointing out that the Lord's divorce of Israel is metaphorical (ibid., 46). Yet the metaphor is meaningful because of its correspondence to literal marriage. Additionally, those holding the permanence position do not hesitate to use the metaphor when it seems to suit their purpose (e.g., arguing for their position from the Lord's faithfulness to his people).

4. Jay Adams, *Marriage, Divorce, and Remarriage in the Bible* (Grand Rapids: Zondervan, 1980), 23.

5. The Mishnah (A.D. 200) describes the positions of the different rabbinic schools. "The School of Shammai say: A man may not divorce his wife unless he has found unchastity in her, for it is written, 'Because he has found in her indecency in anything' (Deut. 24:1). And the School of Hillel say: (He may divorce her) even if she spoiled a dish for him, for it is written, 'Because he has found in her indecency in anything' (m. Git. 9:10)." See Andreas J. Köstenberger with David Jones, *God, Marriage, and Family: Rebuilding the Biblical Foundation*, 2nd ed. (Wheaton, IL: Crossway, 2010), 228.

command anyone to divorce his wife; rather, he *permitted* it, and then only because of the hardness of their hearts (19:8). Jesus goes on to condemn the kinds of frivolous "any-cause" divorces, which were common among the Jews, saying that these divorces and the remarriages that inevitably follow are adulterous (19:9). This is similar to what he teaches elsewhere (Matt. 5:32; Mark 10:11–12; Luke 16:18) and is his emphasis in Matthew 19.

JESUS STATES ONE EXCEPTION
TO THE GENERAL RULE

Jesus, however, offers one qualification: "except for immorality" (also in Matt. 5:32). He thus affirms that one sin so seriously "violates the 'one-flesh' principle underlying marriage"[6] that it gives the innocent party grounds to divorce the adulterer. Those who are against all divorce try to argue that allowing for this exception results in the marriage covenant's being treated less seriously because it can be severed.[7] But in reality, the punishment for the violation of a commandment shows how seriously the Lord takes the breach of his law. For example, in the old covenant, the sixth commandment, "You shall not murder" (Ex. 20:13), was given to protect life. God's institution of the death penalty for murder shows the value of human life in God's image (Gen. 9:5–6). In a similar way, the seventh commandment, "You shall not commit adultery" (Ex. 20:14), was given to protect marriage. The death penalty for adultery demonstrates the seriousness of the sin and acts as a deterrent (Lev. 20:10; Deut. 22:22). The consequence for adultery under the new covenant, the guilty party's being justly divorced by the innocent spouse, is also quite serious, especially in light of how God hates divorce. This penalty could be said to be merciful compared to the Old Testament punishment.[8] Another reason that the

6. Ibid., 275.

7. As opposed to their position that even sexual sin cannot be used as grounds to sever the covenant.

8. John Murray states: "He (Jesus) abrogated the Mosaic penalty for adultery and he legitimated divorce for adultery." *Divorce* (Philadelphia: Presbyterian and

innocent party would have the right to divorce and remarry under the new covenant is that under the old covenant, the adulterer would have been put to death. The innocent party would then have been free to remarry (as a widow or a widower).[9]

WHAT IS THE EXCEPTION (*PORNEIA*)?

So how are we to understand the nature of the exception that Jesus teaches? Those who argue for the permanence view (no divorce or remarriage) acknowledge that their entire argument hinges on the meaning of the Greek word *porneia*, which is translated "immorality." They claim that it must mean something other than adultery; either *porneia* refers to fornication before marriage or it refers to an incestuous disallowed marriage. A fatal problem with the view that Jesus is speaking of fornication during betrothal is that Matthew 19 is addressing grounds for divorce and remarriage—not grounds for breaking an engagement.[10] The texts that Jesus is discussing (Gen. 1–2; Deut. 24) clearly refer to marriage as well. Jesus is condemning the sinful and adulterous actions of the Jews who unlawfully abandoned their wives and entered into new marriages.[11]

In the same way, there is no basis in the context to limit the meaning of *porneia* to the incestuous marriages forbidden in Leviticus 18.[12] *Porneia* is a broad word for sexual immorality, which encompasses adultery, incest, homosexuality, and a variety of other sexual sins.[13] Its meaning may be more precisely determined by context. In

---

Reformed, 1961), 27.

9. The Westminster Confession of Faith (24.5) alludes to this reasoning that the innocent party is free to remarry "as if the offending party were dead."

10. Also, the word *porneia* does not occur in Matthew 1:18–25, in which Joseph ends the betrothal.

11. See also Proverbs 2:17, which describes the adulteress as one who "forgets the covenant of her God."

12. The likelihood of someone's unknowingly marrying a close relative is extremely remote.

13. That is, "of various kinds of 'unsanctioned sexual intercourse,'" according to W. Bauer, F. W. Danker, W. F. Arndt, and F. W. Gingrich, *A Greek-English Lexicon of*

the Septuagint (the Greek translation of the Old Testament), *porneia* is sometimes used interchangeably with the more specific word for divorce, *moichaō* (Jer. 3:8–10; Hos. 2:2–5). The fact that the Lord himself had divorced Israel and Judah on the grounds of adultery (Jer. 3:8) also supports the idea that this is the exception to which Jesus is referring and that students of the Scriptures would have readily understood this as his meaning. In addition, there is strong reason to believe that, in light of the debates over the grounds for divorce going on at the time,[14] Jesus is referring to adulterous sexual immorality as grounds for divorce.

WHAT ABOUT THE TEXTS THAT DON'T MENTION THE EXCEPTION?

Why then do Jesus' other statements forbidding divorce and remarriage (Mark 10:11–12; Luke 16:18) not include the exception? Christ's statements in the other passages briefly include the general rule that divorce and remarriage (especially as it was being practiced at the time through "any-cause divorce") are an adulterous violation of God's design for marriage. General rules, however, can have exceptions that are stated elsewhere.[15] The exception does not negate the general rule. Nor does the general rule negate the exception.[16] For instance, the

---

the New Testament and Other Early Christian Literature, 3rd ed. (Chicago: University of Chicago Press, 2000), 854. This book will hereafter be referred to as BDAG. See also Murray, *Divorce*, 21.

14. In addition to the debates between the followers of Hillel and Shammai over the grounds for divorce, there was the immediate issue of Herod's unlawful marriage to his brother's former wife, Herodias (Matt. 14:3–4).

15. John MacArthur writes, "God has to say a thing only once for it to be true. . . . God doesn't say everything on a subject every time He brings it up." *The Divorce Dilemma* (Leominster, England: Day One Publications, 2009), 23.

16. As Edgar observes, "I disagree with the concept that a passage which does not give an exception may be considered as denying an exception clearly stated in another passage." Thomas R. Edgar, "Response" to J. Carl Laney's essay in *Divorce and Remarriage: Four Christian Views*, ed. H. Wayne House (Downers Grove, IL: InterVarsity Press, 1990), 63.

general rule of God's law is that we should not take human life (Ex. 20:13). Yet there are exceptional situations, such as the enactment of civil justice and war, in which killing is allowed by God (Gen. 9:5–6; Rom. 13:4). Another example would be that although Matthew 5:22 condemns anger without explicit qualification, Jesus, on occasion, was righteously angry (Mark 3:5; John 2:15–17). Another illustration would be speed-limit signs that state the general rule (e.g., don't drive faster than seventy miles per hour on this road), but don't list the exceptions (such as that emergency vehicles can drive faster if it is deemed necessary).

It is also argued that the exceptions Jesus mentions "were obvious and well known to the original audience."[17] His hearers would have assumed, both from current practice and from the Old Testament example (including the Lord's divorce from Israel), that sexual sin provides just cause for divorce without this having to be explicitly stated.[18] Murray additionally points out that the lone exceptive clause "gives prominence to the illegitimacy of any other reason,"[19] thus refuting the lax views of divorce that were prominent in both Jewish and Roman culture.

DOES JESUS ALLOW FOR DIVORCE, BUT NOT REMARRIAGE?

Some have tried to contend that while divorce might be allowed for sexual immorality, remarriage would still be forbidden. In effect, the exception would allow the innocent party only to separate without the right to remarry. One difficulty with this view is that it would have been a fundamental change in the meaning of divorce, which

17. William A. Heth, "Remarriage for Adultery or Desertion," in *Remarriage after Divorce in Today's Church: 3 Views*, ed. Mark L. Strauss (Grand Rapids: Zondervan, 2006), 73.

18. While understanding the cultural background can be helpful in interpreting biblical texts, cultural arguments are not definitive. I am troubled when scholars seem to make the cultural background definitive in interpreting the text.

19. Murray, *Divorce*, 21.

almost always carried with it a right to remarry.[20] More importantly, as Murray and others have shown, the grammatical structure of the sentence in Matthew 19:9 strongly favors the interpretation that the exception clause applies to both "whoever divorces his wife" and "marries another woman," which are coordinate in the text.[21] Murray writes that "the subject dealt with, therefore, is putting away and remarriage in coordination, and this coordination must not be disturbed in any way."[22] Because both verbs (*divorces* and *[re]marries*) apply in the case of the general rule, the violation of which results in adultery, both verbs also must apply to the exception (*except for immorality*).

SUMMARY

According to Jay Adams, "Even though all divorces are the result of sin, not all divorces are sinful."[23] When Jesus addresses the question concerning divorce, he strongly opposes the "divorce for any reason" viewpoint of the more liberal rabbis. While his allowance for divorce and remarriage in the case of sexual sin is similar to the position of the stricter rabbis, his view is more merciful. The rabbis assumed that divorce would take place in such instances, whereas Jesus allows for divorce, but implicitly allows for the possibility of repentance, forgiveness, and reconciliation as well. Jesus does not teach that the act of sexual infidelity in itself ends the marriage covenant, but he does teach that it is a serious enough violation of the covenant that the innocent party has a right to divorce if he or she chooses.

20. Heth, "Remarriage for Adultery or Desertion," 71.
21. Murray, *Divorce*, 36–43.
22. Ibid., 41.
23. Adams, *Marriage, Divorce, and Remarriage in the Bible*, 30.

— Questions for Reflection —

1. How does God's divorce of Israel under the old covenant support the view that adultery is grounds for divorce?
2. Why would the clause mentioning the exception for sexual immorality be left out of the passages forbidding divorce and remarriage in the books of Mark and Luke?
3. Why is it unlikely that Matthew 19:9 refers to the breakup of a betrothal?
4. How would you refute the claim that Jesus allows for divorce in cases of adultery, but not remarriage?
5. How does Jesus' teaching differ from that of the strictest Jewish rabbis?

29

IS ABANDONMENT BY AN UNBELIEVER A VALID GROUND FOR DIVORCE AND REMARRIAGE?

Most of the evangelical scholars who believe Jesus teaches that sexual unfaithfulness is a ground for divorce and remarriage also think Paul teaches that abandonment by an unbelieving spouse is a ground for a Christian to divorce and remarry without committing sin. Moreover, this is acknowledged in the Westminster Confession (24.7).[1]

PAUL, LIKE JESUS, DISCOURAGES DIVORCE

In 1 Corinthians 7, Paul answers various questions relating to singleness, marriage, and sex within marriage. Whereas Jesus primarily addresses Jewish marital practices, Paul is additionally writing in light of prevailing Greco-Roman laws and practices in which divorce and remarriage were rampant.

Regarding the decision about whether to marry, he feels that single people, like him, have the advantage of being able to serve the Lord without distraction (1 Cor. 7:7–8, 33–35), but recognizes that most do not have the gift of singleness and are better off getting married (7:2, 9). He reminds husbands and wives to be careful to fulfill their conjugal duties to each other as well (7:3–5; see also Ex. 21:10–11).

1. http://www.reformed.org/documents/wcf_with_proofs/.

218

Paul then speaks to those who are married and strongly restates the general rule taught by Jesus that husbands and wives should not divorce and that if they do divorce, they would compound their sin by remarrying (1 Cor. 7:10–11). It is clear that Paul is talking about divorce here because the Greek word *chorizō*, which is translated "separate" in 1 Corinthians 7:10–11, is the same Greek word used by Jesus in Matthew 19:6 when Christ forbids divorce, saying, "What therefore God has joined together, let no man separate (*chorizō*)." The fact that Paul prohibits remarriage after an improper divorce corresponds to Jesus' statements in Matthew 19:9 (and elsewhere) that it is adulterous to remarry after an unlawful divorce. Ordinarily, a Christian couple that is separated or divorced should make every effort to pursue reconciliation through the principles and power of the gospel.[2]

STAY MARRIED EVEN IF YOU ARE MARRIED TO AN UNBELIEVER

Then Paul addresses a different situation—one not addressed by Jesus: "But to the rest I say, not the Lord" (1 Cor. 7:12a).[3] What if a believer is married to an unbeliever? While those who were already Christians would have known to marry only in the Lord (7:39), many were converted following marriage to pagans. This would have been a significant question in light of the Old Testament commands not to intermarry with those outside the covenant people: "Furthermore, you shall not intermarry with them; you shall not give your daughters to their sons, nor shall you take their daughters for your sons. For they will turn your sons away from following Me to serve other gods; then the anger of the LORD will be kindled against you and He will quickly destroy you" (Deut. 7:3–4). Intermarriage was such a great evil that in the book of Ezra, the men of Israel put away (divorced) their foreign

2. Questions 38 and 39 will cover this matter.

3. Paul is not saying that his instruction is less authoritative, but rather he—as an apostle of Jesus Christ and under the guidance of the Holy Spirit (1 Cor. 7:40)—is addressing an issue that Jesus does not address.

(pagan) wives (Ezra 10:3, 11). Should the new converts who were already married to unbelievers be concerned about the influence of their pagan spouses on them and their children? Would it be better to take the children away from the unbelieving parents? Should they get divorced like the men of Ezra's day?

Paul's answer is that spiritual differences alone are not reason to end a marriage: "That if any brother has a wife who is an unbeliever, and she consents to live with him, he must not divorce her. And a woman who has an unbelieving husband, and he consents to live with her, she must not send her husband away" (1 Cor. 7:12b–13). In other words, stay in the marriage, and don't initiate divorce. As Köstenberger states, "A mixed marriage . . . is preferable to divorce."[4] Paul also addresses the concern that believers might have about influence on themselves and their children: "For the unbelieving husband is sanctified through his wife, and the unbelieving wife is sanctified through her believing husband; for otherwise your children are unclean, but now they are holy" (7:14). Paul is not promising that the unbelieving spouse (see 7:16) or even the children will be saved, but he is saying that the marital union is legitimate and has God's blessing. You can entrust your children to God.

AGAIN, THERE IS AN EXCEPTION

Just as Jesus emphasized the general rule that divorce and remarriage are sinful before stating the exceptional grounds of sexual sin, Paul has also strongly emphasized that believers should remain in their marriage before coming to the exception. He adds, "Yet if the unbelieving one leaves, let him leave; the brother or the sister is not under bondage in such cases, but God has called us to peace" (1 Cor. 7:15). This understanding follows the teaching of Jesus that while the believer should not be the one to separate what God has joined together in marriage (Matt. 19:6), the other party may unilaterally

4. Andreas J. Köstenberger with David Jones, *God, Marriage, and Family: Rebuilding the Biblical Foundation*, 2nd ed. (Wheaton, IL: Crossway, 2010), 234.

take action that breaks the marriage covenant. Paul employs the same Greek word, *chorizō*, for "leave" in 1 Corinthians 7:15 that Jesus uses for "separate" in Matthew 19:6, thus showing that Paul is alluding to the unbelieving spouse's divorcing (not merely physically separating from) the believer.[5]

The most likely scenario is that the unbelieving spouse would decide to depart from the marriage because of the believer's faith.[6] There were probably cases in the early church, such as we have today, in which the unbelieving partner doesn't like the changes in the new believer's life. Perhaps the believer won't engage in some of the sinful activities in which the couple previously participated. Maybe the unbelieving spouse resents that the believer won't follow his or her religious practices. This person might say, "I didn't sign up for this when I married you!" While the believer should never deliberately attempt to provoke the unbelieving spouse to leave, Paul commands the believer not to cling to a spouse who insists on departing.[7] Though divorce is not the ideal solution, it is the best that can be done under these circumstances. Elsewhere, Paul remarks, "If possible, so far as it depends on you, be at peace with all men" (Rom. 12:18). While it is good to hope that your spouse might change, you can't know that this will happen: "For how do you know, O wife, whether you will save your husband? Or how do you know, O husband, whether you will save your wife?" (1 Cor. 7:16).

MAY THE ABANDONED SPOUSE REMARRY?

Those who take the permanence view think that while the abandoned spouse is free from ordinary marital obligations (e.g., financial

---

5. *Chorizō* was also used in the broader Greco-Roman culture with reference to divorce (BDAG, 1095).

6. Returning to verses 12–13, which describe the unbelieving spouse as consenting to remain in the marriage (in spite of the religious differences), this seems to be a case in which the unbelieving spouse is unwilling to continue in the marriage because of the religious differences.

7. "Let him leave" is an imperative (present passive).

support [other than what is required by civil law], companionship, and conjugal rights) to the departing spouse, their one-flesh bond in some sense remains so that the believer is not free to remarry. They maintain that Paul has already said that all remarriage is forbidden (1 Cor. 7:11). They also claim that the Greek word *douloō*, translated "not under bondage," cannot mean that the believing spouse is free to remarry. Instead, they would say that the person possesses a freedom to pursue singleness.

Given that Scripture allows remarriage for the innocent party in the case of certain other divorces (e.g., for sexual immorality), it is reasonable to assume that the same principle applies to the innocent party in the case of abandonment by an unbeliever. John MacArthur writes, "Simply stated, when divorce is permitted, remarriage is permitted; where divorce is forbidden, remarriage is forbidden."[8] If one is free to remarry after a valid divorce on the grounds of immorality, one should be allowed to remarry for other valid grounds. If one is still (as those with the permanence view hold) in some sense bound in a one-flesh relationship with the former spouse, one is not truly free. The word *douloō*, which is translated "not under bondage" (1 Cor. 7:15), implies the freedom from all obligations of the previous marriage; this then allows the divorced person to assume new obligations of a new marriage.[9] Murray and others argue that the use of *douloō* in 1 Corinthians 7:15 occurs in a way comparable to how *deo* is used in 1 Corinthians 7:39—a widow who was previously bound (*deo*) in marriage is no longer bound and thus free to remarry.[10] Or, as Köstenberger pro-

8. John MacArthur, *The Divorce Dilemma* (Leominster, England: Day One Publications, 2009), 81.

9. Jay Adams, *Marriage, Divorce, and Remarriage in the Bible* (Grand Rapids: Zondervan, 1980), 48.

10. John Murray, *Divorce* (Philadelphia: Presbyterian and Reformed, 1961), 75. Köstenberger notes, "While not identical the terms *douloō* and *deo* do seem to inhabit the same semantic domain . . . so that 1 Corinthians 7:39 seems to be admissible as a relevant parallel to 1 Corinthians 7:15" (*God, Marriage, and Family*, 286). Also, *douloō* is used in Romans 6:18, 22 to speak about how we have been freed from sin, which in the context means that we have no more obligation to sin and are newly united to Christ in the place of sin.

poses, "Paul may be using an analogy, saying that when an unbelieving spouse deserts his or her partner, it is as if that person has died."[11] This meaning of "not under bondage" would also be supported by the fact that both Jewish and Greco-Roman bills of divorce explicitly stated the divorcée's freedom to remarry.[12] Finally, in Paul's statement, "Are you released from a wife? Do not seek a wife. But if you marry, you have not sinned" (1 Cor. 7:27b–28a), the word *released* contains the same Greek root as the word translated as "not under bondage" in 1 Corinthians 7:15. This strongly suggests that someone who has been properly released from a spouse is free to remarry.[13]

According to Charles Hodge, "If the unbeliever broke up the marriage, the Christian partner was thereby liberated from the contract. This is the interpretation that Protestants have almost universally given to this verse. It is a passage of great importance, because it is the foundation of the Protestant doctrine that willful desertion is a legitimate ground of divorce."[14]

WHAT IF YOU ARE DESERTED BY A BELIEVER?

There are frequently cases in which a professing Christian abandons a fellow believer. In such a case, the abandoned spouse is not free to initiate divorce or remarry (1 Cor. 7:10–11). This situation can be addressed, though, by the church's going through the process of church discipline (Matt. 18:15–20). Jesus says that if the disobedient spouse will not repent, then the person is to be treated as an unbeliever: "If he refuses to listen even to the church, let him be to you as a Gentile

---

11. Köstenberger, *God, Marriage, and Family*, 287. In addition, Köstenberger points out that the language used pertaining to the widow's freedom to remarry in 1 Corinthians 7:39 is very close to the language of the standard Jewish bill of divorce.

12. William A. Heth, "Remarriage for Adultery or Desertion," in *Remarriage after Divorce in Today's Church: 3 Views*, ed. Mark L. Strauss (Grand Rapids: Zondervan, 2006), 75.

13. Adams, *Marriage, Divorce, and Remarriage in the Bible*, 84.

14. Charles Hodge, *Commentary on 1 and 2 Corinthians* (Edinburgh: Banner of Truth, 1983), 118.

and a tax collector" (Matt. 18:17). At that point, the innocent spouse could regard himself or herself as abandoned by an unbeliever, and 1 Corinthians 7:15 would apply.[15]

SUMMARY

Paul repeats Jesus' general rule that divorce and remarriage are generally sinful. He then covers a situation that Jesus didn't address as he speaks to believers who are married to unbelievers. Even then the general rule not to divorce applies. But if the unbelieving spouse abandons the marriage, thus forcing divorce on the believer, then the Christian is free from obligation to his or her former spouse and free to remarry.

— QUESTIONS FOR REFLECTION —

1. Does Paul's teaching on marriage, divorce, and remarriage have different authority from that of Jesus (1 Cor. 7:10)?
2. What new situation does Paul address?
3. Why might believers have thought that they should leave their unbelieving spouses?
4. What are a believer's obligations and freedoms if an unbelieving spouse no longer wants to be married?
5. What should a believer do if he or she is abandoned by a spouse who is a professing believer?

---

15. Adams, *Marriage, Divorce, and Remarriage in the Bible*, 89. I recognize that some scholars view this as free from marriage (not freed through divorce). While I believe that the interpretation taken above is preferable, it is not essential to my conclusion that the spouse abandoned by an unbeliever is free to remarry.

30

DOES SCRIPTURE JUSTIFY DIVORCE ON GROUNDS OTHER THAN SEXUAL SIN AND ABANDONMENT?

While the grounds of sexual unfaithfulness and abandonment by an unbeliever are widely accepted by most evangelicals as grounds for divorce and remarriage, some think that there are additional grounds for divorce.

COULD THERE BE MORE EXCEPTIONS?

Some argue that if Jesus teaches one exception to the general rule against divorce and remarriage, and if Paul is able to teach another exception, why can't we, using similar reasoning, add to these exceptions? Could other grounds fit into similar categories? It is asserted that if the breach of covenant responsibilities through adultery is grounds for divorce, other failures to keep the marital covenant should also constitute grounds to end a marriage. Some, including David Instone-Brewer, have affirmed that the failure to meet the expectations of the marriage covenant in Exodus 21:10–11 (provision and conjugal rights) furnishes further grounds for divorce and that Paul had these in mind in 1 Corinthians 7.[1]

---

1. David Instone-Brewer, *Divorce and Remarriage in the Church* (Downers Grove,

A problem with this view is that because we are all sinners, we all fall short of keeping our marriage covenants as we should. What standard of provision is sufficient? What quality and frequency of sexual relations qualify as meeting covenant obligations?[2] John Piper—writing in objection to the position taken by David Instone-Brewer—warns, "To put it bluntly, the implication of this article is that every marriage I am aware of could already have *legitimately* ended in divorce."[3]

DOES UNDERSTANDING FIRST-CENTURY CULTURE BROADEN THE GROUNDS FOR DIVORCE?

Some make the case for broader grounds for divorce based on their understanding of how Jewish and Greco-Roman culture perceived marriage, divorce, and remarriage, saying that the original hearers and readers would have assumed that Paul and Jesus were making allowance for certain practices. While we can benefit from having a better understanding of these first-century practices, we need to be careful not to improperly impose them on the meaning of Scripture. David Instone-Brewer comments that the improper understanding of first-century marriage and divorce practice explains why the church lost its way on this issue after the second century and declares that recent discoveries about first-century culture are key to regaining the correct perspective.[4] These discoveries also lead to his view that the grounds for divorce and remarriage are broader than sexual sin and abandonment by an unbeliever.[5] Piper again cautions, "Beware of what looks

---

IL: InterVarsity Press, 2003), 98. See also David Instone-Brewer, *Divorce and Remarriage in the Bible* (Grand Rapids: Eerdmans, 2002), chap. 7.

2. Instone-Brewer states that the rabbis debated about "the minimum quantities of food and clothing that had to be provided and the amount of 'conjugal love' that was necessary to avoid being charged with neglecting one's partner." *Divorce and Remarriage in the Church*, 97.

3. http://www.desiringgod.org/articles/tragically-widening-the-grounds-of-legitimate -divorce.

4. Instone-Brewer, *Divorce and Remarriage in the Church*, chaps. 12–15.

5. Even when Instone-Brewer argues for the more widely accepted grounds of sexual immorality and desertion by an unbeliever, he seems to rely most heavily on

like scholarly rank-pulling. For example, Brewer says, 'I likely read every surviving writing of the rabbis of Jesus' time. I "got inside their heads."' So when he comes to the texts of the New Testament he says, 'I was now reading them like a first-century Jew would have read them, and this time those confusing passages made more sense.'"[6]

WE MUST BE SWAYED BY
SCRIPTURE, NOT STORIES

I have also seen several cases in which a spouse who is unhappily married looks for grounds to justify leaving, rather than looking for ways that the couple can work to save the marriage.[7] Others have been unduly influenced by their own personal experiences or the stories of people who are close to them. It is hard for them to imagine that God wouldn't allow one of his children to make a choice that would get him or her out of a hard marriage and would seem to offer potential for future happiness. When hearing someone else's story, it is good to be reminded that there may be another side: "The first to plead his case seems right, until another comes and examines him" (Prov. 18:17).

Our beliefs about the grounds for divorce and remarriage must be based on careful study of God's infallible and all-sufficient Word. We must be prepared to read what will challenge our present actions and feelings, and we must submit our will to that of the Lord and trust

---

his understanding of how people in the first century would have understood the words of Jesus and Paul in light of their current laws and practices and not enough on the words of Scripture, which he seems to view as vague without the addition of his outside information. "What about remarriage after divorce? The New Testament is remarkably vague on this important issue, but chapter 9 pointed out that first-century believers would have had no uncertainty because the right to remarry was taken for granted. It was a legal right that was recorded in all Jewish divorce certificates and in Roman law remarriage was actually a legal duty." Instone-Brewer, *Divorce and Remarriage in the Church*, 163.

6. http://www.desiringgod.org/articles/tragically-widening-the-grounds-of-legitimate-divorce.

7. I am not saying that a spouse should remain in a home in which he or she is being abused. This topic will be covered in a later question.

that his ways are best (Prov. 3:5–6). We must even be prepared to temporarily forgo some earthly happiness for the sake of him who left heavenly glory to rescue us from wrath.

THE DANGER OF THE SLIPPERY SLOPE

Once we move beyond a scriptural basis for divorce and remarriage, almost any situation can be justified. John Frame acknowledges the danger that "could open up the floodgates to all sorts of grounds for divorce."[8] Some teachers and scholars, apparently in reaction to situations in which churches have been wrongfully judgmental of people who have divorced and remarried on biblical grounds, seem to have radically swung the other way. They believe that churches should refrain altogether from declaring that any divorce or remarriage is sinful and from taking disciplinary action against those who wrongfully divorce and remarry.

One such scholar, Larry Richards, erroneously removes the right for the church to take a stand on the grounds for divorce and implies that calling any divorce and remarriage sinful is harsh and legalistic. He states, "Jesus' words warn us that pastors and other Christian leaders have no more right to stand in judgment over the dissolution of a marriage than did the Pharisees. His words tell us that theologians have no more right to decree, 'People in this situation can divorce and remarry, but people in that situation cannot.'"[9]

WHAT ABOUT THE TOUGH CASES?

In the following chapters, we will seek to apply the Scriptures to particularly difficult situations, including those of abuse and neglect. In some cases, we will wrestle with the possibility that these situations

8. John M. Frame, *The Doctrine of the Christian Life* (Phillipsburg, NJ: P&R Publishing, 2008), 781.

9. Larry Richards, "Divorce and Remarriage under a Variety of Circumstances," in *Divorce and Remarriage: Four Christian Views*, ed. H. Wayne House (Downers Grove, IL: InterVarsity Press, 1990), 226.

fall within the categories of sexual immorality and abandonment laid out by Jesus and Paul.

SUMMARY

We need to be very careful not to go beyond Scripture in making allowances for divorce and remarriage. Our Lord Jesus spoke and taught about an exception from his own divine authority. Paul, an apostle writing under the inspiration of the Holy Spirit, gave a believer abandoned by an unbeliever freedom to divorce and remarry. Given that God hates divorce and that we are warned not to have any part in separating a couple joined by God in marriage, we should err on the side of caution when considering grounds for divorce and remarriage and not go beyond what is explicitly taught in Scripture.

— QUESTIONS FOR REFLECTION —

1. Why do some think that there could be other exceptions to the general rule against divorce and remarriage in addition to those specifically taught by Jesus and Paul?
2. What role does our understanding of the divorce practices in first-century Jewish and Greco-Roman culture have in comprehending biblical teaching on these subjects?
3. How can people's interpretation of these issues be improperly swayed by their own experience or by the experience of someone close to them?
4. What are the dangers of expanding the grounds for divorce and remarriage?
5. How might some of the other grounds for divorce that people suggest be related to the grounds we have already discussed (sexual sin and desertion)?

31

ARE DIVORCED PEOPLE STILL MARRIED IN GOD'S EYES?

Many who oppose all divorce and remarriage claim that even though a couple has been divorced, they are still married in God's eyes. Even teachers and scholars who believe that there are certain biblical grounds for divorce and remarriage make similar inaccurate statements that lead to confusion.

THE MARRIAGE COVENANT
ENDS WITH DIVORCE

We have already seen in question 28 that the marriage covenant is not unbreakable. While it is ideal that marriage is for life, Jesus does not say that no man *can* separate what God has joined. Rather, he says that it should not happen (Matt. 19:6). Some argue that even if the marriage has ended, a "one-flesh" relationship remains (per Gen. 2:24). But we also read in question 28 that one-flesh relationships are not necessarily permanent, as is the case when a man is joined as "one flesh" to a prostitute (1 Cor. 6:16). A formerly married man and woman are no longer one flesh. When a couple is divorced, they are no longer married to each other. They have been torn asunder.

A DIVORCED PERSON IS REALLY DIVORCED, AND A REMARRIED PERSON IS REALLY REMARRIED

In Deuteronomy 24, when the first husband divorces his wife, who then marries another man, the first man is no longer her husband and they are no longer married. She is now the wife of the second man. If her second husband divorces her or dies, her former husband is not permitted to remarry her. Now, if the first husband and the woman were "still married in God's eyes," or in any sense "one flesh," why would they be forbidden from getting back together? The reality is that they were no longer married. There was no longer any bond between them, and they had no further obligations to each other. There was, however, sin involved in their divorce, which led to the wife's being tainted and resulted in the unlawfulness of her ever returning to her first husband.[1]

In a similar way, when Jesus describes sinful divorce and remarriage (Matt. 5:32; 19:9; Mark 10:11–12; Luke 16:18), he implies that those who wrongfully divorced and remarried were actually divorced and remarried, and were not still married or in a one-flesh relationship with their former spouses. Just as in the case of Deuteronomy 24, a divorce ended the bond between the man and the woman, and a remarriage took place, which created a new one-flesh marriage relationship. The acts of divorcing and remarrying without biblical grounds were sinfully adulterous, just as the divorce in Deuteronomy 24 was due to sin. But the divorces are real, the new marriages are real, and the old marriages no longer exist.

AN OBLIGATION MAY REMAIN

Scripture teaches that improperly divorced people are not free to remarry, which means that some obligation remains in light of their

---

1. All divorce is due to sin. Jesus says that the divorce mentioned in Deuteronomy is due to the hardness of human hearts (Matt. 19:7–8). Some suggest that the sin was in the "indecency" found by the woman's husband (Deut. 24:1). I believe it is more

former marriage. Jesus teaches the general rule that remarriage after divorce is adulterous, and Paul teaches the general rule that a spouse who has wrongfully divorced should either remain unmarried or else be reconciled to his or her former spouse (1 Cor. 7:10–11).[2] Many contend that this restriction proves that these people are still to be regarded as married or in a one-flesh relationship.

While it is not surprising for authors who take the permanence view to assume the position that divorced people are still married in God's eyes, some who affirm the right of divorce and remarriage after sexual sin or abandonment also make (confusing) statements that sound as if the marriage relationship in some sense goes on after divorce. For example, Heth writes concerning Paul's teaching in 1 Corinthians 7:10–11: "So when Paul tells them to remain unmarried or else be reconciled (v. 11), he must be assuming this is an invalid divorce. They should not consider themselves divorced at all."[3] Murray expresses a similarly confusing statement when he addresses the adulterous remarriage that Jesus warned against in Matthew 19:9: "The only reason for which this remarriage can be regarded as adulterous is that the first marriage is still in God's sight regarded as inviolate. The divorce has not dissolved it. Illegitimate divorce does not dissolve the marriage bond and consequently the fact of such divorce does not relieve the parties concerned from any of the obligations incident to marriage. They are still in reality bound to one another

likely that the sin was on the part of the husband who put her away, because this better fits the explanation Jesus gives in the following verse, condemning those who would divorce except for sexual immorality (Matt. 19:9).

2. Paul actually calls the former spouse of the woman who divorced her "husband," by which he means her *former* husband (and the same man to whom he had just referred). Because the two are truly divorced, he does not regain the rights of a husband unless they are formally reconciled. Similar language is used in Matthew 14:3–4, when John the Baptist accuses Herod of taking his brother's wife. It was not that Herodias was at the moment still the wife of Herod's brother Philip (if she was then married to Herod), but that she had been (and still should have been).

3. William A. Heth, "Remarriage for Adultery or Desertion," in *Remarriage after Divorce in Today's Church: 3 Views*, ed. Mark L. Strauss (Grand Rapids: Zondervan, 2006), 77.

in the bonds of matrimony."[4] MacArthur additionally makes what I believe to be a similar error when he speaks of the divorced woman who remarries in Deuteronomy 24: "In God's eyes she was still the wife of the first husband."[5]

I believe that the statements above are inconsistent with scriptural teaching about divorce and can create confusion. The parties *are* divorced and should not consider themselves to still be married. What both Paul and Jesus are teaching is that after a sinful divorce, the parties shouldn't consider themselves free from obligation to seek reconciliation. Nor should they consider themselves free to remarry. But both Jesus and Paul acknowledge that a real divorce and remarriage have taken place, even if they were sinful and adulterous. Former spouses are not still married, even though perhaps they should be. It is more consistent and clear to simply say that because they were sinfully divorced, they may have an obligation before God to pursue reconciliation, but not to call their present status "marriage" or "one flesh."

IF A DIVORCED COUPLE WANT TO CARRY ON LIKE MARRIED PEOPLE, THEY MUST FIRST REMARRY

As long as a former husband and wife continue in their divorced status, they do not have spousal rights over one another. Because the covenant has been formally broken and they are no longer bound in commitment to each other, it would be wrong for them to engage in sexual relations, the sign of a marriage covenant that no longer exists. If a divorced couple were to have sexual relations, they would be guilty of sexual sin. If they decide to reconcile (praise God!), they need to enter into a new marriage covenant, which then would again bring them under the obligations and into the full privileges of being husband and wife.

4. John Murray, *Divorce* (Philadelphia: Presbyterian and Reformed, 1961), 25.
5. John MacArthur, *The Divorce Dilemma* (Leominster, England: Day One Publications, 2009), 42.

DANGEROUS PRACTICAL IMPLICATIONS

The teaching that divorced people are still "married in God's eyes" can lead to some very harmful (and unbiblical) implications. Does this mean that a wife who has been abandoned and divorced by her husband should allow him into her bed when he decides that he wants to visit her every now and then, even though he is living with someone else? Does this mean that a couple who divorced and remarried others should divorce their new spouses and get back together? Does this mean that a man who remarried is now, in effect, a bigamist (or polygamist)—being married in God's eyes to two women? A correct understanding—that even a divorce enacted with a hard heart is truly a divorce and even a remarriage that was adulterous in its inception is still a marriage and must be treated as such—will prevent many misunderstandings.

SUMMARY

Divorce, even if it is sinful, really breaks apart and ends a marriage.[6] Those who are divorced are no longer in any sense married or in a one-flesh relationship. They may, however, have obligation to seek reconciliation to each other or to remain unmarried. A remarriage, even if it is sinfully undertaken, creates a new one-flesh marriage relationship and must be respected as such.

— QUESTIONS FOR REFLECTION —

1. Why do some believe that divorced people are still "married in God's eyes"?
2. How does the Bible disprove the idea that those who are divorced are still, in some sense, "one flesh"?
3. What are possible harmful implications of the teaching

6. Jay Adams, *Marriage, Divorce, and Remarriage in the Bible* (Grand Rapids: Zondervan, 1980), 67.

that divorced people are still married to each other in some sense?

4. Why would it be wrong for a divorced couple to act as if they were still married?

5. What must a divorced couple do if they wish to act as husband and wife toward each other?

C. PRACTICAL QUESTIONS

32

WHAT SEXUAL SINS CONSTITUTE GROUNDS FOR DIVORCE?

Jesus teaches that divorce is permitted when one's spouse has been sexually immoral. But there are still questions regarding exactly what level of sexual sin is sufficient to warrant ending a marriage and what proof of marital unfaithfulness is required.

WHAT DEGREE OF SEXUAL IMMORALITY CAN END A MARRIAGE?

The Greek word *porneia*, which is translated "immorality," has a broad range of meanings and can include various sexual sins, including adultery and homosexuality.[1] It is clear that sexual intercourse with a man or a woman would qualify as *porneia*, as would other acts that involve sexual contact (heterosexual or homosexual), such as oral sex, sexual petting, etc. Pastors and counselors will face many different, heartbreaking situations and will need much wisdom from God as they seek to advise one who has been sinned against sexually.

---

1. "Later Judaism shows how the use of *porneia* broadens out to include not only fornication or adultery, but incest, sodomy, unlawful marriage, and sexual intercourse in general." Geoffrey Bromiley, *Theological Dictionary of the New Testament: Abridged in One Volume* (Grand Rapids: Eerdmans, 1985), 919.

Some acts are clearly sinful, but are not fully sexual. For instance, I counseled a married man who had reconnected with a former high school girlfriend through social media. On two occasions, they met at a public park and "made out," but claimed that they did not have intercourse. His wife kicked him out of the house and filed for divorce. Did she have grounds? While his acts were adulterous, my desire was to try to help them work toward repentance and forgiveness about this issue and to address other problems in their marriage that had led to the breakdown of trust.

In addition, people get into adulterous situations by going to strip clubs (including situations in which there is contact with the performers), receiving massages that are of an inappropriately sexual nature, etc.

Another common problem is the emotional affair, in which one's spouse becomes deeply connected (though not physically) to someone of the opposite sex in a way that threatens the one-flesh intimacy of marriage.[2] A spouse may rightly say, "I believe that your friendship with this other person violates our marriage covenant made under God. I am asking you to choose our marriage over this dangerous relationship."

WHAT ABOUT LUST AND PORNOGRAPHY?

Many years ago, I received a phone call from a woman who had been coming to us with her husband for counseling. She explained, "When we were at the mall, I saw my husband's eyes go toward a younger woman in a short dress. He was lusting after her. Jesus says that is adultery [referring to Matthew 5:28]. I want a divorce." This example illustrates the danger of expanding the grounds for divorce and remarriage. While the instruction of our Lord powerfully makes the point that lust is adulterous and dangerous, he does not teach that every spouse whose partner lusts has a right to divorce as if

---

2. This subject is discussed in question 14: "What Must Be Done to Protect a Marriage?"

one had committed the act of adultery. Otherwise, virtually every spouse would have the right to divorce. Similarly, when Jesus teaches that anger is murder (Matt. 5:21–22), he is not saying that everyone guilty of anger should receive the ultimate penalty that God has prescribed for murderers (death). In the case of the woman on the phone, I was tempted to reply, "You are as much a murderer as your husband is an adulterer. Now go, and show some gospel mercy to each other!"

Technology affords the opportunity for *porneia* through phone sex, video sex, Internet chat rooms, etc.[3] Someone who is truly repentant will address the sins of the heart that lead to such sin (Mark 7:21–23), as well as taking radical steps to cut off temptation (Matt. 5:29–30). Usually when one spouse struggles with private lust, the other should seek to come alongside the struggler as a helper as they seek to fight this sin together, instead of condemning or judging.

On the other hand, there is a difference between a spouse who fights against lust but occasionally stumbles and a person who relentlessly pursues sexual sin through pornography and masturbation without apology or effort to change. I have known men who had no interest in their wives sexually because of their willful addiction to private sexual sin (which may also constitute the sin of abandonment). Some men's pornography habits involve bizarre (or illegal) perversions, including child pornography and torture. For example, one woman was convinced that her husband was guilty of *porneia* after he was caught in acts of voyeurism, including installing a hidden camera in their shower, by which he viewed female houseguests and family members. While every effort should be made to save a marriage affected by sinful lust, I believe there are rare cases so severe that they may qualify as *porneia* and would be grounds for divorce.[4]

---

3. It has also become much more common for women to turn to pornography and masturbation.

4. John M. Frame quotes from the report of the PCA Ad Interim Committee on Divorce or Remarriage, which states that "the committee would argue that masturbation and the destructive sin of pornography per se are not grounds for divorce,

WHAT ABOUT PAST SINS?

Can the innocent spouse divorce if *porneia* (i.e., a pattern of promiscuous fornication) that occurred before marriage and was deliberately and deceitfully hidden has later been exposed? Certainly, the guilty spouse should seek forgiveness for both the sexual sin and even more for the lies (Eph. 4:25). While I would encourage the innocent party to forgive (see the next question), I understand why one would say that this is *porneia* that might provide grounds for divorce.[5]

Another situation that comes up is past sexual sin that took place during the marriage without the knowledge of the innocent spouse. I have had men confess a one-night stand while they were traveling years ago, or past inappropriate sexual contact with a woman at a strip club. They didn't want to tell their wives because it would upset them. My answer was they had committed acts that were in grave violation of the marriage covenant (which Jesus labels *porneia*). These husbands have the duty to seek forgiveness from their wives. Their wives have a right to know and to decide whether to forgive. Of course, it would be my hope that the wives would forgive, but these men must trust God for the outcome.

Moreover, it is entirely possible that the innocent spouses may already know, or that they will find out in the future. I have been amazed to see how sexual sins from many years before have been exposed through God's providence. It would have been much better for the guilty parties to have confessed their unfaithfulness before getting caught, which would have given them opportunity to begin rebuilding trust. By hiding their sin, they only delayed and increased the pain and the consequences.

---

because they do not unmistakably break the one-flesh relationship; but if a person becomes so obsessed with them that they become a substitute for fulfilling the conjugal rights of the spouse, then they could be understood to break the one flesh union." *The Doctrine of the Christian Life* (Phillipsburg, NJ: P&R Publishing, 2008), 775.

5. Deuteronomy 22:13–21, which addresses the proof of virginity, might speak to this question. The woman who claimed to be a virgin, but was not, was put to death, thus ending the husband's marital obligations to her (Deut. 22:20–21).

YOUR SIN WILL FIND YOU OUT

I have encountered several situations in which one spouse suspected the other of infidelity, but did not have ironclad proof. What should be done? For example, a man's wife accused him of infidelity, claiming that her feminine intuition told her that he was having an affair. She had forgiven him for an actual affair years earlier, but was convinced of his guilt this time because she was feeling the same way she had felt when he was in the last sinful relationship. I have counseled others who had reason to suspect that their spouses were being unfaithful because they were acting strangely and were unable to account for large amounts of time. Also, suspicious expenditures were appearing on bank statements and credit-card bills.

Scripture teaches that we cannot treat people as guilty unless we have proof (see Deut. 19:15). Hannah was falsely accused of sin based on appearances (1 Sam. 1:12–16). Scripture tells us that love "believes all things, hopes all things, endures all things" (1 Cor. 13:7); in other words, love assumes the best. This does not, however, prevent a suspicious spouse from gently asking questions and conducting reasonable investigation into the activities of a potentially wayward mate. This should be done not with a motive to discover grounds so that he or she can get out of the marriage, but rather with the hope of restoring a spouse who has wandered from the truth (Gal. 6:1; James 5:20).

Spouses who are involved in sexual immorality typically go to great lengths to hide their sin. Innocent spouses can be tempted to fear that they will forever remain in the dark, but must learn to trust God to bring everything to light in due time. As Moses warns, "Be sure your sin will find you out" (Num. 32:23).

SEEK GODLY COUNSEL

If your spouse has been involved in sexual sin, first turn to the Lord to ask for wisdom and grace. Prayerfully seek answers in his Word. Because these situations are extremely painful and emotional, I strongly advise that you seek godly counsel, ideally from your church leaders, as you seek to sort out whether your spouse has given you grounds for divorce through his or her sexual sin and what you should do next. According to Proverbs, "The way of a fool is right in his own eyes, but a wise man is he who listens to counsel" (Prov. 12:15). Your church leaders have been appointed by God to shepherd your soul, and you are accountable to them (Heb. 13:17). They can help you to evaluate the situation biblically and to avoid making impulsive decisions, which could make things worse. They can help you try to work with your spouse toward some kind of peaceful solution—preferably reconciliation. You will probably have to humble yourself to be open to their advice, which may go against some of your own thoughts and feelings. Their involvement can also protect your future reputation because they will be able to bear witness that you sought to do God's will and listened to wise counsel as you worked through your response to your spouse's sin.

SUMMARY

The word Jesus uses to describe the sexual sins that constitute grounds for divorce covers a range of serious sexual sins. Just because a sin may be potential grounds for divorce does not mean that a divorce must take place. As we will see in the next chapter, God often repairs badly broken marriages.

— QUESTIONS FOR REFLECTION —

1. What sexual sins clearly provide grounds for divorce?
2. What sexual sins are not grounds for divorce?
3. Are you unsure whether certain sexual sins are grounds for divorce? How would you decide?
4. What is the role of the church in helping the spouse who is the victim of sexual sin?
5. Why is it best for the guilty spouse to confess his or her sexual sin, even if the other party doesn't know about it?

33

WHEN AND HOW SHOULD SEXUAL SIN IN MARRIAGE BE FORGIVEN?

We have seen that sexual sin is so serious that it can serve as grounds to end a marriage. Jesus, in contrast to the Jewish rabbis, did not say that a man should or must divorce his wife for sexual immorality, but only that he may do so (Matt. 19:9). This implies that forgiveness and restoration are possible. It has been my privilege to see God work to rebuild numerous marriages that had been badly damaged by sexual sin. How does the innocent spouse decide whether to forgive and to go on with the marriage, or to take advantage of his or her right to obtain a divorce?

SEXUAL SIN DOES NOT END THE MARRIAGE

The sin of *porneia* does not end the marriage, but it gives the innocent party grounds for deciding whether to take legal action toward divorce.[1] When I am invited into these situations as a counselor, my hope is to help the couple through a process of repentance, forgiveness, and restoration.

---

1. Just as fornication between two unmarried people does not automatically make them married, apart from the making of a covenant, adultery does not end the marriage unless the innocent spouse chooses to exercise the right to divorce.

WHERE DO YOU BEGIN?

When counseling in cases of marital unfaithfulness, it is necessary to understand the nature of the sexual sin committed. Was this a one-night stand or an ongoing affair? Were plans and promises made? What was the nature of the sexual sin (intercourse, oral sex, homosexual acts, etc.)? How was the sin exposed? Did the guilty party confess on his or her own (which, in my experience, is very rare), or was the person caught? How was he or she caught? The fact that a person is caught does not mean that repentance is impossible. David was caught and yet truly repented (2 Sam. 12).

In the immediate aftermath of the discovery of adultery, both the guilty party and the victim experience many strong emotions, including anger, fear, guilt, jealousy, shame, shock, and despair. Nothing counselors do is more important than building hope from the earliest stages of counseling. We point both spouses to Jesus, who has compassion for sinners and helps them in their time of need (Heb. 4:14–16). He, too, knows what it is to be betrayed (Jer. 2:13; Luke 22:48). He will stand with them in this trial and will not allow them to be overwhelmed (Ps. 34:17–18; 1 Cor. 10:13). He died to set people free from slavery to sin. He can forgive and transform sinners (Isa. 55:6–7). He is able to do what is humanly impossible (Luke 18:27), such as restoring shattered marriages.

In the early stages of counseling in cases of adultery, I typically don't try to press the innocent spouse to make an immediate decision to forgive the guilty spouse and to give up the right to divorce. Usually, it is hard at this point to know whether the guilty spouse is truly repentant. The innocent spouse may need time to come to grips with what has happened.[2] Instead, I encourage both parties to continue

---

2. There is frequently an initial wave of sympathy on the part of the innocent spouse, who may hope that he or she can "save" the guilty party through love and forgiveness. I have seen cases in which the innocent spouse has offered forgiveness before the guilty spouse appears to be repentant. Often, after a brief "honeymoon period," the reconciliation breaks down because many of the most significant issues haven't been adequately addressed.

to engage in the process and then to see what God may do in the life of the other person and in one's own heart. I also encourage them to each focus on pleasing God, regardless of what the other person does (2 Cor. 5:9). One person can't control a spouse's actions, but he or she can use this as an opportunity to honor the Lord and to grow as a Christian. Furthermore, I have found it to be very significant for the innocent spouse to realize that the sin of the guilty party is primarily against God and reflects the fact that the guilty spouse has wandered far from the Lord. The innocent spouse should recognize that his or her primary role is to seek to help restore the adulterer's relationship with the Lord (Gal. 6:1) and that this may be one of the most important opportunities he or she will ever have to show the kind of rescuing grace to someone else that God has shown to us.[3]

THE ADULTERER MUST REPENT BEFORE GOD

The adulterer must first see that his or her sin is primarily against God. As David writes after his adultery with Bathsheba and murder of her husband, Uriah, "Against You, You only, I have sinned and done what is evil in Your sight" (Ps. 51:4a). It is also important that the person understands and confesses heart sins (e.g., an idolatry of sex and pleasure, living by feelings, not faith) that led to the outward sins (Mark 7:21–23). It may be vital to go back and review the process by which the person drifted from the Lord and toward evil (see James 1:14–15). Rarely do people suddenly fall into such sins. In addition, one must learn to view one's sins as God sees them (Prov. 2:16–19). After being caught, the adulterer may realize that his or her heart has, over time, grown cold and hard toward God and that it may take time for it to become warm and soft again. Repentance is often a process. David's psalms of repentance, written after his sin with Bathsheba was uncovered, can be a great help to the person who is seeking to

---

3. I sometimes refer the innocent spouse to the parable of the good Samaritan, saying that he or she should see the partner as one lying beside the road, beaten and bloodied by sin (Luke 10:25–37).

restore a relationship with the Lord by using these as model prayers (Pss. 32; 51).

The adulterer must make a clean break from his or her sin and confess guilt: "He who conceals his transgressions will not prosper, but he who confesses and forsakes them will find compassion" (Prov. 28:13). All contact with the third party must be broken off, and every bridge must be burned. Scripture reads, "Do not go near the door of her house" (Prov. 5:8). Also, "If your right eye makes you stumble, tear it out and throw it from you; for it is better for you to lose one of the parts of your body, than for your whole body to be thrown into hell" (Matt. 5:29). For example, if the adulterous relationship took place in the context of work, it may be wise to change jobs to eliminate contact with the other party.[4] Every excuse and rationalization for the possibility of future contact ("Can't we just be friends?") must be obliterated.

THE ADULTERER NEEDS TO SEEK FORGIVENESS FROM THE SPOUSE

The guilty spouse has the clear duty at the earliest possible time to seek forgiveness for breaking his or her marriage promises (Matt. 5:23–24). The confession should be thorough—not merely admitting to what has already been discovered, but to all that the innocent spouse has a right to know about the nature of the sexual sin (without explicit or sordid details—Eph. 4:29). Adulterers tend to hold back specifics and minimize sin, thus undermining trust and hope for restoration. The innocent parties suffer as the sin is gradually exposed (like peeling an onion), either through discovery or under duress.

"The Seven A's of Confession" discussed in question 16 provide an excellent guideline for how forgiveness should be sought. A few areas that deserve particular attention include:

Avoid if, but, and maybe. There should not be even a hint of an

---

4. It is best if the adulterer makes his or her own decision (along with the spouse) about what actions to take to apply the principle of radical separation (Matt. 5:29). One wayward husband chose to move his family to a different state for a fresh start.

excuse or justification for the sins committed. The guilty parties will frequently have rationalized their affairs based on their spouses' lack of sexual availability, their failure to take care of themselves physically, or their constant criticism. They must repent of this reasoning.

Admit specifically. Adultery involves far more than sex. I have often heard the innocent spouse say, "I could forgive the sex, but I am not sure I can forgive the lies." Sexual sin breaks the promise made through the marriage covenant and typically involves a multitude of other lies (Eph. 4:25). Sexual sin also has other repercussions, including significant financial waste, subjecting the innocent spouse to risk of sexually transmitted disease, impact on the children, etc.

Acknowledge the hurt. Adultery involves the deepest possible human betrayal. The innocent parties will often question whether they have ever been truly and honestly loved by their spouses. They will also be tempted to feel insecure about themselves physically and sexually, given that the guilty parties felt a need to go elsewhere for sexual satisfaction. The guilty spouses need to realize and confess that their sin was not the fault of their spouses, but rather was due to their own sinful fleshliness as they wandered from the Lord.

GOD HIMSELF MODELS HOW
FORGIVENESS CAN TAKE PLACE

Under the old covenant, the Lord was portrayed as the husband to the nation of Israel, which was repeatedly unfaithful (Jer. 3:6–10; Ezek. 16:1–59; Hos. 2:2–13). Yet, as is beautifully portrayed in the book of Hosea, the Lord drew adulterous Israel back to himself and forgave her when she came to repentance: "Therefore, behold, I will allure her, bring her into the wilderness and speak kindly to her. . . . I will heal their apostasy, I will love them freely, for My anger has turned away from them" (Hos. 2:14; 14:4; see also Ezek. 16:60–63; Hos. 2:16–23). Based on the new covenant, we are taught to forgive others as we have been forgiven by God through the work of Christ (Eph. 4:32).

We encourage the innocent spouse to wait and see if the guilty party gives evidence of being truly repentant before making a decision to forgive. Often I am asked, "How can I know if my spouse is truly repentant? Can you promise me that my spouse won't do it again?" While it is impossible to say for sure that someone (including the innocent party) won't commit a certain sin in the future, Scripture does state the characteristics of true repentance as opposed to worldly sorrow:

> For the sorrow that is according to the will of God produces a repentance without regret, leading to salvation, but the sorrow of the world produces death. For behold what earnestness this very thing, this godly sorrow, has produced in you: what vindication of yourselves, what indignation, what fear, what longing, what zeal, what avenging of wrong! In everything you demonstrated yourselves to be innocent in the matter. (2 Cor. 7:10–11)

Worldly sorrow is self-focused and hates the consequences of sin—for example, after killing his brother, Cain complained that his punishment was too great to bear (Gen. 4:13). Godly sorrow is focused on God and others and hates the sin itself. Worldly sorrow seeks to shift blame and resists accountability. Godly sorrow fully accepts responsibility and welcomes accountability. Worldly sorrow is impatient—demanding to be trusted and restored immediately. True repentance is patient and understanding if the innocent party needs time to grant full forgiveness. It is wise for the innocent spouse to seek counsel from wise church leaders to obtain their perspective about whether the guilty spouse is repentant.

MUST FORGIVENESS BE GRANTED?

In light of the mercy we have received from God (Matt. 6:12), there is a sense in which we should have a forgiving attitude toward those who have wronged us, even if they aren't repentant (Luke 23:34). But full restoration of the relationship cannot take place unless the other person has repented. As Jesus explains to his disciples, "If your brother sins, rebuke him; and if he repents, forgive him" (Luke 17:3).

If someone is not repentant (e.g., the guilty party continues to see the other man or woman), the innocent spouse is not obligated to fully forgive the person by taking him or her back and not using the right to divorce.[5] But as previously discussed, divorce is not required. A spouse may choose to take back an unrepentant partner, though I would not ordinarily advise this.[6]

When adultery is fully forgiven, the innocent spouse makes a decision to continue in the marriage relationship and forgo using the known sexual immorality in the future as grounds for divorce. This forgiveness should be specifically sought and granted. Once this decision has been made, the innocent spouse cannot change his or her mind and file for divorce later on.[7] Forgiveness also implies fully entering into the commitments and responsibilities of marriage.[8] A wife who says, "I will stay in the marriage, but he will have to sleep in a separate room for the rest of his life" has not yet reached the point of truly forgiving as Christ has forgiven all of us.

If the guilty spouse appears to be repentant, must the wronged partner fully forgive him or her? Some believe that the innocent partner must take a repentant spouse back, or that it is only a hard-hearted spouse who can be divorced. Adams comments, "Divorce of a believing spouse who has committed fornication must, therefore, be restricted to

---

5. It may be wise for the innocent spouse to wait for a limited time to see whether the guilty spouse is, by God's grace, brought to repentance before filing for divorce.

6. For example, a Christian may take back an unbelieving spouse who has ended the offending relationship and wishes to continue in the marriage.

7. I once counseled a woman who, because she was very unhappy in her marriage as a result of her husband's quarrelsomeness, tried to use his adultery from twenty years before (which she had at that time forgiven) as grounds to depart from the marriage. I explained that once she had forgiven him and fully reentered the marriage, she had given up her right to divorce for known past sexual sin.

8. I have seen other cases in which the innocent spouse remains in the marriage, but wants to continue to hold the possibility of divorce as a threat for months or even years after discovering the spouse's infidelity. My understanding is that when the innocent spouse chooses to remain in the marriage over an extended time (enjoying the privileges and fulfilling the duties), he or she is effectively choosing to forgive and to remain in the marriage covenant, which could then be broken only by future infidelity. Ideally, this will be clearly communicated between the spouses.

those who refuse to repent of their sin."[9] While I fully agree that reconciliation is the ideal outcome and that every effort should be made to that end, I do not believe the innocent spouse can be compelled (e.g., under the threat of church discipline) not to exercise the right to divorce on the grounds of adultery, even if the adulterer claims to be repentant. Wronged spouses who refuse to fully forgive usually act this way because they are not convinced that the repentance is genuine (e.g., this has happened on multiple occasions). In addition, the sin might have been so serious (e.g., rape, molesting a child) that they do not wish to pursue reconciliation. Or they may have decided that they no longer wish to remain married to a person who has callously broken the covenant or to live with the consequences of the sin (e.g., a sexually transmitted disease). Sometimes forgiven sin still has consequences (Gal. 6:6–7).[10] The consequence could be the end of a marriage. Wronged spouses, however, must guard their hearts. Bitterness and hatred are always sinful (Eph. 4:31–32).

REBUILDING THE MARRIAGE

When reconciliation takes place after sexual sin, the object is not merely that the marriage can go on as before, but rather that the marriage can be renewed according to God's ideals. Both parties need to grow in their own relationship with the Lord. Harmful patterns of the past, including those of the "innocent" spouse (who is also a sinner), need to be transformed. Intimacy must be restored and strengthened on every level. It is a great joy to see broken marriages reconciled and transformed by gospel grace.

9. Jay Adams, *Marriage, Divorce, and Remarriage in the Bible* (Grand Rapids: Zondervan, 1980), 57.

10. The book of Numbers offers an interesting example of forgiveness being granted, but with consequences. When Moses intercedes on behalf of Israel after the people's sinful rebellion, the Lord says, "I have pardoned them according to your word" (Num. 14:20), but also states that those who sinned will experience the consequence of not seeing the land (14:22–24). King David was forgiven of his sin with Bathsheba, but he still had to face consequences (2 Sam. 12:13–14).

SUMMARY

When adultery is uncovered, many marriages seem like a broken egg, which cannot be put back together again, even by all the king's horses and all the king's men. But God's grace can bring a sinner to repentance and can enable the person sinned against not only to forgive, but also to confess his or her own sins. Marriages that had long been weak can become strong as husbands and wives learn to show redeeming love to one another.

— QUESTIONS FOR REFLECTION —

1. Does the act of adultery end the marriage covenant? Explain your answer.
2. How does Jesus' teaching regarding the right of the innocent party to divorce differ from that of even the strictest Jewish rabbis?
3. What should be covered in a first counseling session with a couple in whose marriage adultery has recently been discovered?
4. What biblical reasons would you give for why forgiveness and reconciliation are not just possible but desirable after adultery has taken place?
5. In what cases may the innocent spouse decide not to be reconciled?

34

WHAT CONSTITUTES ABANDONMENT BY AN UNBELIEVING SPOUSE?

While most evangelicals agree that abandonment by an unbelieving spouse provides grounds for divorce and remarriage, there is disagreement about exactly what behavior constitutes desertion. Must the unbelieving spouse physically leave the home and file for divorce, or could other behavior qualify as desertion of the believing spouse?

DEPARTURE AND DIVORCE

When an unbelieving spouse permanently leaves the home, or forces a believer to depart and then files for divorce, the believer is not to fight against the divorce, but rather is freed from the marriage obligation: "Yet if the unbelieving one leaves, let him leave; the brother or the sister is not under bondage in such cases, but God has called us to peace" (1 Cor. 7:15). There are also situations in which the unbeliever physically separates from the believing spouse, making it clear that he or she is done with the marriage, but does not choose to go to the trouble of filing for divorce (perhaps to avoid financial obligations). In this case, the believer would be free to file for divorce to formalize what the unbeliever has initiated. Frame writes, "An unbelieving man may leave his believing wife and go to live with another woman, without filing divorce papers. Where does that leave the innocent, believing spouse? She may accept the situation of a broken marriage, as Paul says. Thus she may regard herself as free from the original marriage obligation. But in order to secure recognition of that freedom, she may need herself to file divorce papers with the state."[1]

CAN SOMEONE ABANDON A MARRIAGE WITHOUT LEAVING THE HOUSE OR FILING FOR DIVORCE?

Some have suggested that a spouse can be guilty of abandoning a marriage through a gross failure to fulfill marital responsibilities, even if the person doesn't physically depart from the house or file for divorce. Under the old covenant, the basic duties of a husband were defined as providing food, clothing, and conjugal rights (Ex. 21:10). Under certain conditions, a wife could be freed from a marriage if her husband refused to do these things for her (21:11). Some would reason that in the same way, when a spouse deliberately and willfully refuses to fulfill one's basic marital duties, the other spouse could be considered free to divorce.[2]

THE TOUGH CASES

Situations I have encountered in which this principle of abandonment might apply include:

1. The wife tells her husband after the first year of marriage that she will never again be willing to have sexual relations and that they will be sleeping in separate bedrooms for the duration of the marriage. She does, however, want to remain legally married.

1. John M. Frame, *The Doctrine of the Christian Life* (Phillipsburg, NJ: P&R Publishing, 2008), 229.

2. David Instone-Brewer states that both Jewish and Greco-Roman courts would have allowed for divorce on such grounds and argues that Paul may have had this in mind when he was writing 1 Corinthians 7 (especially the call to fulfill conjugal duties in verses 3–5 and the reference about duties to meet the needs of one's spouse in verse 33). *Divorce and Remarriage in the Church* (Downers Grove, IL: InterVarsity Press, 2003), 96–102.

2. The wife works as a nurse, making a good income. The husband refuses to work (see 1 Tim. 5:8). He takes the money she earns and buys illegal drugs to party with his friends. By his own choice, he lives in the garage and has very little contact with his wife. He does not want to leave or divorce her, however, because he is living in the house she pays for and spending the money she earns.

3. After ten years of marriage that were blessed with the births of two children, the husband declares that he is a woman trapped inside a man's body and that he intends to have a sex-change operation. He announces that he wants to remain in the marriage with his wife and his children. His wife, weeping, says that she doesn't want to be in a lesbian relationship.

4. The husband, without his wife's knowledge, has been involved in illegal financial activities, including investment scams and tax fraud. He is being sent to prison for the next twenty-five years. The family is bankrupt and on the verge of homelessness.

5. The wife goes away for months at a time, during which she refuses any contact with her husband. Sooner or later, she returns home (usually when she has run out of money) and wants to live with him again. She won't talk about why she left, where she went, or whether she might leave again. This has happened several times over the past five years.

6. The wife sits at home, watching television and drinking liquor all day while the husband is at work. He tried restricting her access to credit cards and cash, but then she actually pawned the silver to get more booze.

PROCEED WITH CAUTION

When dealing with the tough cases, we should first ask, "What can be done to heal this marriage?" before we ask, "Are there grounds for divorce?" Why is one spouse refusing marital intimacy? Did the other partner do something hurtful (Prov. 18:17)? Does the person require help in overcoming the effects of past sexual abuse? Another thing to keep in mind is that these grounds apply only to an unbelieving spouse. When a professing believer is guilty of significant failure to keep the marriage covenant, the person should be confronted through the process defined in Matthew 18:15–20, which ideally would result in repentance, but could result in expulsion from the church and thus being treated as an unbeliever.

Another concern is that once the definition of abandonment is expanded, almost any failure to keep the marriage covenant could be used as an excuse for divorce. Murray warns, "It is, however, of the greatest importance to maintain that . . . the application of this liberty must be limited to the precise conditions specified or implied by the apostle."[3] What if a man is willing to work, but is a very poor provider? How often must a wife make herself available sexually to fulfill her conjugal duties? These are some of the very issues that the Jewish rabbis argued about in Jesus' day.[4] The Greek word *chorizō*, which is translated "leave" in 1 Corinthians 7:15, is the word used for divorce, implying that the unbeliever is willfully abandoning his or her commitment to the other spouse—not merely coming up short in meeting covenant obligations. There is also a difference between being unable (e.g., because of physical disability) to fulfill conjugal duties or the duty to provide, as opposed to a person who is able but unwilling.

In these cases of willful rejection of the marriage covenant by unbelievers, the believing spouses may, after making great effort toward reconciliation, consider themselves abandoned. Frame writes, "The 'separation' in [1 Cor. 7] verse 15 may or may not be geographical. The important thing is that it is a renunciation of one's marriage vows."[5] In doubtful cases, I have found it wise to directly ask unbelieving spouses about their commitment to the marriage and their willingness to make an effort to fulfill their basic duties: "Do you want out

3. John Murray, *Divorce* (Philadelphia: Presbyterian and Reformed, 1961), 76. Murray continues that the desertion that Paul is speaking about is limited to that which is for religious reasons (ibid., 78).

4. Instone-Brewer, *Divorce and Remarriage in the Church*, 74, 101.

5. Frame, *The Doctrine of the Christian Life*, 781.

of this marriage?" If they make it clear that they have no intention to make any effort to fulfill their duties as spouses, the believing spouses may, after making every effort toward reconciliation, consider themselves abandoned.

SUMMARY

While we should be very cautious about expanding the definition of abandonment to include any failure to keep the marriage covenant, there are situations in which a believing spouse may consider himself or herself deserted, even if the unbeliever was not the one who physically moved away from the home and filed for divorce. People facing situations of possible abandonment should seek godly counsel from their church leaders as they strive to honor God through very difficult circumstances.

— QUESTIONS FOR REFLECTION —

1. What are some dangers of expanding the definition of abandonment beyond physical departure and filing for divorce?
2. What biblical basis could be given for saying that a spouse who willfully refuses to fulfill marital duties has abandoned the marriage?
3. Which of the difficult cases described in this chapter would qualify as desertion?
4. What role might church leaders play in helping a believer determine whether his or her spouse has provided grounds for divorce for desertion?
5. What should be done if a professing believer abandons his or her marriage?

35

IS ABUSE GROUNDS FOR DIVORCE?

Abuse as possible grounds for divorce also has significant support among evangelicals. Many have wondered whether, if one ten-minute incident of adultery could be just cause for divorce, ten years of physical violence would not. Instone-Brewer points out that the church father Origen "asked why Jesus did not allow a husband to divorce a wife who had tried to poison him or who had killed one of their children, because 'to endure sins of such heinousness which would seem to be worse than adultery or fornication would appear to be irrational.'"[1]

UNDERSTANDING ABUSE[2]

Abuse, broadly defined, is an improper and harmful treatment of one person by another. There are different kinds of abuse, including physical abuse (behavior that results in the nonaccidental injury of the victim), sexual abuse, verbal abuse, and emotional abuse. Abusive actions and words typically come from fleshly hearts that are ruled by angry desires (Matt. 5:21–22; Gal. 5:19–21; James 4:1–2).

Abuse can be hard to prove in that two parties may give radically different accounts of what transpired, and there are no other witnesses.

---

1. David Instone-Brewer, *Divorce and Remarriage in the Church* (Downers Grove, IL: InterVarsity Press, 2003), 94.
2. See Jim Newheiser, *Help! Someone I Love Has Been Abused* (Wapwallopen, PA: Shepherd Press, 2010).

Sometimes significant sin and provocation occur on both sides of an argument. In one case the wife came in, sporting a black eye. I asked the husband, "How did your wife get the black eye?" He replied, "It happened when I threw my cell phone at her." At that point, the wife chimed in, "That was right after I tried to run him over in the car and broke his leg." It is important to hear from all sides when an accusation of abuse is made. I have seen cases in which one spouse claims to have been terribly mistreated, but when I heard the other side, I realized that I hadn't heard the whole story. "The first to plead his case seems right, until another comes and examines him" (Prov. 18:17).[3] On the other hand, it should not be assumed that there is equal blame on both sides. Abusers are often masters of manipulation, who can make it sound like they were the victims. Finally, it should not be assumed that all abusers are men. I have encountered numerous situations in which the wife repeatedly became violently angry, while the husband would futilely attempt to placate her.

PROTECT THE VICTIMS OF ABUSE

Scripture teaches that God is concerned for the oppressed (Pss. 10:17–18; 82:3–4) and that leaders are responsible to protect those who are afflicted: "Open your mouth for the mute, for the rights of all the unfortunate. Open your mouth, judge righteously, and defend the rights of the afflicted and needy" (Prov. 31:8–9). The church is to reflect the Lord's care for the oppressed (Ps. 9:9; Luke 4:18–19).

Sadly, there have been many cases in which church leaders have failed to protect the victims of abuse. Leaders have not taken the claims of abused spouses seriously. Battered women have been told that if they were more sweet and submissive, the abuse would stop. Sometimes it is implied that it is their fault that their husband is so angry. This counsel

3. William A. Heth writes about his experiences in counseling marriage conflicts: "If we've learned anything from this, it is that our initial judgments about who was at fault in the relationship were almost the opposite of what was really going on." "Remarriage for Adultery or Desertion," in *Remarriage after Divorce in Today's Church: 3 Views*, ed. Mark L. Strauss (Grand Rapids: Zondervan, 2006), 79.

is based on a misinterpretation of 1 Peter 3:1–2, which reads that wives should seek to win their disobedient husbands without a word through their chaste and respectful behavior. While it is true that God may use the gracious submission of a mistreated wife to win her husband to faith, Peter is not saying that she is under obligation to take a daily physical and verbal beating. Nor is Peter saying that the wife can be certain that if she just behaves sweetly enough, her husband will come around. As Paul reminds us, "How do you know, O wife, whether you will save your husband?" (1 Cor. 7:16a). Some men are hard-hearted and will continue to abuse their wives, regardless of what they do. Church leaders who send a woman back into a situation in which she is likely to be beaten have failed to fulfill their call to protect Christ's sheep (Acts 20:28) and are unworthy of their office (Ezek. 34:1–10).

Even those who question whether abuse is grounds for divorce should agree that a wife has a right to be physically safe and that if she is at risk of violence, she is free to find another place to live until it is safe to return home. Holcomb provides several biblical examples of those who took advantage of opportunities to avoid suffering, including Paul's escapes from persecution (Acts 9:25; 22:25–29; 23:12–24).[4] Others note that Paul was willing to use his rights under Roman law to avoid mistreatment. Church leaders should step up to offer protection to battered spouses by providing a safe place to stay, offering compassionate counsel, and furnishing other needed practical help. If the abusive spouses are church members, they are subject to church discipline (Matt. 18:15–20). If the abusive spouses are guilty of criminal physical abuse, the victims may need encouragement to report the matter to the appropriate civil authorities (Rom. 13:4).[5] If children have been physically or sexually abused, church leaders are required by law to report these crimes to the government authorities.

---

4. Justin Holcomb, *Is It My Fault?* (Chicago: Moody, 2014), 129–37.

5. Victims of abuse often fail to report crimes against them because of misunderstanding submission (thinking that it would be unsubmissive to report), fear (of being alone, or of retaliation from the abuser), or false guilt ("If I were a better wife, he wouldn't be this way").

DEGREES OF ABUSE

Angry words (verbal abuse) are very sinful: "With his mouth the godless man destroys his neighbor" (Prov. 11:9a). There is a difference, though, between a man who raises his voice on occasion and the man who physically beats up or berates his wife. Just as we wouldn't encourage divorce in the case of every person who has a lustful thought or look (Matt. 5:28), we wouldn't say that every spouse who has spoken hatefully in anger should be punished as a murderer (5:21–22) or has given grounds for divorce.

One of the most difficult situations that a leader may face is one spouse's relentless verbal (and psychological) abuse of the other. I have seen cases in which the always-angry spouse will follow the partner around the house, railing at him or her, even as the victim just tries to get away. I have encountered controlling husbands who totally micromanage their wives and try to isolate them from others, forbidding them to spend time with family and friends. I have seen abusive spouses who would not let their partners sleep as they continued to berate them throughout the night. While I would be reluctant to tell such people that they have a right to divorce, it is hard to argue that they don't have the right to escape (at least temporarily) the constant verbal attacks.

CAN THE VICTIM OF ABUSE
FILE FOR DIVORCE?

Just as we seek to offer godly counsel—which would ideally lead to repentance, forgiveness, and restoration in cases of marital infidelity—our first hope in cases of spousal abuse is to bring the abuser to true repentance. Then the home would become a safe place for the victim, who could forgive, and the marriage could begin to be rebuilt. Many abusers, however, are arrogant, unrepentant, and manipulative, thus making peaceful reconciliation impossible.

Many believe that severe cases of abuse qualify under the category of abandonment of the marriage, reasoning that if the violent spouse isn't willing to live at peace with the believer, he or she is effectively causing a separation by forcing the innocent spouse to leave. According to Paul, "God has called us to peace" (1 Cor. 7:15b).[6] Crippen writes, "We emphasize once more that abuse is a form of desertion . . . . 'Constructive' desertion occurs when one partner's evil conduct ends the marriage because it causes the other partner to leave."[7] One danger of opening this door is that it could be used to broaden the grounds for divorce to anything that a supposed victim considers to be abusive. Given that we are all sinners who are prone to sinful anger expressed through sinful words and actions, virtually every marriage could be ended on these grounds. On the other hand, there may be extreme cases in which abuse has broken the marriage bonds beyond repair.[8] Consider the following:

1. The husband has repeatedly abused the children physically and sexually, but somehow has escaped prison. Child Protective Services has told the mother that if she lets the husband back into the house, the children will be taken away from her.

2. The wife has engaged in a long-term pattern of verbal and physical abuse against her husband. She will not let him sleep. She constantly yells at him and frequently hits him. The children are traumatized by seeing their parents this way. She has gone to counselors, but hasn't changed. This has been going on for more than ten years.

3. The husband is constantly full of rage and has beaten his wife several times. Once—when he pushed her down—she broke her wrist, but she told the doctors that she had just fallen.

6. This ground would apply only to an unbelieving spouse. But again, a professing Christian who refuses to repent could be considered an unbeliever after the biblical process of church discipline has been followed.

7. Jeff Crippen and Anna Wood, *A Cry for Justice* (Lincroft, NJ: Calvary Press, 2012), 304.

8. John M. Frame quotes a PCA Report that explains that divorce may be necessary "to protect a blameless spouse from intolerable conditions." *The Doctrine of the Christian Life* (Phillipsburg, NJ: P&R Publishing, 2008), 781.

Finally, one night, he came home drunk and beat her so badly that both eyes were blackened and her nose was broken. She wants to know how much more of this she has to take.

4. The husband—after being arrested for beating his wife, burning her with a cigarette, and stabbing her in the arm with a knife—has been sentenced to seven years in prison. Should she consider herself abandoned?

5. The wife attempted to kill her husband and their children with a knife in a fit of anger.

One alternative in such cases of abuse would be to live separately (and safely), while hoping that the Lord would bring the abusive spouses to repentance (1 Cor. 7:10–11). I would not, however, support a church's exercising discipline against the victims who, after a long period of significant abuse with no indication of true repentance on the part of the abusers, chose to regard themselves as abandoned and filed for divorce. I would strongly advise that people considering such a decision work closely with church leaders in evaluating their options biblically.

SUMMARY

Physical, verbal, and emotional types of abuse are contrary to God's design for marriage, which is supposed to reflect love and grace instead of anger and hatred. Victims of abuse have a right to protect their own lives and the lives of their children. Church leaders should carefully investigate claims of abuse and should be faithful to protect the innocent, which may sometimes involve offering shelter or calling the authorities. While some cases of abuse may equate to abandonment by an unbeliever, every effort should be made to rescue the marriage, and great caution should be exercised before granting approval to divorce.

— Questions for Reflection —

1. What behavior constitutes abuse?
2. How have some church leaders failed in their calling to protect victims of abuse?
3. When is it right for the victim of abuse to physically get away from his or her spouse?
4. Why would many consider some forms of abuse to be grounds for divorce? Which of the examples above would provide grounds for divorce?
5. What should church leaders do when they aren't sure where to draw the line about what qualifies as valid grounds for divorce?

36

IS IT BIBLICAL FOR A MARRIED COUPLE TO SEPARATE WITHOUT DIVORCING?

As was briefly discussed in question 23, many in our day choose to separate from their spouses, rather than pursuing divorce. Some separate with the hope that time apart could lead to the healing of the marriage relationship. Others separate because they think that separation is preferable to divorce, being less shameful or sinful.

ONGOING SEPARATION IS CONTRARY TO GOD'S DESIGN FOR MARRIAGE

Given that God's design for marriage is oneness and companionship (Gen. 2:24), physical separation of husband and wife is to be avoided. Physical separation of husbands and wives is sometimes necessary because of war, as was the case with Uriah, who was separated from his wife, Bathsheba, while he was fighting against the Ammonites for his God and his king (2 Sam. 11). The Law prescribed that newly married men should not be forced to go off to war, so that they could bring happiness to their wives (Deut. 24:5). Today, husbands and wives experience temporary and sometimes extended separations because of participation in the military, career obligations, family responsibilities (caring for a sick parent), or even imprisonment (sometimes because of persecution, as was the case of John Bunyan centuries ago and has been true of many church leaders and missionaries in our day).

Paul does say that it is appropriate for a married couple to agree to temporarily abstain from sexual relations for a time for the purpose of prayer, but he also warns married couples that this separation should be brief lest they be tempted to sin from their lack of self-control (1 Cor. 7:5).[1] Some couples don't make sufficient effort to avoid lengthy separations as they put career, children, hobbies, or even ministry ahead of their marriage. Often laziness devolves into disdain as couples grow apart and become independent of each other.

Some couples live separate lives—with separate homes (or rooms), separate vacations, separate finances, and separate friendships—without ever filing for legal separation or divorce. They are still failing to fulfill God's design for marriage and are in breach of the covenant promises they made to each other when they entered into marriage. Their relationship is almost a de facto divorce.

COULD A TEMPORARY SEPARATION HELP?

Some who are miserable within their marriages suppose that spending time apart could benefit the marriage by providing some time to escape the constant conflict, so that each party can cool off and heal. Often, however, separation has the opposite effect as one or both spouses discover that they are happier being apart. Furthermore, the time of separation may cause each to become more independent of the other.

Jay Adams writes, "In the Bible, the modern idea of separation as something less than divorce (whether legal or otherwise) was totally unknown as a viable alternative to divorce."[2] He also warns, "Modern separation settles nothing; it amounts to a refusal to face issues and

---

1. John MacArthur writes, "It is to be by mutual agreement, temporary, and for a spiritual purpose," in *The Divorce Dilemma* (Leominster, England: Day One Publications, 2009), 94.

2. Jay Adams, *Marriage, Divorce, and Remarriage in the Bible* (Grand Rapids: Zondervan, 1980), 33.

set them to rest."[3] People who are living apart cannot resolve their problems. In most situations, a Christian couple would be wise to seek godly counsel as they work on their issues together.

There may be some rare cases in which a brief separation is necessary or appropriate. For example, if one or both spouses are extremely angry and there is a risk of physical or verbal abuse, it might be wise for one of them to go to a separate room or, if necessary, to stay overnight with a friend. In such cases, however, the brief time of separation should be used profitably—not merely as an escape from problems (e.g., by watching television, surfing the Internet, or going to a movie). If the marriage has reached the point that the husband and wife can't live peaceably in the same house together, each should be earnestly requesting God's help through prayer (including confession of personal sin), studying Scripture, and seeking godly counsel (primarily for the purpose of obtaining help in dealing with each mate's own sin—1 Cor. 7:5). When both parties are again walking in the Spirit, they can come back together to work toward reconciliation (see question 16 for further information about conflict resolution).

In addition, there may be cases in which a spouse who has grounds for divorce would choose to physically separate, and/or file for legal separation, while waiting to see whether the guilty spouse will repent and the marriage can be saved.[4]

WHAT ABOUT THE SEPARATION IN 1 CORINTHIANS 7:11?

The one case in Scripture that most resembles a modern legal separation is the situation in 1 Corinthians 7:10–11 in which the wife leaves (divorces) her husband, but is said by Paul not to be free to

3. Ibid.

4. Legal separation may be necessary to protect the financial and property interests of the innocent spouse and to clarify rights and responsibilities of each spouse with the children. If both parties claim to be believers, the terms of the separation could be worked out (perhaps with the help of the church) without having to go to court in an adversarial way (1 Cor. 6).

remarry. This passage raises some challenging questions. If they are both Christians, why doesn't Paul compel them, under threat of church discipline (which was discussed two chapters earlier, in 1 Corinthians 5), to reconcile?[5] Why does he seem to permit the divorce, but then to forbid remarriage? Wouldn't it be strange to have both divorced people in the same church?

I believe that this passage may apply to those circumstances when, while the divorcing spouse doesn't have clear-cut grounds for divorce, things are bad enough that church leaders would be reluctant to discipline the person for moving out. The church's answer in such cases could be, "While we don't approve of your divorce (or separation), we will not enact church discipline against you for it, but based on 1 Corinthians 7:10–11, you are not free to remarry."

SUMMARY

Separation of a husband and wife is contrary to God's design that they be united in marriage as a picture of the Lord's loving relationship with his people. Sometimes temporary separations are unavoidable because of the circumstances of life. It is sinful, though, when spouses deliberately separate from each other in the long term without biblical grounds, whether or not the separation is legally enacted. Temporary separations rarely serve to rescue a marriage in crisis. A couple needs to work together to solve their problems and rebuild their relationship.

— QUESTIONS FOR REFLECTION —

1. How does the Bible speak to the contemporary practice of legal separation?
2. Why is separation of husband and wife contrary to God's design?

---

5. The fact that Paul tells the spouse who wrongfully divorces not to remarry seems to imply that he is still appealing to that person as a Christian, and not as someone who has been put out of the church as an unbeliever.

269

3. How could a temporary physical separation make a troubled marriage worse?
4. When might a temporary physical separation be necessary for a marriage in crisis?
5. How would you counsel a couple who are legally married, but each spouse is living a separate life?

37

WHO DECIDES WHETHER A DIVORCE OR REMARRIAGE IS VALID?

Who has authority to decide who may be divorced and remarried? In this age, human government regulates marriage, divorce, and remarriage through its laws and recordkeeping. Some religious authorities claim that marriage is primarily under their jurisdiction. To which of these authorities must we submit, especially if they contradict one another? Are there times when a Christian is free to go against government or church authority in matters of divorce and remarriage?

GOVERNMENT AUTHORITY

God has established human government authority to maintain order in society (Rom. 13:1–7; 1 Peter 2:13–14). As discussed in question 3, human governments of today have created laws that regulate who can marry under their jurisdiction, what constitutes a valid marriage, which marriages from other jurisdictions they will recognize, grounds for divorce, procedures for divorce, etc.

Laws vary in different jurisdictions. As previously mentioned, the Philippines, which is heavily influenced by the Roman Catholic Church, does not allow for divorce, but legal separations and annulments are available. In some Islamic countries, a husband merely needs

271

to say "I divorce you" three times to obtain an immediate divorce. Some nations have different rights for men than for women when it comes to divorce.[1] Laws also vary regarding waiting periods before a divorce is finalized, division of property, custody of children, child support, and spousal support.[2]

Laws regulating the family are constantly changing. For example, it wasn't so long ago in the United States that a person seeking divorce needed to show grounds, and the one being divorced could contest the divorce and make it hard for the other party to obtain the divorce.[3] In recent years, no-fault divorce has removed the requirement to show grounds or to assess blame.

Government laws may be contrary to Scripture and contrary to justice. They may allow for marriages that the Bible would forbid (including same-sex marriages or polygamy), or they may forbid divorces and remarriages that Scripture would permit.[4] There are jurisdictions (e.g., the Philippines) where people may have grounds for divorce according to Scripture, but the laws of the government do not allow them to divorce.

Governments and courts are often unjust in their handling of

---

1. At the time of this writing, Jewish women in Israel could not get divorced without the agreement of their husbands (http://www.latimes.com/world/middleeast /la-fg-israel-divorce-problems-20130726-story.html).

2. While some jurisdictions have imposed waiting periods after filing for divorce as a means to slow down the process, ostensibly for the protection of the institution of marriage, I see no biblical basis to require people to wait. Furthermore, waiting may be detrimental to the interests of the innocent party, who has a right to be free sooner rather than later.

3. One of the common plotlines in old black-and-white movies concerns the man whose wife has left him but won't grant him a divorce, which means that he can't marry his newfound love.

4. I see no evidence in Scripture for the government's making laws to prevent divorce. Both in Deuteronomy 24 and in the Gospel references to divorce, it is implicit that the law allows people to divorce even if the divorce is sinful. I do not believe that the current government should make laws forbidding divorce, even if the divorce is wrong. The law cannot prevent people from abandoning their marriages. All it can do is to regulate what is inevitable because of the hardness of human hearts. Better divorce laws would protect the innocent and penalize the guilty.

divorce, especially in cases in which one party broke the covenant (through adultery or abandonment), while the other party sought to keep the covenant. Yet the court (applying no-fault divorce laws) treats them equally with regard to financial responsibility, child custody, and property division. There are even cases in which the covenant-breaker is rewarded by the court and the covenant-keeper is penalized. In such cases of injustice, the innocent parties must entrust themselves to God, who will bring justice in due time (1 Peter 2:23).

As discussed in question 3, there may be circumstances when people choose to create their own marriage covenants without registering with the state.[5] In the same way, a rare situation could occur in which a couple regard themselves as divorced and free to remarry, independently of state authority. So far as the government is concerned, those who married without being licensed by the state may be considered as cohabiting, and those who regarded themselves as divorced may be considered by the state as still married. This reality would impact other necessary interactions with the government (tax returns, inheritance laws, spousal rights, etc.).

Some would raise the question whether getting married or divorced without government sanction would be disobeying the civil authorities to which Scripture says people must submit (Rom. 13:1–7). First, in almost every case, the government would not regard these actions as illegal because there are no laws against cohabitation (which is how the relationship would be viewed from a legal standpoint). Furthermore, Christians may determine that under certain circumstances, they will opt to exercise a right that God has given them and be willing to live with any consequences the government might bring.[6]

---

5. For instance, Christians living in certain Islamic states, Christians living as refugees without access to the legal system, or Christians living under any other government that will not allow them to exercise their right to marry or to divorce.

6. For example, for a former Muslim to marry a Christian would be illegal in some Islamic countries, but they may choose to enter into a marriage covenant anyway. Another instance would be that a wife whose husband is living with another woman might choose to consider herself divorced (free from him), even if the government will not grant her a legal divorce.

CHURCH AUTHORITY

Under the old covenant, there was no separation of church and state, a condition that impacted all laws, including the regulation of marriage and divorce. Under the new covenant, there is no valid theocracy, and the legitimate authority of church and state are separate. The Roman Catholic Church, which has a history of trying to unite ecclesiastical and government authority, claims jurisdiction over the marriages of its members on the grounds that marriage is a sacrament of the church. It has also sought to influence family law, especially in nations where the population is largely Roman Catholic. While marriage is sacred as a creation ordinance and a covenant established by God, there is no scriptural warrant for the view that marriage is a sacrament or that the church has formal jurisdiction over marriage.[7]

Pastors of various denominations, as leaders in the community, typically facilitate the making of the covenant in the marriage ceremony. As the community of witnesses, the people of the church are responsible for holding one another accountable to keep their marriage vows.[8] The leaders of the church are called to shepherd the flock, keeping watch over the souls for whom Christ died as those who will give an account to God (1 Peter 5:2; see also Acts 20:28; Heb. 13:17). This pastoral oversight includes the responsibility to help restore troubled marriages and to uphold biblical standards for marriage, divorce, and remarriage for church members.

While the church is not able to prevent a sinful divorce or

---

7. Protestants typically regard the Lord's Supper and baptism to be the only ordinances (or sacraments) of the New Testament church. Whatever role the church would have in regulating marriage would depend on one's ecclesiology. Would it be at the local-church level or the denominational level (for those who believe in denominational authority over that of the local church)? Regardless, Bible-believing evangelicals certainly do not recognize the validity of the Roman Catholic Church, which rejects the sole authority of Scripture and the gospel of salvation by grace alone, through faith alone, in Christ alone.

8. See chapter 3.

remarriage, there may be cases when a spouse who is sinfully breaking the marriage covenant is subject to church discipline, which would result either in restoration or in his or her being put out of the church. It is important for church leaders to have an agreed-upon understanding of what the grounds are (if any) for divorce and remarriage and how they will handle potential situations that arise.

Just as there could be rare cases when a believer chooses to oppose unbiblical government authority in decisions regarding marriage, divorce, and remarriage, there may be cases when a believer chooses to reject unbiblical church authority. For example, a young man who has been abandoned by his wife—who is now cohabiting with another man—may be a member of a church in which the leaders hold to the permanence view of marriage. Through his study of Scripture, he is convinced that after having made significant effort during an extended period to restore the marriage, he has the freedom to file for divorce and to potentially remarry in the future. If he goes through with this decision, the leaders will (in my view, wrongly) place him under church discipline and put him out of the church. He would be accountable to God for his choice and would be free to find another church whose leaders' understanding of divorce and remarriage agree with his own. Finally, he and the leaders of each church will give account to God for their actions.

SUMMARY

Ultimately, marriage is under God's authority. All people are accountable to him, whether they are individuals who marry, divorce, and remarry, or institutions that seek to regulate marriage and divorce. Ordinarily, believers should submit to both civil and church authorities. In some unusual circumstances, however, a Christian may determine to exercise a God-given freedom, based on Scripture, that is contrary to the rules of the church or state.

— Questions for Reflection —

1. How does the regulation of marriage and divorce differ under the old covenant, as opposed to the new covenant?
2. In what ways are the family laws of some governments contrary to God's Word?
3. When, if ever, is it allowable for a Christian to act in a way that is contrary to the government's regulation of marriage and divorce?
4. What role does the church play in regulating marriage and divorce?
5. When, if ever, might Christians choose to marry or divorce against the teachings of their church leaders?

38

WHEN IS REMARRIAGE ADVISABLE?

When may someone remarry? Are there legitimately divorced people who should not remarry? Are there times when remarriage is allowable but not advisable? When is remarriage a good idea?

WIDOWS MAY REMARRY
(AND SOME SHOULD)

The clearest case of allowable remarriage is that of widows and widowers. Paul states, "A wife is bound as long as her husband lives; but if her husband is dead, she is free to be married to whom she wishes, only in the Lord" (1 Cor. 7:39; see also Rom. 7:2–3). The one restriction placed on widows (and widowers) is that they must marry only in the Lord. It is also significant that the widow (not her father or her brothers) may choose (among those Christian men who are interested) whom she marries.

Paul strongly encourages younger widows to remarry: "Therefore, I want younger widows to get married, bear children, keep house, and give the enemy no occasion for reproach" (1 Tim. 5:14). His concern is that younger widows may be tempted to various sins if they remain single (5:11–13, 15). On the other hand, he anticipates that older widows will likely remain unmarried and receive help either from their children (5:3–8) or from the church (5:9–10, 16).

THOSE WHO HAVE BEEN DIVORCED
ON BIBLICAL GROUNDS MAY REMARRY

It has already been shown that the innocent spouse—who is divorced on the grounds of sexual immorality or desertion by an unbeliever—is free to remarry. It may, however, be advisable to wait for some time to see whether God might work in the heart of the former spouse, so that reconciliation is possible. It is also advisable to wait until one is sure that he or she is truly ready to be married again. The time after divorce can be used to examine one's own sins and failures (even on the part of the innocent spouse), which may have contributed to the failure of the marriage, and to address areas of spiritual weakness. There is also a danger that a divorced person, after experiencing rejection from one spouse, will too quickly gravitate to someone new to fill the void. Sometimes divorced people who are rebounding make unwise choices and wind up in marriages that quickly develop some of the same troubles that were experienced in the previous marriage. Lonely hearts can be easily deceived. Those considering remarriage should seek counsel from godly friends and church leaders to ascertain whether others think that they are ready and to help them objectively evaluate any marriage prospects.[1]

Some divorced people may choose to remain single for the foreseeable future. Remaining unmarried may give them greater freedom to serve the Lord. As Paul writes, "Are you released from a wife? Do not seek a wife. . . . But I want you to be free from concern. One who is unmarried is concerned about the things of the Lord, how he may please the Lord; but one who is married is concerned about the things of the world, how he may please his wife" (1 Cor. 7:27b, 32–33). Some also choose to remain single for the sake of their children, not wanting to introduce the complexities of a blended family. Legitimately divorced people are free, though, to remarry—now or in the future. Paul adds, "But if you marry, you have not sinned" (1 Cor. 7:28a).

---

1. See chapters 7–9 to learn more about how to decide whether to marry and how to find the right person to marry.

Just as Paul encourages young widows to remarry, it may be best for most young people who are divorced on biblical grounds to exercise their freedom to remarry, so that they can enjoy the benefits of companionship and not be tempted by sin. I have seen many cases in which people who had been abandoned by unbelieving adulterous spouses found overwhelming joy and blessing in remarriage (see Rom. 8:28).

THOSE WHO ARE DIVORCED WITHOUT BIBLICAL GROUNDS SHOULD NOT REMARRY

Paul makes it clear that believers who wrongfully divorce should not remarry (1 Cor. 7:10–11). Jesus states that sinful remarriages are adulterous (Mark 10:11–12). These marriages are forbidden to believers, even if the laws of the government would allow for remarriage.

One might object that if the widow should remarry, lest she be tempted, how can divorced people resist temptation unless they, too, remarry? The answer from Scripture is that a sinfully divorced person does have another option—seeking reconciliation with his or her former spouse (1 Cor. 7:11).[2] If this spouse refuses to participate in reconciliation, there may in time be valid grounds for divorce and remarriage. In the meantime, lonely men or women must entrust themselves to God, who will not allow them to be tempted beyond what they are able to bear (10:13) as they walk in the Spirit and do not carry out the desires of the flesh (Gal. 5:16–23). Their situation would be similar to that of people who are still bound in their marriages, even though their spouses are physically or mentally disabled. They must remain faithful to God and avoid sin, trusting that he will help them in their hardship and loneliness.

MAY THE "GUILTY PARTY" IN A DIVORCE REMARRY?

While it is clear from the teaching of Paul that the spouse who is the victim of adultery or of desertion by an unbeliever is free to divorce

2. As question 31 explains, reconciliation would include getting married again. The

and to remarry, what are the rights of the guilty party? First, the guilty party should repent before God for the sin and then express repentance by seeking, if possible, to be reconciled with the former spouse.[3] Given that the guilty spouse is to blame for the divorce and the innocent spouse may question the sincerity of the person's repentance, the guilty party should be willing to wait to see whether the former spouse might have a change of heart and take him or her back. If the innocent spouse remarries, then the hope of reconciliation has been dashed, and the guilty party should be allowed to remarry.

There are cases in which both parties in the marriage have committed adultery, thus making each a guilty party and each a victim.[4] In such situations, every effort should be made to bring about biblical repentance, forgiveness, and reconciliation. If restoration of the marriage is impossible, divorce and remarriage would not be forbidden by Scripture. Church leaders who counsel people in such situations, however, should seek to ensure that the heart issues leading to the sinful failures in the last marriage have been addressed before encouraging them to remarry.

WHAT IF AN UNBELIEVING FORMER SPOUSE WANTS TO REMARRY?

What should a believer do if his or her former spouse, who is a non-Christian, wants to get back together (assuming that neither has remarried)? MacArthur and Adams both argue that because Scripture forbids marriage to an unbeliever (1 Cor. 7:39; 9:5), a believer would not be free to remarry a former spouse unless that person is a Christian.[5]

---

couple would not be free to live together as husband and wife until they had made a new marriage covenant.

3. It may also be appropriate for the guilty spouse to take other steps of repentance, such as restitution or paying back child and spousal support.

4. In some cases, one spouse takes revenge on the adulterous spouse by having his or her own adulterous affair.

5. John MacArthur, *The Divorce Dilemma* (Leominster, England: Day One Publications, 2009), 87.

Nor can the believer assume that the unbeliever would become converted after they remarried (7:16). The Christian may choose, though, to remain single for a time to see whether God brings the spouse to repentance and faith. In addition, I would encourage the believer to receive confirmation from church leaders that the conversion seems genuine and wasn't just to get the marriage back.

Others suggest that the believer is free to remarry his or her unbelieving spouse because the marriage covenant should never have been broken (Matt. 19:9), and now there is opportunity for it to be restored.[6] The family can be reunited, and both mother and father can participate in raising any children that God may have given them.

Each church must work out its response to such situations. Many may choose to allow for the believing spouse to make this decision based on the person's own conscience.

ARE THOSE DIVORCED EVER FORBIDDEN FROM REMARRYING THEIR FORMER SPOUSE?

If neither the husband nor the wife has remarried someone else, it may be wonderful for them to remarry each other. If one of them has remarried, then the new marriage should be respected and remarriage is out of the question.

The most complicated case takes place when remarried spouses are freed from a second marriage through death or divorce. Can they then go back to the first spouse? One of my early counseling cases involved a woman who was having conflict with her second husband. Over time he divorced her, and she wanted to remarry her first husband. Does Scripture allow this? Deuteronomy 24:1–4 teaches that a man who divorces his wife—who then marries another man—may

---

6. Wingerd et al. assume this position, which would be consistent with the permanence view of marriage. "When all factors are weighed, it appears to us that it is not sinful for a Christian to marry a former spouse who is still an unbeliever, as long as neither is bound to another living spouse." Daryl Wingerd et al., *Divorce & Remarriage: A Permanence View* (Kansas City: Christian Communicators Worldwide, 2009), 114.

not remarry his first wife, even if the second husband divorces her or dies, because she is "defiled." Some believe that the principle contained in the text still applies today and that remarriage in such cases is not allowed. Most, however, take the position that Deuteronomy 24 refers to a particular type of situation that would have occurred under the old covenant and therefore does not apply today under the new covenant.[7] They would also cite the example of David. Even under the old covenant, he took back Saul's daughter Michal as his wife, although (from no fault of David's) Saul had given her to another man after David was married to her (2 Sam. 3:13–16).[8] Murray writes, "It would appear to be stretching the temporary regulations of the Old Testament beyond warrant to infer that Deuteronomy 24:4 would apply to New Testament divorce when the latter is of a very different character from that permitted in the Old Testament."[9] While I am uneasy with encouraging a remarriage in such circumstances, I would regard it as a matter for a couple to work out in their own consciences with the guidance of their church leaders.

SUMMARY

Those who are widowed or who are divorced on biblical grounds are free to remarry, but they are not compelled to remarry. Some would be wise to remain single, at least for a significant time. Others

7. Heth takes this position and cites research suggesting that the first husband in this case would have a corrupt financial motive for remarrying his former wife. William A. Heth, "Remarriage for Adultery or Desertion," in *Remarriage after Divorce in Today's Church: 3 Views*, ed. Mark L. Strauss (Grand Rapids: Zondervan, 2006), 65. MacArthur reasons that since the sins causing the first divorce have been taken out of the way by the work of Christ, remarriage would be allowed (*The Divorce Dilemma*, 92).

8. It could be argued that 2 Samuel does not evaluate whether David's action was allowed under the Law. It simply reports what happened and that those who understood the Law would recognize that David's action was wrong, just as they would have realized that his taking of many wives violated the law forbidding kings to multiply wives (Deut. 17:17; 1 Sam. 25:43–44; 2 Sam. 3:2–5).

9. John Murray, *Divorce* (Philadelphia: Presbyterian and Reformed, 1961), 113.

would benefit from remarriage if the right opportunity presented itself. Those who are divorced or separated against God's will are not free to remarry and must either pursue reconciliation or remain single as long as their former spouse remains alive and unmarried. In doubtful cases, one should not remarry if it cannot be done in faith and with a clear conscience. Paul reminds us that "whatever is not from faith is sin" (Rom. 14:23b).

— Questions for Reflection —

1. Whom does Scripture encourage to remarry and why?
2. How might a young divorced person's situation be like that of a young widow when considering remarriage?
3. When is remarriage forbidden, according to Scripture?
4. Why might someone who is free to remarry choose to remain single?
5. When should a person remarry his or her former spouse?

39

WHAT SHOULD BE DONE IF SOMEONE HAS DIVORCED AND/OR REMARRIED IMPROPERLY?

After studying what Scripture teaches about divorce and remarriage, many Christians reach the conclusion that they have acted sinfully in the past. Then they wonder, "What should I do now?"

IS RECONCILIATION POSSIBLE?

If a divorce has taken place and if both parties remain single, the possibility of reconciliation should be explored. The couple should seek to deal with the past biblically by addressing the issues that caused the breakup of their marriage and by seeking forgiveness from each other for past sins. The process of investigating the possibility of coming back together would be something like a courtship, during which it would be wise to seek counsel from godly friends and church leaders. Each of them would need to be prepared for the real challenges they would face in the renewed marriage. The reconciliation process could culminate with a simple ceremony, at which the man and the woman would remarry by making covenant vows to each other before family and close friends. Couples who have been separated may also choose to formally renew their marriage vows to each other when they come together again.[1]

On the other hand, one's options may be limited if a former spouse is unwilling to pursue reconciliation. As Paul says in Romans 12:18, "If possible, so far as it depends on you, be at peace with all men." The spouse who desires reconciliation can still seek forgiveness for his or her sins during the marriage, even if the partner won't take the person back. He or she can also offer to wait and see whether the former partner might experience a change of heart. Sometimes the reluctant spouse will be persuaded by ongoing evidence, over a period of months or even years, of God's work in changing the former spouse.

SOME SINS CAN'T BE REVERSED

One of my earliest counseling cases involved a woman named Monica, who had started attending church with her second husband, Lee. Monica's first husband, George, was a committed Christian, but—in Monica's view—was a bit dull. She met Lee at work, and before long, they were involved in a steamy affair. Monica divorced George to marry Lee. By the time she came to me, the steam had gone out of her relationship with Lee. Monica and Lee were always fighting, and she realized that Lee was an angry, ungodly man. Monica admitted, "I made a big mistake. May I leave Lee and go back to George?"

What should be done if one or both former spouses have remarried after divorce? Only a few would say that they should divorce their new spouses and get back together with each other in marriage. According to the overwhelming majority of scholars, even including most who take the permanence view of marriage,[2] once a new marriage has taken place, it should be respected because this couple has been joined

---

1. It has been my joy and privilege to counsel in cases in which couples who had been separated or divorced for a long time formally came back together in marriage, much to the delight of family and friends.

2. Daryl Wingerd et al., *Divorce & Remarriage: A Permanence View* (Kansas City: Christian Communicators Worldwide, 2009), 108–9.

in covenant by God. It is too late to try to undo sins of the past.[3] Attempting to do so would create more sinful divorces and adulterous remarriages. Paul's general principle applies: "Each man must remain in that condition in which he was called" (1 Cor. 7:20).

If anything, former spouses who have since remarried must be especially circumspect in their dealings with each other, so that they will not be a threat to divide the new marriages. Because they were once married and in love, they might be more vulnerable to temptations to inappropriate emotional or physical involvement, which could threaten their new marriages.

Some would ask, "But doesn't Jesus say that the man or woman who divorces and remarries is committing adultery?" (Mark 10:11–12). Does this mean that the remarried couple continues to commit adultery as they continue to come together sexually as man and wife? I have heard of a case in which one spouse, under conviction that the remarriage had been sinful, refused to sleep in the same bed with the other because the person didn't want to keep committing adultery. The verb translated "commits adultery" in Mark 10:11–12 is in the present tense. It most likely refers to the adulterous sin that took place at the time of the remarriage, just as the divorce, which is mentioned in the same passage, took place at a point in time.[4] Once a couple has remarried, they should do their best to fulfill their spousal duties to each other, including in the marriage bed (1 Cor. 7:3–5), and to make every effort to ensure that a new marriage lasts until God, by death, separates them.[5] It would be sinful to do otherwise.

3. Under the old covenant, Deuteronomy 24:1–4 specifically forbids the first husband from remarrying his wife—whom he had divorced—after she has been remarried to another man.

4. "Technically, the present tense Greek verb translated 'commits adultery' can be understood as depicting either present ongoing action or as a single act that occurs at a point in time. The context in the case seems to demand the latter meaning." Wingerd et al., *Divorce & Remarriage*, 108–9. J. Carl Laney also takes the view that the adultery is punctilious at the time of the remarriage and not ongoing. "No Divorce and No Remarriage," in *Divorce and Remarriage: Four Christian Views*, ed. H. Wayne House (Downers Grove, IL: InterVarsity Press, 1990), 39.

5. Jay Adams points out that God blessed even the sinful marriage of David and

DOES IT MAKE A DIFFERENCE WHETHER ONE WAS CONVERTED AT THE TIME OF DIVORCE?

Just as the churches of the New Testament era probably had numerous members who, before their conversion, conformed to their culture in which divorce and remarriage were common, many in churches today have been through multiple marriages and divorces before coming to Christ. There is a sense in which believers can look upon their pre-Christian past with thankfulness that past sins committed in ignorance have been totally forgiven through Christ's work (1 Tim. 1:12–17), rejoicing because they are new creatures in Christ (2 Cor. 5:17). On the other hand, sins—even those committed before a person was saved—frequently have consequences (Gal. 6:7–8). For example, if someone contracted a sexually transmitted disease before becoming a believer, that person will still have to live with the disease after conversion.

Coming to Christ does not release Christians from a hard marriage to an unbeliever (1 Cor. 7:13–14). Nor does it set them free to remarry if they still have an obligation to seek reconciliation with a former spouse (Matt. 19:9; 1 Cor. 7:10–11). In the same way, there may be financial obligations to a former spouse or additional duties with children from a past marriage, which Christians will be eager to fulfill because of their love for Christ (even if it limits their freedom).

On the other hand, it is most troubling when professing Christians sinfully divorce and remarry because they willfully and deliberately go against God's Word (Heb. 10:26). This may be an indication that they may not be truly converted. Those who sin against knowledge are often guilty of presuming on God's grace as they set their will above that of God himself. John writes, "The one who says, 'I have come to know Him,' and does not keep His commandments, is a liar, and the truth is not in him" (1 John 2:4). Moreover, I have known cases in which a professing believer who had sinfully divorced and remarried was later

---

Bathsheba in spite of its sordid beginning. *Marriage, Divorce, and Remarriage in the Bible* (Grand Rapids: Zondervan, 1980), 95.

brought to repentance. While only God can infallibly know the heart, church leaders have a responsibility to ensure that past sins of their members (or potential members) have been handled in a biblical way.

SUMMARY

Those who have sinfully divorced may have the opportunity to be reconciled to their former spouses. Those who have sinfully remarried should repent before God of their past sin and seek forgiveness from the ones who were hurt by their sin. They should not, however, compound their transgressions by breaking apart their new marriage and attempting to restore the old relationship. Rather, they should seek to honor God by being faithful in their new marriage.

— QUESTIONS FOR REFLECTION —

1. When is reconciliation possible after a sinful divorce?
2. What should be done if a former spouse is unwilling to consider reconciliation?
3. Why is reconciliation of the first marriage impossible after one spouse has remarried?
4. Does the fact that someone was divorced before becoming a believer make any difference in terms of his or her obligations and freedoms?
5. Why shouldn't a wrongfully remarried person divorce the new spouse and try to get back together with the former spouse? What should the person do instead?

40

HOW SHOULD THE CHURCH TREAT THOSE WHO HAVE DIVORCED AND REMARRIED?

Forty years ago, when I was a young Christian, I delighted in God's ideals for marriage and assumed that all Christian people would have happy marriages. I didn't know of many, if any, divorced people in my local church. Looking back, I am sure that there were divorced and remarried people in our church. I also think that they probably sought to keep a low profile because of the stigma that divorced and remarried people can experience in evangelical churches.

DIVORCE IS NOT THE UNFORGIVABLE SIN

Some are divorced in spite of their attempts to be faithful to their marriage covenants because of the sinful actions of a spouse. Such people should be viewed with compassion—not judgment. A woman with children who has been abandoned should be viewed as a virtual widow whom the extended family and the church should care for. We should "weep with those who weep" (Rom. 12:15) as we seek to sympathize with those who have been devastated by the betrayal of the one person whom they should have been able to trust most.

The gospel of Jesus Christ gives hope to those who have failed in their marriages. Some in the church may have been, before conversion, responsible for the breakup of a previous marriage, or they may have remarried contrary to Scripture. The Bible tells us that we all have a past deserving of God's wrath (1 Cor. 6:9–10), but that the gospel cleanses and transforms us: "Such were some of you; but you were washed, but you were sanctified, but you were justified in the name of the Lord Jesus Christ and in the Spirit of our God" (6:11). Our new identity is not "adulterer," or "divorcée," or "drunkard," but "Christian" because we are now united to our Savior, who has made us his. As sinners saved solely by God's grace, we should gladly welcome our fellow sinners, just as Barnabas welcomed Paul, the former persecutor of Christians, into the fellowship of the disciples (Acts 9:26–27).

Because the church rightly takes a stance against sinful divorce, many who have been divorced are very sensitive about any perceived criticism or judgment. Those who have not remarried can sometimes feel excluded from events for couples or families. Extra care should be taken to avoid making any comment that could make them feel left out or stigmatized. They should know that they are fully accepted among God's people. As Paul writes, "Therefore, accept one another, just as Christ also accepted us to the glory of God" (Rom. 15:7). If Christ has accepted a person by his grace, we should do so without reservation as well.

SOMETIMES COUNSEL OR
ADMONITION WILL BE NECESSARY

There is a difference, however, between accepting someone who is repentant for past sins and enabling someone who is in the process of willfully sinning. Some teachers erroneously want to go from one extreme—of being sinfully judgmental of all divorced people—to embracing, without judgment, anyone's decision to divorce or remarry. A statement like this by one church leader could be misunderstood or misused: "It is not up to me to decide when someone else's marriage should end or should be healed. Only the wronged spouse in a relationship should make that decision."[1] Church leaders are responsible to oversee the flock, which sometimes involves admonishing those who are sinning (1 Thess. 5:14; 2 Thess. 3:15), and for practicing church discipline on those who willfully defy God's standards, refusing to repent (Matt. 18:15–20; 1 Cor. 5). A professing Christian man who abandons his spouse so that he can marry a woman he met at work is adulterous and must be confronted by church leaders. A Christian woman who has no biblical grounds for divorce but wants to get out of her marriage because she is unhappy and tired must be offered counsel that is both gentle and firm, so that she can endure. If church leaders fail to act, more sinful divorces and remarriages may take place among the church members. Paul warns that "a little leaven leavens the whole lump of dough" (1 Cor. 5:6b).

In addition, church leaders must be certain to investigate a situation carefully before making any judgments (Prov. 18:13, 15, 17). They should patiently try to work with those who are straying before exercising public discipline. They must also be humble and recognize that situations might arise in which they are not certain that discipline is appropriate, in which cases they must hold back. Brian Borgman speaks of rare situations in which he cannot see clear biblical grounds for divorce or remarriage, but neither can he see biblical grounds for prohibiting divorce or remarriage. In such circumstances, we must respect the consciences of the people involved.[2]

CAN DIVORCED PEOPLE
REMARRY IN THE CHURCH?

I have heard of cases in which church leaders would say that a member is permitted to remarry after divorce, but that the couple cannot hold the marriage in the church building. This policy implies

---

1. William A. Heth, "Remarriage for Adultery or Desertion," in *Remarriage after Divorce in Today's Church: 3 Views*, ed. Mark L. Strauss (Grand Rapids: Zondervan, 2006), 80.

2. From Brian Borgman's personal study notes on Marriage, Divorce, and Remarriage.

that, somehow, the new marriage is tainted and would stain the purity of the church facility. If a person has been divorced on biblical grounds and is free—according to God's Word—to remarry, then the marriage should not be treated as being in any way improper. This suggests that the church should treat this marriage like any other legitimate marriage of its members, which would include allowing the use of the facility for a wedding.[3]

In the same way, if a pastor believes that a couple has the right to remarry, based on Scripture, he should feel free to officiate at the wedding. On the other hand, if a pastor has a personal conviction that remarriage is forbidden (e.g., because he takes the permanence view of marriage), he should not be expected to violate his conscience. The couple can find another minister to officiate at their ceremony.

CAN A DIVORCED MAN SERVE AS A CHURCH OFFICER?

Paul teaches that elders and deacons must be "the husband of one wife" or, literally, a "one-woman man" (1 Tim. 3:2, 12; Titus 1:6). There is debate about what limitations this would place on who can serve as a church officer.[4] Some think Paul is saying that a church officer could be married only once in a lifetime, even if his first wife died.[5] Merkle also points out that a similar phrase, "one-man woman," is used for widows who were to be supported by the church. It would not make sense that this means married just once in a lifetime because Paul elsewhere encourages remarriage after a spouse has died (1 Cor.

3. Many couples who remarry after divorce choose to make their ceremony more low-key because it is a second marriage, and there is a recognition that all divorce is a sinful violation of God's design, even if the previous marriage failed primarily because of the other party's sin.

4. See Benjamin L. Merkle, *40 Questions about Elders and Deacons* (Grand Rapids: Kregel, 2008), 124–29.

5. I know about a case in which an elder who remarried after the death of his first wife resigned his office because he had once taught that an elder could have only one spouse in a lifetime.

7:39; 1 Tim. 5:14). Others would say that Paul is simply stating that a man should have only one wife at a time, which would disqualify a polygamist (occasionally an issue in the first century). Most would agree that a man who has been involved in adulterous sin is not a "one-woman man" and is unqualified for office.

In addition, many believe that "husband of one wife" implies that an elder cannot be divorced, or remarried after divorce.[6] While a man's marital history should be examined before he is recognized as an officer in the church, the qualifications deal primarily with the man's present character and status—not his past. When considering the other qualifications, few would say that a man must never have been a drunkard, or pugnacious, or a lover of money. Every believer has a past. A person such as John Newton may have been a pugnacious, covetous drunkard before conversion, but after he was saved, his guilt was wiped away, and God made him into a new man. In the same way, a man who had a sinful pre-Christian past, including a divorce and remarriage, may be transformed into a godly man who is a faithful husband, exhibiting self-control and grace in every area of his life.

One might ask if it makes a difference whether a man was sinfully divorced and remarried or guilty of other serious sin after having become a Christian. Again, because the qualifications refer to a man's present character, a man who was very weak and immature as a young believer (e.g., in his youth), but has been walking faithfully with the Lord for decades and has a proven character, would be qualified for consideration for church office.

Because elder qualifications additionally include "above reproach" and "a good reputation with those outside the church" (1 Tim. 3:2, 7), there could be situations in which a man of good character would not be able to serve because of his past. For example, if a sizable percentage of the church members object to having a divorced elder, it would not

6. For example, Piper writes, "Persons remarried after divorce will forgo positions of official leadership at Bethlehem which correspond to the roles of elders or deacons" ("A Statement on Divorce & Remarriage in the Life of Bethlehem Baptist Church," http://www.desiringgod.org/articles/a-statement-on-divorce-remarriage-in-the-life -of-bethlehem-baptist-church).

be wise to impose him on the congregation, even if the other leaders believe that he is qualified. There also could be a case in which a person's past sins were of such a scandalous public nature that the church might choose not to recognize the person as an officer. Those who are not in office may still serve Christ and his church by using the gifts they have been given to the glory of God (1 Peter 4:10–11).

SUMMARY

The church consists of sinners who have been saved by God's grace, which include people who have divorced and remarried. We should never stigmatize or shun those who have turned from their sin to Christ. Just as we have been shown mercy through Christ, who has fully accepted us, we should accept one another.

— QUESTIONS FOR REFLECTION —

1. Why is it wrong for Christians to stigmatize those who have been divorced and/or remarried?
2. Should people who wish to be remarried be allowed to hold their wedding in a church with a minister officiating?
3. What should the church do if a member is planning to divorce or remarry, even though that person has no biblical grounds for doing so?
4. What would you say to someone who is overwhelmed with guilt for past marital failures and sins?
5. Should a divorced person be allowed to serve as a church officer? Explain your answer.

SELECTED BIBLIOGRAPHY

Adams, Jay E. *Marriage, Divorce, and Remarriage in the Bible.* Grand Rapids: Zondervan, 1980.

Frame, John M. *The Doctrine of the Christian Life.* Phillipsburg, NJ: P&R Publishing, 2008.

Harvey, Dave. *When Sinners Say "I Do."* Wapwallopen, PA: Shepherd Press, 2007.

House, H. Wayne, ed. *Divorce and Remarriage: Four Christian Views.* Downers Grove, IL: InterVarsity Press, 1990.

Instone-Brewer, David. *Divorce and Remarriage in the Bible: The Social and Literary Context.* Grand Rapids: Eerdmans, 2002.

Instone-Brewer, David. *Divorce and Remarriage in the Church: Biblical Solutions for Pastoral Realities.* Downers Grove, IL: InterVarsity Press, 2003.

Keller, Timothy, and Kathy Keller. *The Meaning of Marriage.* New York: Penguin Group, 2011.

Köstenberger, Andreas J., with David W. Jones. *God, Marriage, and Family: Rebuilding the Biblical Foundation.* 2nd ed. Wheaton, IL: Crossway, 2010.

MacArthur, John. *The Divorce Dilemma: God's Last Word on Lasting Commitment.* Leominster, England: Day One Publications, 2009.

Mack, Wayne. *Preparing for Marriage God's Way.* Phillipsburg, NJ: P&R Publishing, 2014.

Murray, John. *Divorce.* Philadelphia: Presbyterian and Reformed, 1961.

Ortlund, Ray. *Marriage and the Mystery of the Gospel.* Wheaton, IL: Crossway, 2016.

Peace, Martha. *The Excellent Wife.* Bemidji, MN: Focus, 1999.

Sande, Ken, and Kevin Johnson. *Resolving Everyday Conflict.* Grand Rapids: Baker, 2011.

Strauss, Mark L., ed. *Remarriage after Divorce in Today's Church: 3 Views.* Grand Rapids: Zondervan, 2006.

Wingerd, Daryl, et al. *Divorce & Remarriage: A Permanence View.* Kansas City: Christian Communicators Worldwide, 2009.

INDEX OF SCRIPTURE

297

7:46—118
8:41—200
8:44—110
9:21—65
13:3–4—87
14:15—170–71
15:5—11, 104
17:14—96

Acts
5:29b—99
9:25—261
9:26–27—290
15:20—201
15:29—201
20:28—261, 274
22:25–29—261
23:12–24—261

Romans
1:26–27—31, 33, 144
1:32a—31
1:32b—31
2:4—81, 155
5:1—121
5:8—86, 167
5:10—86
6:1–2—170
6:18—222n10
6:22—222n10
7:2—9
7:2–3—171, 205, 277
7:3—27n1
8:5–8—31
8:28—168, 279
12:1–2—47, 147
12:2—45, 166
12:15—289

12:18—65, 140, 221, 285
13:1—96
13:1–7—21, 100, 271, 273
13:4—215, 261
13:14—43
14:23—157
14:23b—283
15:1–2—16
15:2–3a—111
15:7—290

1 Corinthians
1:4–8—131
1:30–31—132
2:14—31
5—269, 291
5:1—201
5:6b—291
6—268n4
6:1–8—181
6:9—33, 144
6:9–10—290
6:9–11—34
6:11—290
6:16—42, 210, 230
6:20—47
7—47, 218, 225
7:1b—47
7:2—48, 218
7:3–4—61, 150, 157
7:3–5—16, 23, 111, 218, 255n2, 286
7:5—154, 267, 268
7:7—48
7:7–8—218

7:8–9—48
7:9—44, 73, 218
7:10—181, 224
7:10–11—171, 180, 203, 219, 223, 232, 264, 268–69, 279, 287
7:11—222, 279
7:12a—219
7:12–13—166, 221n6
7:12b–13—220
7:12–14—204
7:13—181
7:13–14—287
7:14—167, 220
7:14b—98
7:15—140, 191, 204, 204n3, 208, 220–22, 222n10, 223–24, 254, 257
7:15b—263
7:16—55, 220–21, 281
7:16a—261
7:20—286
7:27b—278
7:27b–28a—223
7:28—48
7:28a—278
7:32—49
7:32–33—278
7:32–34—48, 65
7:33—255n2
7:33–35—218
7:34—101
7:35–39—48

7:36—64

7:39—9, 55, 65, 171, 191, 204n3, 205, 219, 222, 222n10, 223n11, 277, 280, 292–93

7:40—219n3

9:5—48n1, 55, 280

10:10—115

10:12—43

10:13—33, 82, 125, 134, 246, 279

11:3—96

11:8–9—32, 95

13—83

13:4–7—83, 138

13:5—62, 116

13:7—177, 243

15:33—170

2 Corinthians

5:9—247

5:17—34, 110, 287

6:14–18—54

7:10–11—126, 250

8:9—127

Galatians

3:28—91, 95

5:15—123, 134

5:16—81, 134

5:16–17—111

5:16–23—104, 279

5:16–24—134

5:17—82

5:19–21—55, 81, 123, 259

5:20—134

5:22–23—55, 111, 134

5:22–24—82

6:1—81, 100, 133–34, 138, 243, 247

6:2—134

6:6–7—252

6:7—42, 169–70

6:7–8—287

6:7–8a—146

Ephesians

1:3–6—79

1:7–9—89

1:7–14—79

2:1–10—79

2:5–6—90

2:10—132

2:11–22—79

3:1–13—79

3:6—90

3:12—90

3:14–19—80

4:11—90

4:11–16—104

4:20–23—90

4:25—66, 105, 115, 242, 249

4:26–27—105

4:29—113, 248

4:31–32—16, 126, 140, 252

4:32—249

5:1–2—66, 81

5:2—168

5:3—44

5:22—94

5:22–24—87, 96

5:22–33—57

5:24b—96

5:25—79, 85, 157n7

5:25–27—14, 94

5:25–30—96, 185

5:26–27—88–89, 130

5:28–30—89

5:29a—89

5:32—14, 79, 142, 150

6:1—96

6:2—64

6:4a—65

6:5–9—27n2

Philippians

1:6—68

2:3–4—62, 138, 157

2:3–5—87, 112

2:5–8—123

2:14—115

4:2–3—138

4:4—169

4:8—114

4:13—11

Colossians

1:3–8—132

3:12–14—108

3:18—96

1 Thessalonians

1:2–10—132

4:3–5—145

5:14—291

2 Thessalonians

3:15—291

INDEX OF SUBJECTS AND NAMES

305